DO YOU SPEAK FOOTBALL?

DO YOU
SPEAK
FOOTBALL?

A Glossary of Football Words and Phrases from Around the World

Do YOU SPEAK FOOTBALL?

A Glossary of Football Words and Phrases from Around the World

TOM WILLIAMS

BLOOMSBURY SPORT

LONDON · OXFORD · NEW YORK · NEW DELHI · SYDNEY

BLOOMSBURY SPORT
Bloomsbury Publishing Plc
50 Bedford Square, London, WC1B 3DP, UK

BLOOMSBURY, BLOOMSBURY SPORT and the Diana logo
are trademarks of Bloomsbury Publishing Plc

First published in Great Britain 2018

Bloomsbury Publishing Plc does not have any control over, or responsibility for,
any third-party websites referred to or in this book. All internet addresses given
in this book were correct at the time of going to press. The author and publisher
regret any inconvenience caused if addresses have changed or sites have
ceased to exist, but can accept no responsibility for any such changes

A catalogue record for this book is available from the British Library

Library of Congress Cataloging-in-Publication data has been applied for

ISBN: HB: 978-1-4729-4721-5; eBook: 978-1-4729-4720-8

2 4 6 8 10 9 7 5 3 1

Typeset in Life by Deanta Global Publishing Services, Chennai, India
Printed and bound in Great Britain by CPI Group (UK) Ltd. Croydon, CRO 4YY

To find out more about our authors and books visit www.bloomsbury.com
and sign up for our newsletters

For my dad,
who showed me how to love football,
and my mum,
who hates it

CONTENTS

'Those who know nothing of foreign languages know nothing of their own.'
Johann Wolfgang von Goethe

INTRODUCTION

Football, it's often said, is a universal language, but while you might not need any specialist vocabulary to play it or watch it, how about to discuss it? Would you know what an Italian meant if they told you someone had scored with a 'spoon'? Why a Ukrainian's mouth might water at the prospect of a 'biscuit with raisins'? Why you really wouldn't want to be called a 'Dundee United' by someone from Nigeria?

The story of football is the tale of a sport spawned on the muddy school playing fields of Victorian England that carried itself into the hearts of people in every country on the planet. The words in this book are the words of that tale. No country's football story is the same, each nation's experience of the game being refracted through the unique prism of its language. Hold each prism to your eye and football reveals itself in strange, amusing and unexpected ways.

The language of Spanish football bears traces of the bullring. We find fragments of cricket in England, while American football, baseball and basketball loom large in the United States. Animals lope, slither and fly across our path everywhere we go: bears in Finland, snakes in Kenya, elephants in Indonesia, zebras (somewhat incongruously) in Brazil. In Argentina, a diving header is known as a 'little pigeon'. In the Indian state of Kerala, a crafty forward is likened to a specific local species of fish.

A technically limited player might have a 'wooden leg' (Brazil), a 'wooden foot' (Paraguay) or be made of wood entirely (Serbia). In Spain a bulky defender is a 'wardrobe', in Tanzania a 'padlock' and in Saudi Arabia a 'safety valve'.

The home and, in particular, the kitchen provide a plentiful supply of metaphors. Depending on where you are in the world, a spectacular long-range shot could be likened to a banana, a cucumber, a potato or a croissant. A Dutch player who attempts a shot with his weaker foot is said to have used his 'chocolate leg'. Thanks to Roy Keane, corporate fans in Britain are known as the 'prawn sandwich brigade'. In France, home of the world's finest gastronomy, what else would you call a perfectly delivered through ball that begs to be gobbled up but *un caviar*?

The language of football springs from many sources. Lots of terms have leaped from neighbourhood pitches and school playgrounds. Some owe their existence to iconic players, historic goals or notorious incidents. We also hear echoes of the voices of influential journalists and commentators, such as Ricardo Lorenzo Rodríguez, better known as Borocotó, whose editorship of sports magazine *El Gráfico* shaped Argentina's attitude towards football in the first half of the 20th century. Or Gianni Brera, who mapped every hill, valley, highway and byway in the landscape of post-war Italian football.

Every football culture under the sun has a word for the singularly humiliating act of sticking the ball between an opponent's legs, which is known as a 'nutmeg' in the English-speaking world, a *panna* ('gate') in the Netherlands and variously as an 'egg', a 'bridge', a 'pen', a 'violin', a 'salad' or a 'gherkin' – to cite but six examples – elsewhere. The same is true to a slightly lesser extent of the goal's top corners (often described in terms of spiders and cobwebs) and jittery goalkeepers ('lettuce hand' in Brazil, 'porridge fingers' in Estonia, 'flying buffalo' in Turkey).

Referees, naturally, get it in the neck everywhere. A referee suspected of being crooked is branded a 'black whistle' in China. A hopeless match official in Malaysia will be told that he's a 'blockhead'. In the Soviet Union, fans aggrieved at a referee's performance would call for the man in black to be turned into a bar of soap – a sinister nod to the Soviet practice of using the bodies of stray dogs to make cosmetic products.

Several countries, among them Italy, Spain and Russia, employ a term from the card table – *poker* – when a player puts the ball into the net four times in the same game. Nicknames for the ball itself abound, although they tend to be rather more poetic in South America – *gorduchinha*, meaning 'little pudgy one', is one example from Brazil – than in Europe, where 'the leather' is often the default metaphor.

The internet is changing the way that new terminologies emerge, and has concurrently engendered an increase in the use of English as a conduit for new coinages. If Britain laid down football's linguistic foundations ('corner', 'free-kick', 'offside', even 'football' itself) and then stepped away as foreign cultures arrived to carry out the brickwork (*rabona, panenka, sombrero*), the status of English as the lingua franca of the online world has brought the sport's native language back to the building site.

The phenomenon can be seen in freestyle football and street football, where many of the new tricks and moves that have emerged over the past 15 years – curated in widely viewed YouTube videos and disseminated via social media – have been assigned English names. Manoeuvres like the 'mouse trap', the 'air akka' and the 'mesmomeg' are too convoluted even for the most skilful elite players to attempt in a match, but altogether they represent a new column in football's linguistic development, where elements of the game's future vocabulary already exist and are just waiting for the sport to catch up.

Since football fans are uniquely sensitive to the language used to describe their sport, it should be acknowledged that some of the terms in this book may have alternative meanings in different regions or countries. Language drifts like smoke across borders and all countries pinch terms, magpie-like, from beyond their own frontiers, so it's for the sake of convenience that some words and phrases have been listed beneath the flag of a certain country.

Much of the language of Spanish football, for example, will be familiar to people from Hispanic America, and vice versa. There is inevitable crossover between the football vocabularies of Portugal and Brazil, Belgium and the Netherlands, France and Francophone Africa, Britain and her former colonies, and among the many nations of the Arab world.

This is by no means an exhaustive glossary, and you're invited to flag up omissions by joining the conversation at the hashtag #doyouspeakfootball (where you'll also find related pictures and videos). The aim of the book is merely to offer a flavour of the myriad ways in which football is talked about around the world. As you will discover in the pages that follow, to truly speak football is to speak a language of a thousand tongues.

Tom Williams
@tomwfootball

SOUTH AMERICA

A riot of noise, colour and skill, South American football is characterised by both the steely guile of Argentina and the vivacious technical artistry of Brazil. From Uruguay's 1924 Olympic champions to the fabled Brazil XI that elevated the sport to unparalleled heights at the 1970 World Cup, South America has furnished football with some of its most magnificent teams, and in men like Pelé, Diego Maradona, Ronaldo and Lionel Messi, it has gifted us the game's very greatest players.

Spanish is the first language in most of the countries of South America – the legacy of Spain's colonisation of the Americas – but the huge population of Brazil (208 million at the last count) means that Portuguese is the continent's majority language.

ARGENTINA

What is Argentinian football? A dribble, certainly. A beautifully weighted through ball. A roar. But also a sly dig. A crafty handball. Smoke and dust, tickertape and toilet roll, venom and violence. Blood on the terraces, poetry on the pitch.

Football came early to Argentina, the country's first recorded match taking place less than four years after the English Football Association codified the rules in 1863 and almost 30 years before the sport arrived in neighbouring Brazil. That was largely because of the huge British migrant presence in Argentina – by 1880, there were some 40,000 Britons in Buenos Aires – but in the decades that followed the country's native footballers sought to slough off the British influence in search of a playing style that they could call their own.

What emerged was a gloriously expressive but also intrinsically cunning interpretation of the sport, and with it, in tandem with the development of the game in Uruguay, came a language that was to provide the basis of a football vernacular for an entire continent.

aguante – *endurance*

From the verb *aguantar*, meaning 'to endure' or 'to bear', *aguante* refers to fans' capacity to support their club through lean times, however long they might last. Supporters who don't stick with their team through thick and thin, turning on their players when results don't go their way, might be labelled *amargos* ('bitter').

anti-fútbol

Having swept to glory at the 1957 Campeonato Sudamericano (their 11th success in the competition and fifth in 12 years), Argentina travelled to Sweden for the following year's World Cup confident of winning the tournament for the first time. Instead a badly disorganised side met with disaster, a 6-1 thrashing by Czechoslovakia in Helsingborg ending their tournament just a week after it had started. The team's group-stage exit, and the humiliating manner of it, sparked a sea change in Argentinian football. Where idealism had previously reigned, cynicism took over, and the new attitude found its truest expression in the notorious Estudiantes team of the late 1960s. Under coach Osvaldo Zubeldía, an arch-pragmatist, the side from the city of La Plata upset the established hierarchy to win the 1967 league title and followed it up with three consecutive triumphs in the Copa Libertadores. But despite their remarkable success, it's for their brutality that they're most remembered. Estudiantes were prepared to do whatever it took to gain an edge over their opponents, from physical violence to callous and carefully targeted psychological abuse. There were even stories of players carrying pins onto the pitch. Their style became known as *anti-fútbol* and it was showcased during two infamous Intercontinental Cup contests. Bobby Charlton and Denis Law were left requiring stitches after they played for Manchester United against Estudiantes in 1968, while George Best and José Hugo Medina were sent off for swinging punches at each other in the second leg at Old Trafford. United midfielder Paddy Crerand described Estudiantes as 'the dirtiest team I've played against'. Further violence during a shameful second-leg match against Milan in Buenos Aires the following year saw two Estudiantes players sent off, and culminated in Aguirre Suárez, Eduardo Manera and goalkeeper Alberto Poletti being sentenced to 30 days in jail. Poletti was also banned for life for punching Milan golden boy Gianni Rivera, although he was later pardoned. The Milan match became known as *la vergüenza de La Plata* ('the shame of La Plata') and was partly responsible for the refusal of several European teams to compete for the trophy in the years that followed. Nowadays the term *anti-fútbol* is used to deride teams who pair a defensive strategy with brazen spoiling tactics. Lionel Messi accused Rangers of playing *anti-fútbol* after

Barcelona were held to a 0-0 draw at Ibrox in the Champions League in October 2007 and Johan Cruyff employed the expression to criticise the Netherlands following their loss to Spain in the 2010 World Cup final in South Africa.

See also: *bunker* (United States), *zaburkvam betona* (Bulgaria), *park the bus* (England), *catenaccio* (Italy), *Cholismo* (Spain)

banderazo – *big flag*
A huge, pre-planned show of support for a player or team during which giant flags are waved and coloured flares set off.

barra bravas – *wild gangs*
The name given to the violent organised supporter groups whose tentacular influence spreads through all of Argentina's major clubs. Part hired muscle, part mafia gang, the *barra bravas* enjoy close ties to club directors, corrupt police officers and local politicians, enabling them to amass huge sums of money from illegal activities such as ticketing and car-parking rackets, money laundering and drug-dealing. Violence between *barras* from rival clubs has claimed hundreds of lives since their emergence in the 1950s, but in recent years clashes have increasingly been between warring factions seeking influence and control over income streams at the same club.

See also: *torcedores* (Brazil), *ultràs* (Italy), *fanaty* (Russia)

bicicleta – *stepover*
The stepover – when a player feigns a change of direction by flicking his foot around the ball – is one of football's most familiar tricks and is said to have been invented by Argentinian winger Pedro Calomino, who made his debut for Boca Juniors in June 1911. Allowed to play in pumps because he didn't like wearing football boots, Calomino was one of Boca's first idols, helping the club to four league titles. His trademark move, dubbed *la bicicleta*, delighted supporters and confounded opposition full-backs. Bologna and Italy winger Amedeo Biavati popularised the technique in Italy, where it became known as a *doppio passo* ('double step'), in the 1930s. More recently, the trick was taken to new heights by players such as Ronaldo, Denílson, Robinho and Cristiano Ronaldo, who introduced spectators to the dizzying concept of the multiple stepover.

See also: *pedaladas* (Brazil), *khawya f amra* (Morocco), *caap waa* (China), *marwaha* (Saudi Arabia)

Bilardismo

Known as *El Narigón* ('Big Nose'), Carlos Bilardo was one of the enforcers in Osvaldo Zubeldía's Estudiantes midfield (the stories about carrying pins onto the pitch were generally about him) and after retiring from playing in 1970, he succeeded Zubeldía as manager. Appointed national team coach in 1983, he brought his *anti-fútbol* principles with him. His predecessor César Luis Menotti, architect of Argentina's 1978 World Cup triumph, was an idealist. Bilardo was not. 'Football is about winning and nothing else,' he once said. Nevertheless, it was his innovative 3-5-1-1 system that freed Diego Maradona to inspire Argentina to glory at the 1986 World Cup in Mexico. Argentina also reached the final under Bilardo four years later in Italy, losing 1-0 to West Germany in a wretched game during which they had two players sent off. Argentina's two World Cup-winning managers have been pitted against each other on an ideological level ever since, with every coach that has followed in their footsteps inevitably assigned a position somewhere on the *Bilardismo–Menottismo* spectrum.

See also: *Menottismo* (Argentina)

boba – *drag-back*

One of several players to have been cursed with the 'New Maradona' tag, one-time Portsmouth man Andrés D'Alessandro at least succeeded in introducing a new trick to the game. His move *la boba* (which literally means 'the fool') involves him placing his left foot on top of the ball, rolling the ball to his left and then immediately shifting it back the other way before sprinting off. Unwitting defenders, lured in by his showy first touch, are caught flat-footed and often have to suffer the added indignity of having the ball slipped between their legs.

botineras – *wives and girlfriends*

Botineras is the Argentinian equivalent of the British term 'wives and girlfriends' (usually shortened to 'WAGs') and describes the female partners of professional footballers. The word comes from *botín* ('boot'), which can refer to a boot of either the high-heeled or football variety. *Botineras* was the name of a football-themed soap opera that ran on Argentinian television between 2009 and 2010.

cinco – *five*

Much like everywhere else in the world, the 4-2-4 formation took hold in Argentina after Brazil prevailed with the system at the 1958 World Cup. An outmoded 2-3-5 configuration had previously held sway and while the two wing-halves (who wore shirt numbers 4 and 6) dropped back to create a back four, the centre-half (who wore the number 5 shirt) remained in place as a holding midfielder. *Cinco* is therefore used in Argentina as a name for a defensive midfielder. The roll call of greats to have worn the shirt at international level includes Luis Monti, who represented Argentina and Italy, Néstor 'Pipo' Rossi, dubbed 'The Howler of the Americas' for his noisy on-pitch organising, Antonio Rattín, battling captain of the 1960s, and the impossibly elegant former Real Madrid midfielder Fernando Redondo. At the 1978 World Cup, one of three at which Argentina decided to arrange their squad list in alphabetical order, the number 5 shirt went to goalkeeper Ubaldo Fillol. When Manuel Pellegrini started playing with two holding midfielders during his time as coach of San Lorenzo and River Plate, the system was baptised *doble cinco* ('double five'). The term *cinco grandes* ('big five'), meanwhile, refers to the country's five giant clubs: River Plate, Boca Juniors, Independiente, Racing Club and San Lorenzo.

See also: *volante* (Brazil), *Makélélé role* (England), *pihkatappi* (Finland), *sentinelle* (France), *stofzuiger* (Netherlands), *trinco* (Portugal)

enganche – *hook*

The playmaker or number 10 is afforded special status all over the world, most notably in Eastern Europe and the Latin countries, but nowhere are they worshipped quite as ardently as in Argentina. Known as an *enganche* (literally meaning 'hook'), the Argentinian playmaker is responsible not only for knitting together midfield and attack, but also for setting his team's passing rhythm and giving them an identity on the pitch. Maradona and Messi are Argentina's most celebrated number 10s, but the country's most classic *enganches* have been men like Ricardo Bochini, Maradona's idol, and Juan Román Riquelme, the brooding Boca star. Neither player was blessed with great physical attributes, but both had the ability to reduce an entire defence to ruins with a simple, devastating through pass.

See also: *ponta de lança* (Brazil)

gambeta – *dribble*

Synonymous with Maradona and Messi, *gambeta* is the name given to the jinking, weaving dribble that has been an Argentinian speciality almost since the moment the game arrived there. It's believed to come from *gaucho* literature and to refer to the distinctive running motion of an ostrich. (An alternative theory is that it stems from the Italian world *gamba*, meaning 'leg', which seeped into Argentinian parlance via *Lunfardo*, the Italian-influenced slang of tango and the

Buenos Aires underworld.) The most famous *gambeta* of them all was the one that carried Maradona through the heart of the England defence en route to scoring *el gol del siglo* ('the goal of the century') at the 1986 World Cup.

golazo – *great goal*

The term for a stunning strike, roared by commentators throughout Latin America and in many parts of southern Europe. The stem is *gol*, from the English 'goal', and the suffix *-azo* carries the basic meaning of 'big' but also conveys the sense of a hit or strike.

gol de vestuario – *changing-room goal*

A goal scored in the opening seconds of a match.

See also: *hol v rozdyahal'nyu* (Ukraine)

gol olímpico – *Olympic goal*

Uruguay's triumph at the 1924 Olympic Games in Paris was a breakthrough moment for rioplatense football, but amid the admiration, there were covetous glances from neighbours Argentina, who had not made the trip to France. Argentina challenged Uruguay to a two-legged play-off on their return and following a closely fought 1-1 draw in Montevideo (and a return leg that had to be abandoned because of crowd trouble), the teams met in Buenos Aires on 2 October. After 15 minutes, Hurácan left-winger Cesáreo Onzari opened the scoring with one of the most famous goals in South American football history when his corner from the left curled straight into the net. The International FA Board had only modified the rules to allow goals to be scored direct from corners less than four months previously. Argentina were awarded victory after Uruguay's players walked off the pitch at 2-1 down following skirmishes with stone-throwing fans and Onzari's goal was burnished into history as a reminder of the day his country bested the Olympic champions. To this day, goals scored direct from corners are known across Latin America as 'Olympic goals'. Colombia's Marcos Coll is the only player to have scored a *gol olímpico* at a World Cup after he embarrassed the great Lev Yashin during a 4-4 group-stage draw against the Soviet Union at the 1962 tournament in Chile. The USA's Megan Rapinoe brought things full circle in London in 2012 when she curled a left-wing corner inside the near post against Canada to become the first player to score a *gol olímpico* at the actual Olympics.

See also: *sukhoi list* (Russia)

A goal scored direct from a corner is known in Latin America as a *gol olímpico*

hacer la cama – *to make the bed*

When a squad of players is believed to be conspiring to get their coach the sack, they will be accused of *haciendo la cama* ('making the bed'). Players suspected of involvement in coach sackings are known as *camarilleros* (a slang term effectively meaning 'bed-makers'). *Hacer la cama* can also refer to the actions of a player who ducks out of an aerial challenge with a leaping opponent, flattening his back into a ledge and sending his adversary toppling to the ground. It's known in Brazil as *cama de gato* ('cat's cradle') and in Italy as a *ponte* ('bridge').

ladrón – *thief*

Bellowed at a teammate who has an opponent creeping up behind him, this is the Argentinian equivalent of 'man on'. It's used throughout Hispanic America, as well as in Brazil (*ladrão*). A Mexican variation is *tienes cola*, meaning 'you have a tail'.

See also: *mala leđa* (Montenegro), *polícia* (Portugal), *house* (Republic of Ireland), *gorísh* (Russia), *yau gwai* (China)

la nuestra – *our way*

Expatriates from Britain brought football to Argentina in 1867, but as the game took hold its new practitioners came to rebel against the muscular, physical British style in favour of something subtler and more authentically

Argentinian. Where British teams favoured long balls, hard running and high crosses, Argentinian football was all about *gambetas*, short passes, individual expression and guile. It came to be known as *la nuestra* ('our way') and it found its most enduring form in the great River Plate team of the 1940s, nicknamed *la Máquina* ('the Machine'), whose players were famed almost as much for their free-wheeling behaviour off the pitch as for their free-scoring football on it. So much of what defines Argentina's attitude towards football – the emphasis on dribbling, creativity and mischief, the central symbolism of the *enganche* – has its roots in the belief that there's a certain style of play to which all Argentinian players and all Argentinian teams must aspire. 'Once you lose your style, it's like giving up your soul,' said Norberto 'Beto' Alonso, River Plate's fêted number 10. 'You can play well in any style, but you can only play well in the Argentinian way with one style: *la nuestra*.'

la pausa – *the pause*

Timing, they say, is everything and that certainly holds true on the football pitches of Argentina. *La pausa* is a quintessentially Argentinian expression that describes the moment when a playmaker delays a pass just long enough to allow a teammate to get into the ideal position before releasing the ball. It's the football equivalent of a sniper timing a shot between heartbeats, and players like Bochini, Maradona and Riquelme have turned it into an art form.

Mano de Dios – *Hand of God*

Has a piece of blatant cheating ever been given a more lyrical description? Maradona enraged England and scandalised the world by punching Argentina's opening goal past Peter Shilton in the 1986 World Cup quarter-final at Mexico City's Estadio Azteca. Asked how he had scored the goal, Maradona said it had been '*un poco con la cabeza de Maradona, y un poco con la Mano de Dios*' ('a little with the head of Maradona, and a little with the hand of God'). Both teams had avoided talking about the Falklands War in the build-up to the game, but years later Maradona said his first goal had been a form of revenge for the 1982 conflict, which claimed 649 Argentinian lives. 'Before the match, we said football had nothing to do with the Malvinas war,' he wrote in his 2004 autobiography *El Diego*. 'But we knew a lot of Argentine kids died, shot down like little birds. This was revenge.' When Thierry Henry used his hand to tee up William Gallas for the decisive goal in France's World Cup qualifying play-off against Ireland in November 2009, it was variously dubbed *the Hand of Gaul*, *le Hand of God* and *the Hand of Frog*.

manos de manteca – *butter hands*
As belonging to a clumsy goalkeeper.

marianela
Juan Evaristo won Olympic silver with Argentina in 1928 and played alongside his younger brother, Mario, in the 1930 World Cup final. The wing-half was credited with inventing a trick known as the *marianela*, which has since disappeared from the game. Typically used by a defender who found himself crowded out by opponents, the trick resembled a *rabona*, but at the point of contact with the ball, the player balletically twirled to face backwards and used his toes to scoop the ball back to a teammate in a deeper position.

See also: *rabona* (Argentina)

Menottismo
The *yang* to Carlos Bilardo's *yin*, César Luis Menotti was a left-wing intellectual who felt that his business as a football coach was nothing less than to bring joy to the masses. A slender, long-haired chain-smoker, Menotti believed that by guiding an attacking Argentina team to their first World Cup success as hosts of the 1978 tournament, he had helped to restore a sense of the old, carefree Argentina at a time when the country was in the murderous grip of dictator Jorge Rafael Videla's right-wing military *junta*. Argentina's triumph was, though, less than spotless, with other teams complaining of intimidation and uneven refereeing. Eyebrows were also raised when, needing to beat Peru by four goals to reach the final, the hosts cantered to a 6-0 victory, although the Peruvians rejected accusations that they had been bought off. Menotti, known as *El Flaco* ('The Thin One'), became an outspoken critic of his successor, Bilardo, and said the negative football played by Argentina at the 1990 World Cup made him 'ashamed as an Argentinian'. The philosophical conflict between the two men remains a running theme in Argentinian football.

See also: *Bilardismo* (Argentina)

morfón – *ball-hog*
A *Lunfardo* (Buenos Aires slang) term derived from the Italian *morfa*, which means 'mouth'. When inveterate dribbler Mauro Zárate joined Internazionale

on loan from Lazio in 2011, his contract contained an unusual assist bonus, which was described in Argentina as an *'anti-morfón* clause'. A similar term, *mamón*, meaning 'sucker', is used in Costa Rica.

See also: *amarrabola* (Peru), *ballverliebt* (Germany), *chupón* (Spain)

palomita – *little pigeon*

Diving headers in Argentina are known as *palomitas*, the most famous of which was scored by Aldo Pedro Poy. Playing for Rosario Central against their local rivals Newell's Old Boys in the semi-finals of the Argentinian championship in December 1971, Poy scored with a flying header to secure a 1-0 victory. Rosario beat San Lorenzo in the final, making them the first team from outside Buenos Aires province to become champions of Argentina. The club's fans mark the goal's anniversary every year by getting together with Poy to recreate it. In Spain, *palomita* also refers to a goalkeeper's diving save.

See also: *gol de peixinho* (Brazil), *een Beb Bakhuys* (Netherlands)

papá

In the peculiar language of Argentinian fandom, to get the better of a rival is to become their *papá*, and it's a theme revisited time and time again in the country's football chants. When Argentina reached the World Cup final in Brazil in 2014, a taunting ode to their hosts, sung to the tune of 'Bad Moon Rising', became the tournament's unofficial theme tune. *'Brasil, decime que se sienté,'* ('Brazil, tell me how it feels'), they sang, *'Tener en casa a tu papá'* ('To have your papa in your home'). To the immense relief of Brazilians everywhere, Germany decided that Argentina had been up well past their bedtime, beating them 1-0 through Mario Götze's extra-time goal.

¿Para qué te traje? – *Why did I bring you?*

Popularised by Argentinian commentator Juan Manuel 'Bambino' Pons, who typically delivers it in an exaggerated wail, this phrase is uttered in exasperation when a player misplaces a pass or slices an attempt in the direction of the corner flag. Pons says he picked up the expression from a coach called Ricardo Trillin. It has become so popular that it has fallen into use colloquially as a term for an embarrassing blunder – a striker who spoons the ball over an open goal or a goalkeeper who fails to keep out a tame shot will be said to have committed a *para qué te traje*.

pecho frío – *cold chest*

A term used to describe a player who goes missing when his team need him, thought to have been a *gaucho* expression for a work-shy horse. It was often used against Riquelme (chiefly, it has to be said, by River fans), who won everything with Boca but ultimately failed to deliver for the national team.

See also: *pipoqueiro* (Brazil)

pibe – *kid*

Incarnating Argentinian football's inherent romanticism is the *pibe* (meaning 'kid' or 'urchin'), an impish child footballer self-schooled on rough dirt pitches amid the shadows cast by city tower blocks, impudent, irrepressible and breathtakingly skilful. In 1928 the renowned Argentinian football writer Borocotó, editor of sports magazine *El Gráfico*, proposed a statue in honour of the *pibe*, who he wrote should have 'a dirty face, a mane of hair rebelling against the comb', 'intelligent, roving, trickster' eyes and a 'rag ball' at his feet. There have been many *pibes*, and there are likely to be many more, but the most celebrated of them all is Maradona, who was dubbed *El Pibe de Oro* ('The Golden Kid'). Another famous *pibe* was Colombia's pom-pom-haired playmaker Carlos Valderrama, known simply as *El Pibe*.

potrero

Central to the Argentinian conception of football, *potreros* are the mythologised baked-earth pitches where the country's greats are formed. They occupy a special place in the popular imagination as the sites where a fledgling player grazes his knees for the first time and learns, in overcrowded games on dusty, uneven surfaces, the trickery and slipperiness fundamental to *la nuestra*. Originally the word *potrero* referred to areas of the *pampa* ('prairie') managed by *gauchos* where horses and livestock were free to graze. It began to be used in a football context when Borocotó conflated it with the *baldío* ('wasteland'), the name given to the vacant urban lots that lay between buildings in Buenos Aires where chaotic informal football matches would be played. In Borocotó's eyes, whereas British football was something that was taught on the 'blackboard', Argentinian football could only be learned on the *potrero*, a lawless eternal playground where *pibes* never had to worry about growing up.

See also: *tanner ba' player* (Scotland), *kora sharab* (Egypt), *sakora park* (Ghana)

promedio – *average*
After San Lorenzo were relegated in 1981, it was decided that demotion from Argentina's Primera División would be determined by teams' points-per-game averages over the two most recent seasons (increased to three in 1984). The move was effectively made to help protect Argentina's *cinco grandes* from going down, but it has not always been successful, as demonstrated by River's shock relegation in 2011.

rabona
Like many of football's most durable skill moves, the *rabona* probably has many inventors, but in Argentina it's known as the creation of Ricardo Infante. The Estudiantes striker used the technique to score a stupendous goal from 35 yards during a game against Rosario Central in September 1948, wrapping his kicking foot behind his standing leg to strike the ball and lob the goalkeeper. *El Gráfico* dressed the Argentina international up as a schoolboy for a front-cover picture (a play both on his surname and the fact that 'Estudiantes' means 'Students'), accompanied by the punning headline: *'El infante que se hizo la rabona'*, meaning 'The child who played hooky' (or skipped school). *Rabona* became the default word for the trick and has also lent its name to a tango step. The move was popularised in Italy in the 1970s by winger Giovanni 'Cocò' Roccotelli, who played for Cagliari, Ascoli and Torino. In Italy it was known as an *incrociata* ('crossed kick').

See also: *marianela* (Argentina), *chaleira* (Brazil)

ratonera – *mouse nest*
A shot that flies into one of the goal's bottom corners will be said to have ended up in *la ratonera*.

sotana – *cassock*
The most common term for a nutmeg in Argentina is *caño* (meaning 'pipe'), but *sotana* is also used. It comes from something that might have been teasingly said to a player who'd just been nutmegged: *'La próxima vez, ponete una sotana!'* ('Next time, wear a cassock!'). In time the taunt came to be used as a synonym for the skill itself.

See also: *dimije* (Bosnia and Herzegovina), *kupite mu pregaču* (Croatia), *foul thawb* (Qatar)

tiki-tiki

Huracán lost out to Vélez Sarsfield in the 2009 Clausura title race, but the sparkling football played by Ángel Cappa's side left a lasting impression. Players like Javier Pastore and Matías Defederico helped to produce a fresh and fizzing style of play based on nutmegs, back-heels and first-time passes, which became known as *tiki-tiki*.

See also: *tiki-taka* (Spain)

tronco – trunk

A tall player with very basic technique.

See also: *perna de pau* (Brazil), *pieds carrés* (France), *duffer* (Republic of Ireland), *derevo* (Russia), *drvo* (Serbia), *tuercebotas* (Spain)

viveza – sharpness

Sometimes referred to as *viveza criolla* ('creole cunning'), this term describes a rule-bending wiliness that sits at the heart of Argentinian culture and, by extension, Argentinian football. Also known as *picardía* ('craftiness'), it refers to a way of life based on cadging and swindling, surviving on your wits and taking advantage of honest fools. In football it has informed a host of controversies, such as the claim that Brazil left-back Branco was duped into drinking drugged water during Argentina's semi-final victory over their neighbours at the 1990 World Cup. For Maradona, a paragon of *picardía*, scoring with his hand against England was not cheating, but 'sticking my hand in the pocket of an Englishman and removing the money that did not belong to them'.

See also: *malandragem* (Brazil)

BOLIVIA

One of only two landlocked countries in the Americas (the other being neighbouring Paraguay), Bolivia has sent a team to three World Cups (1930, 1950 and 1994) and tasted glory as the host nation of the Campeonato Sudamericano de Fútbol in 1963.

The national team's nickname, *Los Altiplanicos* ('The Highlanders'), reflects the high altitude at which they play their home games in La Paz, where Maradona's Argentina memorably succumbed to a 6-1 defeat in April 2009.

gol de apenitas – *just barely goal*

In Bolivia, when a goal is scored with no margin for error – a chip that evades the goalkeeper's outstretched hands by millimetres, for example, or a shot squeezed through a phalanx of defenders – it's known colloquially as a *gol de apenitas*, which is drawn from the word *apenas*, meaning 'barely'. If it's allied to a supreme display of technique in the build-up, it might go down as a *gol de lujo* ('delux goal'). A fortuitous goal, such as one that depends on an unpredictable ricochet, is a *gol de chiripa* ('fluke goal').

BRAZIL

If football in the first half of the 20th century was a sport played in black and white, it was Brazil that thrust the game into luminous Technicolor.

Initially the preserve of the metropolitan elites, football spread rapidly through Brazil's impoverished suburbs, shanty towns and *favelas* in the 1920s and it was here that the country's inimitable football culture was born. Brazilian football was playful and flamboyant, highly individualistic and ceaselessly inventive. It came to define the country like nothing else.

Beginning in 1970, colour TV broadcasts of the World Cup served to imprint the dashing skills and canary-yellow shirts of Pelé, Zico and their teammates upon the global consciousness. Yet it was radio commentary that soundtracked the burgeoning love affair between the people of Brazil and *o jogo bonito* ('the beautiful game') in the 1940s and 1950s. Reporters such as Rebelo Júnior (the first man to cry '*Goooooool!*' from the commentary box), Édson Leite and Ary Barroso developed a rich, intricate lexicon teeming with creative metaphors and curious analogies. The language reflected the country's singular attachment to the game and informed the beguilingly quirky tapestry of words and images that is Brazil's modern football dictionary.

caneta – *pen*

Nutmeg a Brazilian and you're spoilt for choice in terms of the taunts you could hit them with. The art of slipping the ball between an opponent's legs is variously likened to giving someone a pen (*caneta*), a little egg (*ovinho*), a little window (*janelinha*), a little roll (*rolinho*) and a little skirt (*sainha*).

See also: *huacha* (Peru), *salad* (Jamaica), *Gurkerl* (Austria), *jesle* (Czech Republic), *nutmeg* (England), *klobbi* (Iceland), *panna* (Netherlands), *cueca* (Portugal), *bayda* (Morocco), *yalli* (Senegal), *shibobo* (South Africa), *deya* (Zimbabwe), *lawd daak* (Thailand)

chaleira

Known as a *rabona* elsewhere in the world, in Brazil the move that involves hooking your foot behind your standing leg to strike the ball is called a *chaleira*. It has a complicated etymology that begins with Charles Miller, the former Southampton schoolboy who's seen as the father of Brazilian football. Born in Brazil to a Scottish father and Brazilian mother, Miller helped to establish the sport in São Paulo following his return from studying in England in 1894 and was credited with inventing a skill that involved flicking the ball forwards using the heel. It became known as the *charles* (or *Charles Miller*) and, intriguingly, it was more closely associated with defenders than forwards. When Brazil played their first international game in 1914, a combined Rio/São Paulo selection beating a touring Exeter City team 2-0, it was Píndaro, Brazil's right-back, who was hailed in contemporary reports for his adroit use of the *charles*. Over time, *charles* morphed into *chaleira* (which has an alternative meaning of 'kettle') and came to be understood to refer to a *rabona*, although there's not 100 per cent unanimity about what it means. For some people in Brazil it refers not to a *rabona*, but to the move known in English as a 'rainbow flick': when a player grips the ball between his feet and then flicks it over an opponent's head (which in Brazil is generally called a *lambreta*). When a player lifts one foot into the air and uses the heel of their other foot to strike the ball (a variation on the *chaleira*), it's known as a *letra* ('letter'). A player might look to score with a *letra* from a low cross that has been played slightly behind him.

See also: *rabona* (Argentina)

chapéu – hat

There's nothing in football quite as emasculating, quite as violating, as a nutmeg, but having the ball breezily lifted over your head by an opponent comes pretty close. In Brazil it's known as a *chapéu*. Perhaps the most famous *chapéu* in Brazilian football was pulled off by a 17-year-old Pelé en route to scoring the first of his two goals in the 1958 World Cup final against hosts Sweden. The Santos starlet chested down Nílton Santos's left-wing cross, hoisted the ball high over Bengt Gustavsson and then (having eluded Gustavsson's crude, thigh-high lunge) speared a low volley past goalkeeper Kalle Svensson. Reflecting the mongrel nature of Brazil's football vocabulary, *chapéu* is taken from the French *chapeau*. The move is also known as a *lençol* ('sheet') or *balão* ('balloon').

See also: *sombrero* (Spain), *baptiser* (Cameroon), *kanzu* (Kenya), *height* (Nigeria), *deff ko watt* (Senegal), *kanyumba* (Zambia)

Brazilian showman Ronaldinho gives an opponent a *chapéu* ('hat') – a trick also known as a *sombrero*

chute por cobertura – *roof shot*

A finish particularly favoured by Brazilian forwards – notably Romário and Robinho – the *chute por cobertura* is a chip or lob that sends the ball in a graceful arc over the head of a stranded goalkeeper and into the net (putting a 'roof' over the keeper's head).

See also: *pichenette* (France), *cherpak* (Russia), *vaselina* (Spain)

craque – *ace*

Didi. Pelé. Garrincha. Zico. Romário. Ronaldo. Ronaldinho. Neymar. It's little surprise that Brazil is obsessed by the concept of the star player or *craque*. The stars of Brazil's five World Cup wins trip off the tongue – Didi and Pelé in 1958, Garrincha in 1962, Pelé in 1970, Romário in 1994, Ronaldo in 2002 – and the country's football supporters cling tightly to the notion that the national team is not complete without a shining figurehead who embodies the virtues of *futebol arte*. The *craque* can be a winger, a playmaker or a striker, but he must be a virtuoso, a player capable of changing the course of a match or even a tournament with an audacious flash of inspiration. Before games were televised, a player who starred in a match might be called a *craque do dia seguinte* ('next day ace'), meaning he could expect to be eulogised in the following day's papers. The word derives from the English military term 'crack', once used to denote an elite soldier, but is believed to have filtered into Brazil's football language from horse racing (a 'crack' being a champion horse).

See also: *Primgeiger* (Austria)

dar um chocolate – to give (someone) a chocolate

Following a crushing 4-0 win for Vasco da Gama against Internacional at the Maracanã in January 1981, radio journalist Washington Rodrigues decided to play the song *El Bodeguero*, which contains the snappy Spanish refrain: *'Toma chocolate, paga lo que debes'* ('Take some chocolate, pay what you owe'). One-sided thrashings subsequently became known as *chocolates*.

de três dedos – with three toes

This expression describes a shot or pass played with the outside of the foot, a skill most famously exhibited when Roberto Carlos scored his jaw-dropping banana free-kick against France in 1997. When the inside of the foot is used, the expression is *bater na orelha da bola* ('to hit the ball's ear').

See also: *papegøje* (Denmark), *trivela* (Portugal), *shvedka* (Russia), *NASA pass* (Nigeria), *outfoot* (Pakistan)

drible da foquinha – seal dribble

Completely new technical innovations are rare in football and when they do occur, they don't always endure. So when word got out that a 17-year-old Brazilian player was flicking the ball into the air and then running along bouncing it on his brow, the football world immediately took notice. Kerlon Moura Souza, known as Kerlon, devised the technique and would regularly employ it in matches, whether for his club side Cruzeiro or the Brazil Under-17 team. Once he had the ball in the air – often achieved by simply scooping it from ground level to head height with his foot – he was difficult to stop, and despite being obliged to keep both eyes on the ball as he juggled it, he was capable of making sudden changes in direction. It was christened the *drible da foquinha* and it brought its inventor worldwide fame. Confronted by a problem that they'd never encountered before, defenders more often than not employed foul means to stop Kerlon, either barging into him or, as in the case of one opponent in an Under-17 match against Colombia, simply booting him in the chest. One assailant, Atlético Mineiro right-back Dyego Rocha Coelho, was given a 120-day ban – subsequently reduced to five games – after flattening him with a cynical forearm smash during a match in September 2007. Coelho expressed remorse, but was not universally seen as the guilty party (Brazil coach Dunga wondered aloud whether Kerlon would have tried the trick had his team been losing at the time). Kerlon's party piece made him one of football's first YouTube stars, but injuries prevented him from making an impact in Europe and he drifted from team to team in Japan, the United States, Malta and Slovakia. 'I did a pre-season with José Mourinho at Inter, but I never tried the dribble,' Kerlon said of his time at Internazionale. 'If [Marco] Materazzi hit me, I would fly away.' His career is destined never to recapture its teenage heights, but Kerlon's name continues to resonate as a testament to the pioneering spirit of Brazilian football.

drible de vaca – *cow dribble*
Drible de vaca describes the skill employed by a player who knocks the ball past an opponent on one side and collects it on the other. It may have originated in informal matches played on scrubland, where encountering livestock was an occupational hazard. Sometimes referred to as a *meia-lua* ('half-moon'), it's a close cousin of the *drible de Pelé*, the name given to the outlandish manoeuvre performed by Brazil's number 10 against Uruguay in the dying seconds of the 1970 World Cup semi-final in Guadalajara. Racing onto Tostão's pass from the inside-left channel, Pelé took advancing goalkeeper Ladislao Mazurkiewicz out of the game with an outrageous dummy, letting the ball pass between himself and Mazurkiewicz before running around him. Kenneth Wolstenholme, commentating for the BBC, could scarcely believe what he was seeing. 'Pelé, sprinting in at speed!' he cried. 'And he's going to get a fourth! Oh what, what *genius!*' The pace on the ball took Pelé wide of the goal to the right and with a defender racing back to cover he overcooked his attempt to accommodate for the angle, firing a fraction wide of the far post. 'The dummy was a moment, just something you do,' Pelé said. 'You can't plan it. It happens, it's a reaction. But I really don't know why I missed. When I went round the keeper, I thought, "OK, I'm going to put the ball in before the defender." But then I saw he was

going very quickly and I thought, "I'd better be quick before him," and maybe I rushed it.' The move has since been perfected by players including Zico, River Plate icon Norberto 'Beto' Alonso and former Manchester United winger Jesper Blomqvist, all of whom went one better than Pelé by dummying the keeper and scoring.

See also: *grand pont* (France)

elástico – *elastic band*

Viewers of the 1998 UEFA Cup final between Internazionale and Lazio were treated to a truly exceptional display of skill by Ronaldo that took several slow-motion replays to decipher. Minutes after putting Inter 3-0 up at Parc des Princes, Ronaldo had the ball headed to his feet by teammate Javier Zanetti. The Inter number 10 evaded one challenge from Guerino Gottardi by shifting the ball from left foot to right and when the Lazio substitute launched himself into a second tackle, close to Inter's left-hand touchline, Ronaldo seemed somehow to glue the ball to the toe of his right boot, swishing it one way and then the other before sprinting down the touchline, leaving the incredulous Gottardi sprawled in his wake. It looked like witchcraft, but the replays revealed that Gottardi had in fact succumbed to a piece of skill known in Brazil as an *elástico*, which the country's footballers have mastered like nobody else. Also known as a *culebrita* ('little snake'), or, in English, a 'flip-flap', the move (when performed by a right-footer) involves a player using his toes to tease the ball from left to right, before suddenly snapping it back in the opposite direction, sending the ball quickly one way and then the other, and inevitably leaving the nearest defender clutching at thin air. Popularised in recent years by Ronaldinho and Cristiano Ronaldo, the move is most closely connected with Roberto Rivellino, the moustachioed and effortlessly gifted left-winger from Brazil's 1970 world champions. Rivellino was initially credited as its inventor, but he actually learned it from a Japanese-Brazilian teammate called Sergio Echigo, with whom he played at Corinthians in 1964. 'I saw him do it once and I said, "Hey, Japanese, what's that trick?"' Rivellino explained. 'He said, "It's easy Rive, I'll teach you it." He says now that he invented it, but I perfected it.'

See also: *culebrita* (El Salvador), *el ghoraf* (Algeria)

embaixadinhas – keepy-uppies

Brazil may be the fatherland of *o jogo bonito*, but there are strict unspoken rules about where and when it's acceptable to showboat. A piece of skill will be tolerated if it's used to beat or even embarrass an opponent, but when skill becomes superfluous, when it's used purely to goad or humiliate, the consequences can be painful. Kerlon learned the hard way what can happen when a young buck tries to teach grisly old pros new tricks in Brazil. Another player to fall foul of the showboat police was Edílson, who produced a notorious display of *embaixadinhas* amid the dying embers of the 1999 Paulista state championship final. With victory for Corinthians over his previous club Palmeiras already secure, Edílson collected the ball in front of the dug-outs and began juggling it, flicking it into the air five times and then provocatively allowing it to roll down his back. Incensed, Palmeiras players Júnior and Paulo Nunes assailed Edílson with flying kicks and chased him down the pitch, sparking a mass brawl that brought the match to an immediate end. The result stood, but the incident cost Edílson – appropriately nicknamed *Capetinha* or 'Little Devil' – his place in Brazil's triumphant 1999 Copa América squad, which went to a 19-year-old Ronaldinho. Asked in 2011 if he regretted what he had done, Edílson replied: 'No way! The keepy-uppies marked my career. They were part of my life. To this day I am hailed by Corinthians fans.' In a May 2014 exhibition match to mark the opening of Corinthians' new stadium, the Itaquerão, Edílson produced an impromptu repeat performance, drawing roars of approval from the crowd. Off the pitch, ball-juggling skills are held in high regard. Several Brazilians have held world records for keepy-uppies, including Milene Domingues, model and ex-wife of Ronaldo. Aged 17, she kept a ball airborne for nine hours and six minutes (making a total of 55,187 touches), cradling it on the back of her neck when she had to eat, drink or go to the toilet. *Embaixadinhas* is probably derived from the verb *baixar*, which means 'to lower' or 'to let fall'.

fazer cera – to make wax

When a player whose team are winning lingers over a throw-in or a goalkeeper takes an age to take a goal-kick, he will be accused of *fazendo cera* ('making wax'), which is not an enterprise you should think about undertaking if you're pushed for time.

See also: *melina* (Italy)

ficar sem pai nem mãe *– to be left without father or mother*
While they can be sniffy about excessive displays of skill, Brazilians nonetheless take deep delight in seeing a defender torn to pieces by an enterprising attacker. A forlorn player beaten all ends up by an opponent may be said to have been left *sem pai nem mãe*. Which is a bit dark.

folha seca *– dry leaf*
Players like Cristiano Ronaldo (when his efforts do not sail into Row Z) and the former Lyon midfielder Juninho Pernambucano have acquainted modern football audiences with free-kicks that confound goalkeepers by suddenly dipping as they approach the goal, but the man credited with inventing the technique was Didi, inspiration behind Brazil's World Cup triumphs in 1958 and 1962. The graceful midfielder's style of free-kick, which involved hitting across the ball with the outside of his foot, became known as *folha seca*, due to the way the ball imitated the descent of a falling leaf, and brought him five of his 21 international goals.

See also: *banaanipotku* (Finland), *la maledetta* (Italy), *mukaitenshūto* (Japan)

frango *– chicken*
As the opening scene in the 2002 Brazilian crime epic *City of God* testifies, a chicken can be a slippery thing. Appropriately, then, when a goalkeeper allows the ball to squirm from his grasp and into the net, it's known as a 'chicken'. A goalkeeper prone to blunders may be dubbed a *frangueiro* or, alternatively, a *mão de alface* ('lettuce hand'). Brazil has a long and rather unpleasant history of castigating goalkeepers for mistakes. Most famously, Moacir Barbosa became a national pariah after being blamed for the goal that gave Uruguay a shock win over hosts Brazil in the deciding match of the 1950 World Cup. One of Barbosa's successors, Manga, found himself immortalised in the term *mangueiradas* (a name given to goalkeeping blunders) after his error allowed Portugal to score their opening goal in a 3-1 win that eliminated Brazil from the 1966 World Cup at Goodison Park, the Botafogo goalkeeper slapping Eusébio's left-wing cross right onto the grateful head of António Simões.

See also: *but casquette* (France), *birthuz* (Israel)

gandula *– ball boy*
In the popular imagination, this is a corruption of the surname of Bernardo Gandulla, an Argentinian forward who moved to Vasco da Gama amid great

fanfare in 1939 but spent most of his time fielding stray balls from the sidelines. However, there's evidence that the term was being used to describe ball boys well before Gandulla's arrival in Rio de Janeiro, with his experience at Vasco serving only to reinforce its meaning. It probably comes from the archaic Portuguese word *gandulo*, meaning 'slacker' or 'beggar'.

gol de peixinho – *little fish goal*

Several countries equate diving headers with fish, the common denominator being horizontal, head-first movement, but in Brazil the *gol de peixinho* owes its name to Peixinho, a former São Paulo winger who scored the first ever goal at Éstadio do Morumbi. Born Arnaldo Poffo Garcia, he was dubbed Peixinho ('Little Fish') in honour of his father, Peixe ('Fish'), who played for Santos – whose nickname, confusingly, is 'Peixe' – in the 1940s. Peixinho was in the starting line-up when São Paulo played Sporting Lisbon in a friendly to inaugurate the Morumbi on 2 October 1960. In the 12th minute he made history by flinging himself at a right-wing cross from teammate Jonas to head home the only goal of the game. Unlike with a true comic-book diving header, Peixinho managed to land on his feet after propelling the ball into the net, but his name has nonetheless become a reference point in the domain.

See also: *palomita* (Argentina), *een Beb Bakhuys* (Netherlands)

gol de placa – *plaque goal*

Brazilian football fans, traditionally, have been suspicious of the instant replay. Football in Brazil occupies a territory that lies somewhere between fact and fantasy. Details quite simply spoil the fun, so rather than a definitive account of what happened, the video replay is felt to provide only one possible interpretation among many. As Nelson Rodrigues, the playwright and football writer, was fond of saying: 'If the videotape shows it's a penalty, then all the worse for the videotape.' The goal considered the greatest ever scored at Rio's iconic Maracanã was seen by only those who were there to witness it with their own eyes. In a match on 5 March 1961 that wasn't filmed by television cameras, Santos were 1-0 up against Fluminense when Pelé, who had earlier opened the scoring, picked up the ball on the edge of his own penalty area following a save by goalkeeper Laercio. Setting off downfield, he weaved through a swarm of opponents with a series of jinks and feints before breaking into the penalty area and drilling a crisp shot into the bottom-left corner. The following day's edition of *O Globo* newspaper reported that the strike drew a standing ovation lasting 'nearly two full minutes'. Even Fluminense's fans felt moved to join in. Journalist Joelmir Beting, covering the game for *O Esporte*, successfully mounted a campaign to have the goal commemorated with a bronze plaque, and days later Pelé returned to the stadium for the official unveiling. The plaque, which remains in place, reads: 'On this pitch on 5/3/1961, Pelé scored the greatest goal in the history of the Maracanã.' It became known as the *gol de placa* – the goal worthy of a plaque. Yet Pelé felt that his best goal had come two years earlier when, in a Paulista state championship match against Juventus, he controlled a cross from Dorval on his chest, lifted the ball over three defenders in succession and then nodded it into the net. The cameras weren't there for that one either.

gol do meio da rua – *goal from the middle of the street*
An expression that brings to mind the humble origins of many of Brazil's greatest players, a goal scored from exceptionally long range might be said to have been scored from *o meio da rua*. In Brazil, the most famous *gol do meio da rua* is a *gol* that wasn't: Pelé's 66-yard skyrocket against Czechoslovakia at the 1970 World Cup, which sailed a foot wide of the right-hand post. When a player succeeds in scoring from the halfway line, Brazilians will say that they've scored *o gol que Pelé não fez* ('the goal that Pelé didn't score').

gorduchinha – *little pudgy one*
In Brazil, love of football naturally finds expression in love of the ball itself. As the Portuguese word for a ball is a feminine noun (*a bola*), it's exclusively referred to in female terms. Its many nicknames include *menina* ('girl') and *gorduchinha* ('little pudgy one'), and it was also referred to in the past using women's names like Maria or Margarida. Coined by famous radio commentator Osmar Santos in the 1970s, *gorduchinha* was touted as a potential name for the official 2014 World Cup ball, only for *brazuca* (a slang term for people from Brazil) to get the nod.

See also: *la pecosa* (Colombia), *la bendita* (Ecuador), *bubamara* (Bosnia and Herzegovina)

jogar de salto alto – *to play in high heels*
Used to describe players or teams who turn up for a game believing victory is already assured.

See also: *zvyozdnaya bolezn'* (Russia)

lambreta – *scooter*

One of football's most complicated – and brash – skill moves, the *lambreta* involves cradling the ball against one heel with your other foot before flicking it over your opponent's head and running past them to collect it. It's also known in Brazil as a *carretilha* ('reel') and in the English-speaking world as a 'rainbow flick'. A trick beloved of Neymar, who often lands himself in hot water with his opponents for trying it, its inventor in Brazil is held to be another Santos showboater. Alexandre de Carvalho Kaneco, a right-winger of Japanese descent, caused a major stir when he pulled the move off during a night game against Botafogo (the São Paulo version) in the Campeonato Paulista in March 1968. Picking up possession on the right side of the penalty area, Kaneco gripped the ball between his feet and flicked it over Botafogo left-back Carlucci before crossing from the byline for Toninho Guerreiro to score with a back-heeled volley (or *letra*) at the near post. A more Brazilian goal you will struggle to find.

See also: *milo* (Ghana)

malandragem

Effectively meaning 'street smarts', *malandragem* represents one of the foundation stones of Brazilian football. Slavery was only abolished in Brazil in 1888 and football in the country was an exclusively non-black pastime in its formative years, with membership of clubs in Rio and São Paulo restricted to wealthy whites and foreigners. But as the growing metropolitan clubs sought to gain an edge over each other, so they began to find room for talented black and *mulatto* players, who brought with them innovative skills developed in matches on the streets and scrublands of the run-down suburbs. Players accustomed to kicking around bundles of rags on scraps of land strewn with stones and broken bricks found that manipulating a nice, round leather ball on a nice, flat pitch was child's play. *Malandragem* became part of Brazilian football and it would become one of its defining characteristics. Brazilian sociologist Gilberto Freyre drew upon the example of football in the 1930s to argue that the country's mixed racial heritage should be viewed in a positive light, rather than seen as something to be ashamed of. Freyre, and others, posited that Brazil's African heritage – typified by the *capoeira* martial art, formerly practised by Angolan slaves – had helped to give Brazilian football a sense of spontaneity and artistry that was both unique and symbolic of the country's mixed ethnic identity. In *capoeira*, an elegant meeting point between dance and martial arts, *malandragem* describes the ability to read an opponent's intentions and react accordingly by deceiving him. In the lyrics of samba songs popularised by singers such as Noel Rosa and

Bezerra da Silva, it describes an idealised life of roguery, idleness and petty crime. In football it encapsulates the cunning and elusiveness of bandy-legged street footballers like Garrincha and Rivaldo, whose quick-witted, irrepressible style of play helped to make Brazil the envy of the world.

See also: *viveza* (Argentina)

Maracanazo

One of the most evocative words in World Cup history, *Maracanazo* was the name given to Brazil's sensational defeat by Uruguay in the deciding match of the 1950 tournament. Brazil had thrashed Sweden 7-1 and crushed Spain 6-1 in their first two games of the final round-robin group phase, and needed only to avoid defeat in their last game against Uruguay at Rio's newly built Maracanã to win the tournament for the first time. The hosts were overwhelming favourites. On the day of the game, Brazilian newspaper *O Mundo*'s early edition carried a picture of the Brazil squad accompanied by the caption: 'These are the world champions.' Special medals for each of Brazil's 22 players had already been made and a victory song, 'Brasil Os Vencedores' ('Brazil the Victors'), composed. But though Friaça put Brazil ahead early in the second half, Juan Alberto Schiaffino equalised before Alcides Ghiggia netted a historic 79th-minute winner, skidding a low shot between Barbosa and his near post to bring Uruguay glory and plunge Brazil into a state of national mourning. Fans at the ground were inconsolable and there were even reports of suicides. Nelson Rodrigues, Brazil's greatest playwright, described it as 'our Hiroshima'. The calamity was evoked again during the 2014 World Cup when Brazil, again the hosts, collapsed to an unbelievable 7-1 loss to Germany in the semi-finals at Belo Horizonte's Estádio Mineirão. It was quickly dubbed the *Mineirazo*.

marmelada – *marmalade*

When the outcome of a match raises suspicions of collusion between players on opposite teams, it's known as a *marmelada*. The term is believed to refer to the surreptitious tactic devised by penny-pinching food manufacturers of blending cheap (and flavourless) chayote with quince fruit in order to produce greater quantities of quince paste, which is known as *marmelada* in Brazil and Portugal. Just as shoppers who unwittingly bought diluted *marmelada* were short-changed, so are spectators who turn up to watch a match in which the result has been agreed in advance.

See also: *biscotto* (Italy), *hombre del maletín* (Spain)

mata-mata – *kill-kill*

It's kill or be killed in Brazil, where direct knockout games are known as *mata-mata*. 'Sudden death' is the nearest English expression.

morrinho artilheiro – *little hill gunner*

When a ball travelling towards goal hits a bump or mound that sends it flying past the goalkeeper, the divot is given credit for the goal by being described as an *artilheiro* ('gunner'), an epithet usually reserved for lethal strikers.

na banheira – *in the bathtub*

A player caught offside may be said to be *na banheira*.

See also: *milpa* (Costa Rica), *camsefyll* (Wales)

onde dorme a coruja – *where the owl sleeps*

An effort that whistles into the top corner of the goal, such as Josimar's 30-yard bullet into the top-left corner against Northern Ireland at the 1986 World Cup, might be described as having entered the goal *onde dorme a coruja*.

See also: *jep nest* (Trinidad and Tobago), *upper 90* (United States), *rašlje* (Croatia), *postage stamp* (England), *lucarne* (France), *sette* (Italy), *winkelhaak* (Netherlands), *devyatka* (Russia), *donde anidan las arañas* (Spain), *wayn yeskon shaytan* (Algeria), *fil maqass* (Egypt)

Neymar places a shot *onde dorme a coruja* ('where the owl sleeps')

oxo

Nothing to do with gravy. As an 'x' is used to separate the teams in Brazilian football results, a 0-0 draw (0x0) will sometimes be referred to as an *oxo*. Television commentator Walter Abrahão is credited with inventing the expression.

See also: *barankad* (Estonia), *brilstand* (Netherlands)

paradinha – *little stop*

In the months leading up to the 2010 World Cup, a controversial craze swept through the penalty areas of Brazil's football stadiums. Players taking penalties were running up to the ball, then abruptly stopping, waiting to see which way the goalkeeper dived and rolling the ball into the opposite corner. Ronaldo did it. Neymar did it. Fred did it, adding a showy fake shot for good measure before tucking the ball into the net. Goalkeepers were furious. After being hoodwinked by a *paradinha* ('little stop') penalty by Neymar in the derby against Santos, São Paulo goalkeeper Rogério Ceni warned: 'He should take advantage of doing this while it's still permitted in Brazil, because when he goes to Europe he won't be able to do it.' (It didn't, however, stop Rogério, a renowned penalty specialist in his own right, from trying it himself on occasion.) Kaká tweeted: 'Only in Brazil!' But FIFA president Sepp Blatter didn't see the funny side. 'This is cheating,' he complained. Pelé had used the trick during his career, having first seen Didi do it in a Brazil training session in 1959, but it had fallen out of use. Now it was back with a vengeance, and it claimed another victim in March 2010 when Wender, a goalkeeper for minor side Brusque, dislocated his left elbow as he tried to change direction following a *paradinha* by Joinville's Lima in a Catarinense championship match. 'It's so cruel,' said Wender, who was sidelined for three months as a result. 'They do everything to harm the goalkeepers. If there was a vote to ban it, I'd be first in line.' His wish was granted two months later – just in time for the World Cup – when the International FA Board outlawed the *paradinha*, branding it 'unsporting behaviour' and making it a yellow card offence.

See also: *stutter step* (United States), *panenka* (Czech Republic), *cucchiaio* (Italy)

pedaladas – *pedals*

One stepover is never enough in Brazil and when an attacker attempts to flummox an opponent with a flurry of blurred limbs, the word employed is *pedaladas*. The most famous display of stepovers in Brazil's history was produced by Robinho – the self-proclaimed *Rei das Pedaladas* ('King of

Pedals') – in the final of the national championship in December 2002. Aged 18 and touted – like any exciting teenage Santos forward – as the 'New Pelé', Robinho was the attacking jewel in a team that also boasted the creative talents of Elano and Diego. Santos had beaten their Paulista rivals Corinthians 2-0 in the first leg of the final, and 37 minutes into the second leg, Robinho produced his moment of magic. Barrelling fearlessly towards goal from the Santos left, the slender number seven in the black and white stripes backed experienced Corinthians full-back Rogério into his own penalty area with a disorienting series of *pedaladas* – six in total – before feinting to go right and then knocking the ball left, prompting the bewildered defender to jut out his right knee in desperation and bring him down. (Robinho's official website claims that there were eight stepovers. Consultation of the footage reveals that the true number was in fact six.) Robinho stroked in the resulting penalty, and although goals from Deivid and Anderson gave Corinthians hope, late efforts by Elano and Léo secured Santos's first top-flight title since Pelé had won his sixth and last national crown with the club in 1968. A player who uses *pedaladas* to no discernible effect risks being dubbed a *jogador triatleta* or 'triathlon player'. The joke behind the expression is the phrase: *'Corre, pedala e nada!' Corre* means 'runs', *pedala* means 'pedals' (i.e. stepovers) and *nada* can mean either 'swims' or – as is the implication here – 'nothing'.

See also: *bicicleta* (Argentina), *khawya f amra* (Morocco), *caap waa* (China), *marwaha* (Saudi Arabia)

perna de pau – *wooden leg*
If you're a player who traps the ball further than most players can kick it, chances are you'll be dubbed a *perna de pau* in Brazil. In Paraguay the expression is *pysatronco* ('wooden foot').

See also: *tronco* (Argentina), *pieds carrés* (France), *duffer* (Republic of Ireland), *derevo* (Russia), *drvo* (Serbia), *tuercebotas* (Spain)

pipoqueiro – *popcorn man*
Mocking moniker given to players who allow big games to pass them by. A player who fails to influence a match is likened to a stadium popcorn seller – resplendent in his uniform and present for the whole game, but unable to do a single thing about the result.

See also: *pecho frío* (Argentina)

In Brazil, a player who lets big games pass him by might be dubbed a *pipoqueiro* ('popcorn man')

pombo sem asa – *pigeon without wings*

A long-distance strike that flies past the goalkeeper is referred to as a *pombo sem asa*.

See also: *pushka strashnaya* (Russia), *evrogol* (Serbia), *intercontinental ballistic missile* (Nigeria), *bballaejul katteun shoot* (South Korea)

ponta de lança – *spearhead*

Typically used as an alternative to 'striker' these days, the term *ponta de lança* initially referred to a very specific role. When Flávio Costa took over as coach of Flamengo in 1938, he inherited a form of the W-M formation (effectively a 3-2-2-3 system) that had been introduced by his predecessor, Dori Kürschner. Costa's masterstroke was to tilt the square formed by the four players in the centre of the pitch, drawing one of his wing-halves back to a position in front of the defence and pushing one of his inside-forwards up in support of the centre-forward. The more advanced inside-forward became known as the *ponta de lança* and was given chief responsibility for coordinating his side's attacks. The first great *ponta de lança* was Ademir, who starred for Vasco da Gama and Fluminense in the 1940s and 1950s, and was the top scorer at the 1950 World Cup. His elusive performances in the withdrawn role so confounded opposing teams that he's credited in some quarters with having unwittingly expedited the birth of the four-man defence. Pelé announced himself to the world at the 1958 World Cup while operating as a *ponta de lança* in support of Vavá.

See also: *enganche* (Argentina)

torcedores – supporters

Brazilian football supporters are known as *torcedores*, which comes from the verb *torcer*, meaning 'to twist', the idea being that supporting a team requires the commitment and flexibility of a contortionist. Organised fan groups – the rough equivalent of Argentina's *barra bravas* – are known as *torcidas organizadas*.

See also: *barra bravas* (Argentina), *ultràs* (Italy), *fanaty* (Russia)

véu da noiva – bride's veil

Alternative name for the goal-net.

volante – holding midfielder

The player who sits in front of the back four is known in Brazil as a *volante*, which literally means 'steering wheel'. There's a theory in Brazil that it refers to an Argentinian midfielder called Carlos Martín Volante, who was a pioneering figure in the development of the position during his time with Flávio Costa's Flamengo between 1938 and 1943. But it's more likely to derive from the fact that the position was originally known as a *médio-volante* or 'flying midfielder', because the player occupying the role 'flew' across the space in front of his defence. The term is also used in Japan, where it's written as *boranchi* (ボランチ). A particularly bruising *volante* will be known as a *volante brucutu* ('caveman holding midfielder'). The expression comes from *Brucutu*, the Brazilian version of the *Alley Oop* American comic strip about a time-travelling caveman, which was created in the 1930s.

See also: *cinco* (Argentina), *Makélélé role* (England), *pihkatappi* (Finland), *sentinelle* (France), *stofzuiger* (Netherlands), *trinco* (Portugal)

zebra

In another example of the whimsically inward-looking nature of Brazilian football's linguistic palate, a shock result is known as a *zebra*. This refers to the illegal people's lottery *Jogo do Bicho* ('The Animal Game'), in which numbers are associated with 25 different animals (butterfly, camel, rooster, peacock, etc.). There's no zebra on the list. In 1964, before a match between his Portuguesa team and Rio giants Vasco, manager Gentil Cardoso said that beating Vasco would be 'like drawing a zebra' in *Jogo do Bicho*. Portuguesa duly won 2-1 and the expression stuck.

CHILE

Although the Federación de Fútbol de Chile was founded in 1895, making it the second-oldest football association on the continent after its Argentinian equivalent, it took Chile until 2015 to win the first of their two South American titles.

The archetypal Chilean footballer is the explosive, rough-edged forward, incarnated by Carlos Caszely, Marcelo Salas, Iván Zamorano and Alexis Sánchez.

chilena – overhead bicycle kick

The man widely credited with inventing the overhead bicycle kick, football's most spectacular manoeuvre, was Ramón Unzaga Asla, a naturalised Chilean who moved to Chile from Bilbao at the age of 12. He's said to have unleashed his bicycle kick upon the world for the first time while playing for Talcahuano club Estrella de Mar in 1914. Capped by Chile, he trotted out his party piece during the inaugural Copa América (then known as the Campeonato Sudamericano de Fútbol) in Buenos Aires in 1916, moving the local press to dub it the *chilena*. Another Chilean footballer, David Arellano, introduced the move to European audiences during a tour of Spain with Colo-Colo in 1927. Arellano, the club's founder and captain, was to meet a tragic end on the same tour when he died of peritonitis after taking a blow to the stomach during a match against Real Unión Deportiva in Valladolid. The horizontal black band that sits above the Colo-Colo crest was added in his honour.

See also: *chalaca* (Peru), *Fallrückzieher* (Germany), *hjólhestaspyrna* (Iceland), *rovesciata* (Italy), *ngả bàn đèn* (Vietnam)

Condoro

The Maracanã, September 1989. Chile are 1-0 down against Brazil in a World Cup qualifying match that they have to win when a white firecracker is thrown onto the pitch near Chile goalkeeper Roberto Rojas and he plunges to the ground clutching his head. As his teammates rush over to him, blood begins to stream down his face. With Brazil's players standing around looking bemused, Rojas's teammates pick him up and carry him down the tunnel, never to return. Brazil are left staring at possible disqualification, until a photograph taken by photographer Ricardo Alfieri emerges that proves the flare had landed a full metre from where Rojas, nicknamed 'Cóndor', had been standing. An investigation reveals that Rojas had used a razorblade hidden in one of his gloves to cut himself, in the hope that his side would be given a walkover victory. (His initial plan had been to pretend that he had been struck by a stone thrown from the crowd.) Instead, Brazil were awarded a 2-0 win, ending Chile's qualification hopes, and Chile were also banned from the 1994 World Cup. Rojas received a life ban, along with coach Orlando Aravena and team doctor Daniel Rodriguez, who was found to have submitted a fraudulent medical report. Rojas's ban was eventually lifted in 2001, by which time he was 43 and too old to resume playing. But he was given a way back into the game by São Paulo, his former club, and worked for them as a goalkeeping coach before settling in Brazil. The flare had been thrown by a young Brazilian woman, Rosenery Mello do Nascimento, who appeared on the cover of Brazilian *Playboy* two months later. The word *Condoro*, drawn from Rojas's nickname, subsequently entered Chilean parlance as a means of describing a major calamity, along with a second expression. While Rojas lay prone on the Maracanã turf being heckled by the crowd, Chile forward Pato Yáñez made an obscene gesture by aggressively grabbing his genitals and motioning to Brazil's fans. That's now known in Chile as *haciendo un Pato Yáñez* ('doing a Pato Yáñez').

el bautizazo – the baptism scandal

In November 2011, days before a World Cup qualifier against Uruguay, five Chile players were sent home from the team's training camp after breaking curfew. Jorge Valdivia had been celebrating his son's christening in the company of teammates Arturo Vidal, Jean Beausejour, Carlos Carmona and Gonzalo Jara. All five arrived back at the team hotel 45 minutes after the 10p.m. curfew and coach Claudio Borghi said they had been 'not in a fit state', although they denied reports that they were drunk. The incident became known as *el bautizazo*. One Uruguayan newspaper suggested a gift should be sent to Valdivia's new-born son to thank him for inadvertently robbing Chile of some of their most important players. In the quintet's absence, Chile sank to a 4-0 loss in Montevideo, their heaviest qualifying defeat in six years, with Luis Suárez scoring all four goals.

patas con sangre – *bloody legs*
A term used to describe a dirty player. To emphasise the point, the word for animal legs (*patas*) is used instead of *piernas*, the word for human legs.

See also: *chirurgul* (Romania)

ratón – *mouse*
A defensive coach or team might be likened to a mouse in Chile, the implication being that they are prisoners of their own timidity.

COLOMBIA

To Colombian ears, the Spanish spoken in their country (and particularly the capital Bogotá) is the purest in the region, which is purportedly due to a lack of strong linguistic influences in neighbouring countries.

Though Colombia have tended to flatter to deceive at international level, in players like René Higuita, Carlos Valderrama and Faustino Asprilla they have produced some of South American football's most fondly regarded characters.

bartolo – *clogger*
A term commonly used in Bogotá to describe a player, typically a defender, whose first thought is always to hoof the ball as far from danger as possible. It comes from one of Bogotá's first football teams, the San Bartolomé school, who were famed for their long-ball tactics.

Dimayorada
The División Mayor del Fútbol Colombiano (Major Division of Colombian Football), known as Dimayor, is responsible for administering Colombia's league and cup competitions. It's become so renowned for baffling decisions and rule changes that a word was coined to describe the phenomenon: *Dimayorada*. In 1997 the organisation decided that it had had enough of draws. As victory was worth three points and a draw only two (one for each team), the Dimayor decided that drawn matches would be followed by penalty shootouts to decide which of the teams picked up the 'lost' third point. The initiative was abandoned a year later. In 1995 the Colombian top flight switched to a

European-style autumn-to-spring format, only for the Dimayor to announce a year later that they were going to revert to the traditional spring-to-autumn system after attendances plummeted. The result was that the 1996/97 season lasted for over 15 months, with América de Cali ultimately crowned champions in late December 1997 following an absurd 76-match campaign.

el scorpión – *the scorpion*

England's goalless draw against Colombia at Wembley in September 1995 would have been forgotten as quickly as most England friendlies had it not been for a memorable display of acrobatics by visiting goalkeeper René 'El Loco' Higuita. As an over-hit cross from England debutant Jamie Redknapp floated harmlessly towards him at chest height, Higuita threw himself forwards and flung up his heels to club the ball clear of danger. A collective 'Woah!' echoed around the stadium, while England assistant coach Bryan Robson and substitute John Barnes could be seen cackling on the bench. Back home in Colombia it was christened *el scorpión* and it ensured that Higuita would not only be remembered for having his pocket picked by Cameroon's Roger Milla at the 1990 World Cup. Higuita may have been the first goalkeeper to use the technique, but its inventor is said to be Paraguay great Arsenio Erico, who used the method to score a goal for Argentinian club Independiente against Boca Juniors in August 1934. His goal was dubbed *el balancín* ('the see-saw').

Colombia's René Higuita springs *el scorpión* upon an unsuspecting world in 1995

el toque – *the touch*

Graceful, languid, one-touch passing style associated with the Colombia team of the early-1990s, inevitably orchestrated by the imperious Carlos Valderrama. Their high watermark was a historic 5-0 rout of Argentina in a September 1993 World Cup qualifier at El Monumental in Buenos Aires. The result secured Colombia's place at the following year's World Cup, while Argentina, who were the South American champions and had never previously lost at home in qualifying, were obliged to beat Australia in a play-off. But Colombia couldn't live up to the hype as they crashed out in the group phase, the misery of elimination compounded by the senseless murder of Andrés Escobar for scoring the own goal that precipitated their 2-1 loss to hosts the United States.

la pecosa – *the freckled one*

Used at the 1970 World Cup in Mexico, the Adidas Telstar was perhaps the most stylish football of all time. Designed by former Denmark goalkeeper Eigil Nielsen, it was the first 32-panel – or truncated icosahedron – ball to be used at a World Cup. Its white and black panelling was a nod to the Telstar satellite, after which it was named, but in Colombia it had a different name: *la pecosa*.

See also: *gorduchinha* (Brazil), *la bendita* (Ecuador), *bubamara* (Bosnia and Herzegovina)

palo'e mango – *mango tree*

A goal attempt that clears the bar by miles. Made famous by Colombia's most popular commentator, William Vinasco, who would yelp the phrase whenever an effort on goal looked destined for Row Z.

See also: *caau fei gei* (China), *yaseed hamaam* (Saudi Arabia)

ECUADOR

Along with Venezuela, Ecuador are one of the two major South American national teams never to have won the Copa América. After turning down an invitation to participate in the inaugural World Cup in Uruguay in 1930, they had to wait until 2002 to make their first appearance at the tournament.

estar en capilla – *to be in chapel*
To be on the brink of suspension. Alternatively, this term can be used to describe a player whose place in the starting XI is under threat from a teammate.

la bendita – *the blessed one*
Popularly known as *La Voz del Pueblo* ('The Voice of the People'), Ecuadorian radio commentator Carlos Efraín Machado bequeathed the term *la bendita* to his country's football dictionary as an alternative name for the ball. Other names given to the ball in Ecuador include *la cariñosa* ('the affectionate one') and *la caprichosa* ('the capricious one').

See also: *gorduchinha* (Brazil), *la pecosa* (Colombia), *bubamara* (Bosnia and Herzegovina)

táctica del murciélago – *bat tactics*
If a team find themselves defending so deep that all their players are camped inside their own penalty area, they're likened to bats hanging upside-down from the crossbar.

See also: *Obrona Częstochowy* (Poland), *ući golmanu u krilo* (Serbia), *mball camp yi* (Senegal)

PARAGUAY

Football was introduced to Paraguay in the latter years of the 19th century by a Dutch PE teacher called Williams Paats, who moved to Asunción from the Netherlands in the 1890s.

Despite a population of around seven million people that is dwarfed by many of their continental rivals, Paraguay have twice prevailed in the Copa América (1953 and 1979).

gol queso – *cheese goal*
Paraguay's national cheese, *queso Paraguay*, is creamy and liable to melt in the sunshine. When a Paraguayan team concede a soft goal, it's known as a 'cheese goal'.

pelota jagua – *dog ball*

The Pep Guardiola era at Barcelona familiarised the football world with the concept of the *rondo*, that intense piggy-in-the-middle drill used to finely hone players' first-time passing. The Paraguayan equivalent is *pelota jagua*.

See also: *rondo* (Spain)

vakapipopo – *football*

Paraguay has two official languages: Spanish and Guaraní, an indigenous language spoken by around 90 per cent of the population. Football in Guaraní is quite magnificently known as *vakapipopo*, which translates as 'bouncing cow skin' (*vaka* meaning 'cow', *pi* meaning 'skin' and *popo* meaning 'bouncing').

See also: *nogomet* (Croatia), *calcio* (Italy)

PERU

A white shirt with a diagonal red sash stretching from the left shoulder to the right hip, the Peru jersey is one of the most recognisable in international football. The national team's high point came in the 1970s, when a side featuring Teófilo Cubillas, Hugo Sotil and Héctor Chumpitaz qualified for three World Cups (1970, 1978 and 1982) and won the 1975 Copa América.

amarrabola – *ball lover*

When a Peruvian player gets so attached to the ball he decides he'd rather not pass it to anyone else, he's known as an *amarrabola*.

See also: *morfón* (Argentina), *ballverliebt* (Germany), *chupón* (Spain)

chalaca – *overhead bicycle kick*

An overhead kick may be known as a *chilena* in much of the Spanish-speaking world, but woe betide the person who utters the word in Peru, where it's called a *chalaca*. Alejandro Villanueva, one of the first stars of the Peruvian game, was credited with inventing the move in 1928 and it was initially known as a *tiro caracol* ('snail shot'). But research by Argentinian journalist and football historian Jorge Barraza led him to assert that the technique's Peruvian origins could actually be traced back to the final years of the 19th century. Barraza found evidence that British sailors working at the Peruvian port city of Callao had asked locals of African descent to make up the numbers in their quayside kickabouts. During these informal matches, the local players wowed their visitors by performing acrobatic mid-air volleys. The move was christened a *chalaca* after people from Callao, who are known as *chalacos*. Barraza speculated that Chile's footballers had copied the *chalaca* after witnessing it during matches between players from Callao and the Chilean port of Valparaíso, making Peru – and not Chile – the true home of the overhead bicycle kick.

See also: *chilena* (Chile), *Fallrückzieher* (Germany), *hjólhestaspyrna* (Iceland), *rovesciata* (Italy), *ngả bàn đèn* (Vietnam)

huacha – *washer*

The Peruvian name for a nutmeg is *huacha* (also known as a *huachita*), which is a corruption of the English 'washer', a thin, metal disk with a hole in the middle used to tighten screws and bolts.

See also: *caneta* (Brazil), *salad* (Jamaica), *Gurkerl* (Austria), *jesle* (Czech Republic), *nutmeg* (England), *klobbi* (Iceland), *panna* (Netherlands), *cueca* (Portugal), *bayda* (Morocco), *yalli* (Senegal), *shibobo* (South Africa), *deya* (Zimbabwe), *lawd daak* (Thailand)

URUGUAY

The enduring miracle of South American football, the Uruguayan national team have belied their country's status as the smallest of the continent's major nations – both in terms of size and population – to win two World Cups (making them, by some distance, the smallest nation ever to have won the tournament) and a record 15 Copa América titles.

It was through Uruguay's rivalry with neighbours Argentina in the 1920s and 1930s that the historic culture – and language – of rioplatense football was formed.

cortita y al pie – *short and to the foot*

When Peñarol (then known as the Central Uruguay Railway Cricket Club) played a friendly against Ferro Carril Oeste in Buenos Aires in 1908, it was to prove a defining moment in the development of Uruguayan football. While Peñarol cruised to a 5-0 victory, the club's officials were greatly impressed by Ferro's composed Scottish centre-half John Harley, a Glasgow-born railway engineer. He was persuaded to join Peñarol the following year and his arrival triggered sharp changes in the Montevideo club's playing style. Previously, long-ball tactics had prevailed at Peñarol, the legacy of the English influence, but Harley, versed in Scotland's short-passing game, helped to introduce a style of slick, coordinated passing that became known as *cortita y al pie*. He would go on to both play for and manage the Uruguayan national team, helping to instil a methodical, possession-based approach that laid the foundations for Uruguay's successes at the 1924 and 1928 Olympics and the inaugural 1930 World Cup.

garra charrúa – *charrúa claw*

Named after the Charrúa Indians who called Uruguay home before being hounded from their lands by the conquering Spanish, *la garra charrúa* describes the grit and fighting spirit that have enabled Uruguay to punch above their weight on the international football stage. Also known as *la garra celeste*, it's inevitably evoked whenever *la Celeste* ('the Sky Blues') contrive to snatch victory from the jaws of defeat, and was popularised as a means of explaining how a country of just three million people had managed to win two World Cups. In particular, it was said to have been a decisive factor in Uruguay's victories over Argentina in the finals of the 1928 Olympics and 1930 World Cup, triumphs that helped to spawn the mocking phrase: *'Ataca Argentina, gol de Uruguay!'* ('Argentina attack, Uruguay score!') The most resonant example of *garra charrúa* was Uruguay's extraordinary victory over Brazil in the final game of the 1950 World Cup. However, the concept has also served as a means of legitimising the thuggishness of some of the less talented Uruguay teams that have emerged since.

hinchas – *fans*

The word for supporters that's used throughout Latin America is thought to have been coined by fans of Uruguayan giants Nacional. The story goes that in the early 20th century Nacional were supported by a burly, moustachioed man by the name of Prudencio Miguel Reyes, whose principal responsibility was to inflate the club's footballs. He also used his prodigious lungs to hurl encouragement at Nacional from the sidelines, which – at a time when British attitudes regarding decorum still held sway in Uruguayan sport – was something of a revelation. Acknowledging his prominence, fellow supporters dubbed Reyes *El Hincha* (meaning 'The Inflator') and the expression soon became shorthand for any passionate fan.

tuya, Héctor – _yours, Héctor_
With Uruguay and Argentina drawing 1-1 in the replay of the 1928 Olympic final in Amsterdam (the teams' first meeting having ended in a 1-1 draw), a cross from the left was played towards Uruguay's Tito Borjas. Spotting teammate Héctor Scarone's run behind him, Borjas yelled '_¡Tuya, Héctor!_' ('Yours, Héctor!'), before deftly heading the ball into the Nacional inside-right's path. Scarone lashed a shot into the roof of the net to earn Uruguay a 2-1 victory and Borjas's phrase passed into everyday language as a way of inviting someone to finish off a task.

vuelta olímpica – _Olympic lap_
After beating Switzerland 3-0 in the 1924 Olympic final in Paris, Uruguay's players performed a circuit of the pitch to salute the crowd in what is claimed to be the first recorded lap of honour. The practice is now known in Uruguay as a _vuelta olímpica_. Defensor Sporting defied convention by performing a clockwise _vuelta olímpica_ after winning the Uruguayan championship in 1976, which was the first time neither Nacional nor Peñarol had won the title in the post-1932 professional area. Defensor were known for their left-wing convictions and their unusual _vuelta_ was reportedly a protest against the brutal dictatorship of the time.

VENEZUELA

Uniquely among South American nations, football in Venezuela plays second fiddle to baseball due to the influence of American oil workers who came to the country in the early years of the 20th century. It partially explains why Venezuela are the only major national team from the continent never to have played at a World Cup, although they achieved an impressive fourth-place finish at the 2011 Copa América.

cabeza de dimple – _dimple header_
Dimple is a blended Scotch whisky sold in a distinctive, oval-shaped bottle that's popular in Venezuela. A miscued header that sends the ball looping in an unexpected direction is known as a _cabeza de dimple_, the idea being that it's as if the ball has bounced off one of the rounded shoulders of a Dimple bottle.

dar un joropo – *to give (someone) a joropo*

When a Venezuelan team have been given a pasting, they're imagined to have been danced around the pitch in the manner of a *joropo*, a popular folk dance similar to the fandango.

tirar un ladrillo – *to throw a brick*

To give a teammate a pass so forceful that it's impossible for them to control the ball. An alternative expression with the same meaning is *lanzo una nevera*, which means 'to launch a fridge'.

vinotintoso – *faded claret*

Venezuela's national team are known as the *Vinotinto*, which refers to the red-wine colour of their shirts. If a player who excels for his club team is unable to reproduce his form for the national side, he's said to be *vinotintoso*.

PUTTING IT ON A PLATE – WHEN FOOTBALL MEETS FOOD

Whether it's a chicken balti pie at half-time, Manchester United's official noodle partner or some metaphorical egg on the face of a blundering goalkeeper, football and food are never far apart. Here are some foodstuffs that have blended themselves into the language of the game.

Bananenflanke – *banana cross (Germany)*
Germany sees your common or garden banana shot and raises you a banana *cross*.

biscotto – *biscuit (Italy)*
Italians use the term *biscotto* to describe a suspicious result that mutually benefits both teams.

boabe – *beans (Romania)*
Calling to mind the English expression 'bean-counter', which is used in a football sense to describe a stats-obsessed striker, 'beans' serves as a colloquial term for goals in Romania.

caviar *(France)*
In France, gastronomic centre of the known universe, a *caviar* is a defence-splitting pass.

cherry-picking *(United States)*
This is the American equivalent of the British term 'goal-hanging' and describes the activities of an attacking player determined to keep as close to the opposition goal as possible.

chocoladebeen – *chocolate leg (Netherlands)*
A Dutch player uses his *chocoladebeen* when he takes a swing at the ball with his weaker foot.

ciasteczko – *little cookie (Poland)*
The Polish player who creates a shooting chance that can't be missed is imagined to have handed his teammate a biscuit.

croqueta – *croquette (Spain)*
Mastered in modern times by Andrés Iniesta, the *croqueta* is a piece of skill where a player rapidly flips the ball from one foot to the other in order to squeeze through a narrow gap.

dar um chocolate – *to give (someone) a chocolate (Brazil)*
On the football pitches of Brazil, to give a team a chocolate is to give them a spanking.

gol queso – *cheese goal (Paraguay)*
A soft goal.

Gurkenpass – *cucumber pass (Germany)*
One of several examples of cucumbers being used in a pejorative sense in the German language, a *Gurkenpass* is a pass that fails to reach its intended destination.

kaaskijkers – *cheese-watchers (Netherlands)*
Kaaskijkers are fans who watch their team passively without actively supporting them. The term was cooked up by Co Adriaanse during his time as coach of AZ in the cheese-producing city of Alkmaar.

kai deak *(ไข่ แตก)* – *to break the egg (Thailand)*
A Thai footballer who notches his team's first goal cracks the 'egg' of the zero in their half of the scoreline.

kifli – *crescent (Hungary)*
A *kifli* is a central European pastry that resembles a croissant. The word is employed in Hungary as a metaphor for a curling shot.

patate – *potato (France)*
In France, *patate* is the name given to a thunderous long-range goal.

potet – *potato (Norway)*
Conversely, in Norwegian football the humble potato is put to use as an alternative name for a versatile player who can slot into any position.

prawn sandwich brigade *(England)*
First described by a scowling Roy Keane, the *prawn sandwich brigade* refers to people who come to matches and pay more attention to the food in the hospitality box than the action on the pitch.

slice of cheese *(Australia)*
A cult phrase invented by three amateur commentators during an Australian cup match in August 2014, *slice of cheese* is a deliberately naff synonym for a yellow card.

smörpassning – *butter pass (Sweden)*
A slick pass that arrives right at the receiving player's feet.

sukhar (сухар) – *biscuit (Ukraine)*
In Ukraine, a 'biscuit' is a clean sheet. Sprinkle a penalty save on top and it becomes a *sukhar z rodzynkamy* (сухар з родзинками) or 'biscuit with raisins'.

NORTH AND CENTRAL AMERICA

The region administered by the Confederation of North, Central American and Caribbean Association Football (CONCACAF) stretches from the icy northern shores of Alaska to the steamy swampland of the Panama–Colombia border and includes three South American outposts in the form of Guyana, Suriname and French Guiana. Propelled by the twin motors of Mexico and the United States, CONCACAF is the third most successful FIFA confederation in terms of World Cup performance.

From a linguistic perspective, the region encompasses the English spoken in Canada and the United States, the Spanish and indigenous languages of Mexico and Central America, and the panoply of Spanish, English, French, Dutch and various creoles found in the Caribbean.

CANADA

Though cast into the shade by the national obsession with ice hockey, the Canadian men's football team have experienced occasional spots of success, qualifying for the 1986 World Cup and pulling off a massive upset to win the 2000 CONCACAF Gold Cup.

The biggest match in Canadian club football is an interlingual affair between Toronto FC and Montreal Impact, de facto representatives of anglophone and francophone Canada. It's known as the '401 Derby' after Highway 401, the 514-mile highway that runs through Toronto to the Ontario–Québec border.

deke

Pronounced DEEK and borrowed from ice hockey, this is a Canadian word for a body feint. To successfully beat an opponent is to *deke them out*.

Gordie Howe hat-trick

This expression describes the performance of a player who scores, sets up a goal and gets involved in a fight in the same match, and is named after bruising NHL Hall of Famer Gordie Howe, who was known as 'Mr Hockey' for his exploits with the Detroit Red Wings. Danny Dichio was credited with a partial *Gordie Howe hat-trick* in May 2007 when, after scoring the first goal in Toronto FC's history in a 3-1 win over the Chicago Fire, he was sent off following a scuffle with Diego Gutiérrez.

COSTA RICA

Football-mad Costa Rica is the most successful country in Central America, the national team having won three continental titles (1963, 1969 and 1989) and qualified for five World Cups (1990, 2002, 2006, 2014 and 2018). They reached the last 16 on their World Cup debut in 1990 and made it to the quarter-finals in 2014 after remarkably finishing top of a 'Group of Death' that included England, Italy and Uruguay.

caballo – horse

A physically imposing player prone to doling out painful kicks.

See also: *armario* (Spain), *kitasa* (Tanzania), *samaam al amaan* (Saudi Arabia)

mejenga – kickabout

An integral part of local life in Costa Rica, where football is king, a *mejenga* is an informal pick-up match between friends. The first recorded use of the word, according to Arturo Agüero Chaves's *Diccionario de costarriqueñismos* ('Dictionary of Costa Rican Jargon'), came in the first part of the 19th century, when it was used to refer to a drinking spree or a disorderly fight. It was subsequently employed to describe an unruly kickabout and now serves as a name for any kind of match across a variety of sports.

milpa – *cornfield*

This is the Costa Rican term for offside and it has an etymology that can be traced back to the old Estadio Nacional, which stood west of downtown San José. In the late 1940s the stadium was unfinished and there was no stand behind the western goal, so the arena's security guard asked the country's General Directorate of Sports if he could use the vacant space to grow radishes, tomatoes and corn that he would sell to supplement his income. His wish granted, his vegetable patch duly took shape and remained in place over the years that followed. When a team playing at the stadium wanted to emphasise the extent to which a player was offside, they would proclaim to the referee: '*Está en milpa!*' or 'He's in the cornfield!' The joke was relayed around the country by match commentators and in time it became the default term for offside.

See also: *na banheira* (Brazil), *camsefyll* (Wales)

EL SALVADOR

El Salvador became the first country from Central America to qualify for a World Cup when they reached the 1970 tournament, and the first team from the region to score at a World Cup in 1982. Unfortunately, Luis Ramírez Zapata's goal at the 1982 finals came during a 10-1 group-stage loss to Hungary in the Spanish town of Elche that established an unwanted competition record.

culebrita – *little snake*

Culebrita is one of the Spanish names for the *elástico* trick and in El Salvador it's closely associated with Jorge 'Mágico' González, revered as the country's greatest player. He was able to perform the manoeuvre at high speed and in two directions (right–left and left–right), enabling him to spring past opponents on both sides. His interpretation of the technique was so devastating that it came to be known as a *culebrita macheteada* ('ankle-breaking little snake'). González counted Diego Maradona among his army of fans and played for El Salvador at the 1982 World Cup in Spain.

See also: *elástico* (Brazil), *el ghoraf* (Algeria)

HONDURAS

CONCACAF champions in 1981, Honduras made their first World Cup appearance the following year and achieved a surprising third-place finish at the 2001 Copa América in Colombia after being drafted in as 11th-hour replacements for Argentina, who withdrew from the tournament citing security fears.

Honduras and neighbouring El Salvador fought what became known as the 'Football War' in 1969 after a heated World Cup qualifying play-off ignited existing diplomatic tensions between the countries, sparking a brief but bloody four-day conflict.

costlyña

Standing 6ft 3in and carrying a bulky frame, former Honduras striker (and one-time Birmingham City loanee) Carlo Costly is not an obvious skill merchant, but he carries in his locker one of the most delightful tricks in the modern game. It's typically implemented when Costly is on the left side of the pitch with a defender alongside him on his inside. He will drop his pace to no more than a jog and then languidly swing his left foot up and backwards in a fake back-heel. At this point the defender invariably takes a step forwards, seeking to cut out the back-heel, only for Costly to suddenly hit the gas and surge away. The trick is known as the *costlyña* and, as several YouTube videos demonstrate, its capacity for rendering opposing defenders flatfooted is uncanny.

JAMAICA

While cricket and athletics have traditionally been the most popular sports in Jamaica, football was a favourite pastime of the country's most iconic cultural figure, Bob Marley, who fell in love with Pelé's Santos and was often photographed with a ball at his feet.

Jamaica's yellow-shirted 'Reggae Boyz' made their first and, to date, only World Cup appearance at the 1998 tournament in France.

salad

They appreciate a skill move in Jamaica. To beat a player with a piece of skill is to *shif* them, when someone lifts the ball over an opponent's head it's known as a *pile* and a nutmeg is a *salad*. The latter term is said to have been coined in honour of Peter Knowles during Wolves' tour of the Caribbean in 1964, when the 18-year-old winger nutmegged a succession of opponents during an 8-4 friendly win over the Jamaican national team. An England Under-23 international, Knowles was tipped for stardom, but in 1969 he stunned the football world by turning his back on the game in order to become a Jehovah's Witness. Wolves kept him under contract until 1982, by which time he was 36, before manager Graham Hawkins conceded defeat and released him.

See also: *caneta* (Brazil), *huacha* (Peru), *Gurkerl* (Austria), *jesle* (Czech Republic), *nutmeg* (England), *klobbi* (Iceland), *panna* (Netherlands), *cueca* (Portugal), *bayda* (Morocco), *yalli* (Senegal), *shibobo* (South Africa), *deya* (Zimbabwe), *lawd daak* (Thailand)

UB40s

With Jamaica toiling mid-way through the final round of qualifying for the 1998 World Cup, Brazilian coach René Simões looked to Britain in the hope of injecting his team of talented but callow semi-professional players with some top-level know-how. He drafted in four England-born players with Jamaican roots – Portsmouth pair Paul Hall and Fitzroy Simpson, Wimbledon's Robbie Earle and Derby's Deon Burton – and the results were instant. Goals from Burton earned Jamaica 1-0 victories over Canada and Costa Rica and a 1-1 draw away to the United States, before draws against El Salvador and Mexico carried the 'Reggae Boyz' to their first World Cup. The English contingent were dubbed the *UB40s* after Birmingham-based reggae group UB40 (whose name was a reference to a document – Unemployment Benefit Form 40 – that was issued to people claiming unemployment benefit in the UK). By the time the World Cup rolled around there were seven *UB40s*, Wimbledon's Marcus Gayle, Chelsea defender Frank Sinclair and Burton's Derby teammate Darryl Powell having joined the ranks. Jamaica were eliminated in the group phase in France after one-sided losses to Croatia and Argentina, but claimed a historic 2-1 win over Japan in their final game.

See also: *farbowane lisy* (Poland), *mujannisoon* (Qatar)

MEXICO

One of the two powerhouses of the CONCACAF region (alongside the United States), Mexico have won 10 continental titles, twice finished second as a guest team at the Copa América and qualified for more World Cups than any nation except Brazil, Germany, Italy and Argentina.

In addition to the achievements of *El Tri* (short for *El Tricolor*, after the green, white and red national flag), Mexico also provided the setting for the coronations of Pelé's Brazil and Maradona's Argentina at the 1970 and 1986 World Cups.

apedriando el rancho – throwing stones at the ranch
When a Mexican team are laying siege to their opponents' goal, they're pictured to be *apedriando el rancho*.

chanfle – swerve
Chanfle is the term used in several Latin American countries to describe the effect put on the ball by a player who strikes it in such a way as to make it swerve or curl in the air. The word is attributed to the great Mexican comedian Roberto Gómez Bolaños, known as 'Chespirito', who was obsessed with words that began with the letters 'ch'. His comedies, widely broadcast throughout the Spanish-speaking world, featured characters who would express shock or irritation by exclaiming '*Chanfle!*' and in time it caught on as a football expression. Chespirito wrote and starred in a 1979 film called *El Chanfle* in which he played a bumbling Club América kitman.

cuauhtemiña
During Mexico's opening game against South Korea at the 1998 World Cup, Cuauhtémoc Blanco unveiled an innovation that instantly won him global acclaim. Twice during the second half of the match at Lyon's Stade de Gerland, Blanco collected possession wide on the left, allowed two defenders to close in on him and then gripped the ball between his feet and leaped through the gap between them. In Britain it was dubbed 'the bunny-hop'. The French called it the *saut de crapaud* ('toad jump'). Mexicans came to know it as the *cuauhtemiña* (effectively, 'little Cuauhtémoc move'). It was ungainly but effective and it brought a smile to the face – much like Blanco

himself. He was an improbable international footballer – stooped and a little paunchy, with a ragged running style – but he delighted in using his body in strange and unusual ways on the pitch. His other tricks included the *jorobiña* ('little hunchback flick') and the *nalguiña* ('little arse flick'). In March 2016 Blanco came out of retirement at the age of 43 to play a farewell game for his formative team Club América. Naturally, he squeezed in one last *cuauhtemiña* for the road.

la ola – *Mexican wave*

There are various theories about where the Mexican wave originated (many of which cite the United States as its true country of origin), but what's commonly accepted is that it came to global prominence during the 1986 World Cup in Mexico – hence its name. In Mexico it's known simply as *la ola*. Ironically, given its association with festiveness and celebration, it's usually a sign that fans at a game are bored to tears.

síndrome del Jamaicón – *Jamaicón syndrome*

In the days before Rafael Márquez and Javier 'Chicharito' Hernández, Mexican footballers had a reputation for not travelling well and the phenomenon came to be known as *síndrome del Jamaicón* after José 'Jamaicón' Villegas. He played at left-back for the all-conquering Chivas team of the 1950s and 1960s and was said to have been one of the few players to have got the better of Garrincha, but when he was obliged to play abroad, his game went to pot. According to one story, during a training camp with the Mexican national team in Lisbon prior to the 1958 World Cup in Sweden, he crept out of a team meal and was found by the team's manager, Nacho Trelles, hugging his knees beneath a tree in the hotel grounds and looking forlornly at the sky. Asked what was wrong, he replied: 'How can I have dinner when they've prepared such rotten food? What I want are my *chalupas* [filled tostadas], a few good *sopes* [thick tortillas with toppings] or a *pozole* [stew] and not this crap that isn't even from Mexico.' After an 8-0 thrashing by England at Wembley in 1961, Villegas offered a similar excuse for his poor display, explaining gloomily that he missed his mum's cooking. Villegas's 'Jamaicón' nickname, given to him by his mother in reference to his fondness for *agua de Jamaica* (hibiscus tea), came to stand for the difficulties encountered by Mexican stars who failed to take their talent with them when they travelled overseas.

PANAMA

Known as *Los Canaleros* ('The Canal Men') in honour of the country's famous waterway, Panama qualified for their first World Cup in October 2017 when defender Román Torres's 88th-minute goal secured a 2-1 victory over Costa Rica that sent Hernán Darío Gómez's side to the tournament at the expense of the United States.

It was a sweet reversal of roles. Four years previously, the US had scored two stoppage-time goals to condemn Panama to a 3-2 defeat that prevented them from reaching a qualifying play-off for the 2014 World Cup.

llevar a alguien a la escuelita – *to take someone to pre-school*

In Panama, this is one of the phrases employed when a player's feint is so successful that it sends his opponent diligently trotting off in completely the wrong direction. In another term redolent of the school playground, a weak shot is known as a *pistolita de agua* ('water pistol').

See also: *poslati ga po burek* (Bosnia and Herzegovina), *da go pratya za bira* (Bulgaria), *kohvile saatma* (Estonia), *het bos ingestuurd* (Netherlands), *sendt opp i pølsebua* (Norway), *att köpa korv* (Sweden), *pazara göndermek* (Turkey), *kupelekwa shopping* (Kenya)

quechón – *catcher*

Panama's first professional baseball league was founded in 1946 and there's evidence that the sport was first played there in the 1850s, when it was introduced to the country by American tradesmen and workers from the Panama Railroad Company. In Panamanian football, a lazy striker who spends all his time waiting for the ball to be played to him is likened to a baseball catcher crouching behind home plate in anticipation of the next pitch.

See also: *cherry-picking* (United States), *goal hanger* (England), *ficar na mama* (Portugal), *atetɛ nkura* (Ghana), *pettu kidakunnavan* (India)

TRINIDAD AND TOBAGO

Trinidad and Tobago became the smallest country ever to qualify for the World Cup when they reached the 2006 tournament, ceding that crown to Iceland in 2017. Their most famous players are Dwight Yorke, the former Manchester United striker, and Stern John, whose record of 70 goals in 115 appearances between 1995 and 2011 makes him one of the most prolific goal-getters in the history of international football.

ball jumbie

Someone who lives and breathes football, to the point of obsession. A *jumbie* (also spelt *jumbee*) is a supernatural spirit or ghost.

jep nest

The top corner of the goal. A *jep* or *jack spaniard* is a type of wasp found in Trinidad and Tobago that typically nests beneath the eaves of houses.

See also: *onde dorme a coruja* (Brazil), *upper 90* (United States), *rašlje* (Croatia), *postage stamp* (England), *lucarne* (France), *sette* (Italy), *winkelhaak* (Netherlands), *devyatka* (Russia), *donde anidan las arañas* (Spain), *wayn yeskon shaytan* (Algeria), *fil maqass* (Egypt)

UNITED STATES

Listening to football commentary from America can be a dislocating experience, familiar things like boots and penalty kicks made to sound strange and foreign by virtue of having been re-rendered in transatlantic sportsese. But if Brazil and Finland and Papua New Guinea can have their own ways of talking about football, why not the United States?

Versions of football were being played at America's top universities before 1840 and when the United States reached the semi-finals of the inaugural 1930 World Cup, England were still 20 years away from their tournament debut. American soccer-speak is the fruit of a long, unsteady process of linguistic evolution, just like in every football culture in the world, and if it betrays evidence of cross-pollination with the vernaculars of the country's well-established native sports, that can hardly be a surprise.

Beckham Rule

Nickname for Major League Soccer's Designated Player rule, which allows teams to pay wages in excess of what the league's salary cap usually permits to up to three players. David Beckham became the league's first Designated Player (or DP) when he joined Los Angeles Galaxy from Real Madrid in 2007 on a five-year deal worth a guaranteed annual wage of $6.5 million.

bunker

An expression used to describe teams who defend deep (*bunker defence* or *to bunker in*). It's heard more often in women's football than in the men's game, having been popularised by Anson Dorrance, the inspirational University of North Carolina women's coach who led the USA to glory in the inaugural Women's World Cup in 1991. US goalkeeper Hope Solo took exception to Sweden's *bunker* tactics after her side were eliminated from the 2016 Olympics in Brazil, complaining: 'I think we played a bunch of cowards.' It earned her a six-month ban.

See also: *anti-fútbol* (Argentina), *zaburkvam betona* (Bulgaria), *park the bus* (England), *catenaccio* (Italy)

cherry-picking

A term lifted from basketball, *cherry-picking* is the US equivalent of 'goal hanging'.

See also: *quechón* (Panama), *goal hanger* (England), *ficar na mama* (Portugal), *atete nkura* (Ghana), *pettu kidakunnavan* (India)

cleats

American words for sporting equipment can take some getting used to. Football boots are known as *cleats* (a synecdoche, literally meaning 'studs'), kits as *uniforms* and bibs as *pinnies*. It's a similar story on the pitch, which becomes the *field*. In echoes of American football terminology, the byline is known as the *end line* and the touchline as the *sideline*. A clean sheet is a *shutout*, while a penalty kick is a *PK*.

CONCACAF'd

The name given to the perception held in the United States (and Canada) that their teams are unfairly treated during games against Latin American opposition in competitions administered by regional governing body CONCACAF. Both the US men's national team and the country's club sides have learned to be apprehensive about trips to Spanish-speaking countries in the region, where poor pitches, fan hostility, debatable refereeing decisions and alleged play-acting by their opponents have fuelled conspiracy theories. Examples of American grievances include a 2010 CONCACAF Champions League group game between Real Salt Lake and Arabe Unido during which the Panamanian side's players, unsuccessfully seeking to hold on for a 1-1 draw, flopped to the ground repeatedly, bringing stretcher-bearers onto the pitch with almost comical regularity. Costa Rica's Joel Campbell, meanwhile, was reprimanded by FIFA in October 2013 for getting Matt Besler booked by flinging himself to the ground and rolling around in mock agony after the American centre-back accidentally stepped on the tip of his boot during a World Cup qualifier. The USA do not always have reason to consider themselves hard done by, however. They reached the final of the 2007 Gold Cup at Canada's expense after Atiba Hutchinson was denied a stoppage-time equaliser by an offside call that ignored the fact the ball had been headed into his path by American defender Oguchi Onyewu. More generally, *CONCACAF'd* is used to refer to shoddy officiating in CONCACAF tournaments.

en fuego – *on fire*

America's huge Latino population has helped several Spanish phrases to filter into the country's football argot. They include *chilena, golazo* and *en fuego*, which is used – as in English – to describe a player who's on a hot streak.

In-form American players are said to be *en fuego* ('on fire') – an expression imported from Spanish

in the six

In the six-yard box. Another expression for the area directly in front of the goal is *on the doorstep*. *Top of the D* is an American term for the widest point of the 'D' (otherwise known as the penalty arc), where a player might loiter in anticipation of a cut-back from a teammate foraging down one of the flanks.

on frame

As any footballer knows, the frame of the goal is not what you're aiming for when you're trying to score, but the waters are muddied somewhat in America, where an effort that hits the target is described as *on frame*.

ponytailed hooligans

Nickname given to the passionate teenage followers of the US women's football team. Where men's football in the US has had to compete for attention with the sporting behemoths of the NFL, the NBA and Major League Baseball, the women's game has encountered fewer obstacles, enabling it to flourish there as in no other country. Interest in women's football reached fever pitch in the build-up to the 1999 Women's World Cup, which was staged on home soil. The home nation prevailed following a penalty shootout victory over China at Pasadena's Rose Bowl, defender Brandi Chastain netting the decisive spot-kick and then creating a timeless image by tearing off her white jersey to reveal a black sports bra and sinking to her knees in jubilation. 'There's a legacy now,' said US Soccer's general secretary Hank Steinbrecher. 'In 10 to 20 years, those ponytailed hooligans, those young girls [watching at the Rose Bowl] will be on that field of play.' The women's game in the US has made uneven progress in the years since, with a succession of national leagues forced to fold, but Steinbrecher's vision continues to resonate. One of the 90,185 spectators who packed into the Rose Bowl to watch the final on that sunny July day was a 10-year-old Californian girl called Christen Press. Sixteen years later, she was a member of the US squad which triumphed at the 2015 Women's World Cup in Canada.

See also: *soccer mom* (United States)

riding pine

Sitting on the substitutes' bench. A term borrowed from baseball.

soccer mom

The expression *soccer mom* has acquired negative connotations in recent years, conjuring up images of overbearing mothers bundling reluctant children out of the passenger doors of SUVs and into football matches in which they'd rather not play, but the original soccer moms played a pivotal role in the establishment of football as a major American pastime in the 1980s and 1990s. As David Goldblatt observes in *The Ball is Round: A Global History of Football*, football bucked a trend in the US by becoming a middle-class (rather than a working-class) sport, and it was middle-income working mothers who took the lead by organising the game at grass-roots level. Soccer moms permeated the national consciousness during the build-up to the 1996 US presidential election when they were identified as a key demographic for Democratic incumbent Bill Clinton. Following Clinton's victory over his Republican rival Bob Dole, *soccer mom* was voted 'Word of the Year' by the American Dialect Society.

stutter step

When a player checks his run-up before taking a penalty in an attempt to unsettle the goalkeeper, it's known as a *stutter step*.

See also: *paradinha* (Brazil), *panenka* (Czech Republic), *cucchiaio* (Italy)

upper 90

'And Landon Donovan has lodged that one . . . *right* in the upper 90!' One of American soccer's most distinctive terms, *upper 90* refers to the top corner of the goal and derives from the 90° angle formed by the meeting point of post and bar. The *lower 90* is its less glamorous cousin.

See also: *onde dorme a coruja* (Brazil), *jep nest* (Trinidad and Tobago), *rašlje* (Croatia), *postage stamp* (England), *lucarne* (France), *sette* (Italy), *winkelhaak* (Netherlands), *devyatka* (Russia), *donde anidan las arañas* (Spain), *wayn yeskon shaytan* (Algeria), *fil maqass* (Egypt)

NEAR UNSTOPPABLE – TOP CORNER TERMINOLOGY

With the possible exception of a shot that crashes into the net off the crossbar, there's no sweeter sight in football than that of the ball flying into the top corner. This is how that hallowed patch of air between post and bar is known around the world.

devyatka (девятка) – *nine (Russia)*
A Russian player who places a shot into the top corner is said to have struck the *devyatka*, after a shooting drill that awards nine points for efforts that end up there.

donde anidan las arañas – *where the spiders nest (Spain)*
In Spain, a high shot that evades the goalkeeper's fingertips sends imaginary arachnids scrambling for cover.

fil maqass (في المقص) – *in the scissors (Egypt)*
The Egyptian name for the goal's top corners reimagines post and crossbar as the outspread blades of a pair of scissors.

gamma (γάμμα Γ) – *gamma (Greece)*
Handily, the third letter of the Greek alphabet (Γ) doubles as a neat depiction of a post and crossbar.

jep nest *(Trinidad and Tobago)*
Wasps are known as *jeps* in Trinidad and Tobago and their nests are commonly found in the eaves of houses, tucked away out of reach like an unstoppable shot.

lucarne – *dormer (France)*
A dormer, which is the name for a gabled window that projects out from a sloping roof, is where top-corner shots end up in France.

onde dorme a coruja – *where the owl sleeps (Brazil)*
With characteristic lyricism, the goal's loftiest extremities in Brazil are imagined to be the sort of appropriately out-of-reach place where you might come across a dozing owl.

postage stamp *(England)*
Popularised by Andy Gray, in England planting a shot top-right is likened to sticking a stamp on an envelope.

sette *– seven (Italy)*
In Italy, the top corner of the goal brings to mind the shape of the number seven. Which doesn't say much for the straightness of the average Italian goalpost.

šibenice *– gallows (Czech Republic)*
For the gloomy Czechs, the meeting point of post and bar recalls the frame of a gallows.

skinuti paučinu *– to take down the cobwebs (Croatia)*
A Croatian player who finds the top corner is declared to have carried out a spot of spring cleaning.

upper 90 *(United States)*
The American term for the top corners refers to the 90° angle found where post and crossbar meet.

wayn yeskon shaytan (وين يسكن شيطان) *– where Satan lives (Algeria)*
Antar Yahia said he put the goal that sent Algeria to the 2010 World Cup at Egypt's expense 'where the devil couldn't reach' and the expression continues to be used.

winkelhaak *– try square (Netherlands)*
To Dutch eyes, the goal's top corners are reminiscent of a try square, which is an instrument for measuring straightness in woodwork and metalwork.

EUROPE

Nobility nestles alongside novelty in the topography of European football, where the grand old nations of the sport such as England, Italy and Germany rub shoulders with newcomers like Montenegro, Kosovo and Gibraltar. Whether it's the white shirts of Real Madrid, the red jerseys of Manchester United or the black and white stripes of Juventus that are gleaming beneath the floodlights, the European game is steeped in grandeur and tradition, its stories and scandals, triumphs and tragedies known by heart by football fans the world over.

In Europe's collective football language we detect voices from the gentlemen's clubs of Victorian London and the coffee houses of inter-war Vienna, from the newspaper offices of 1950s Milan and the television studios of 1970s Paris, the street football games of 1980s Rotterdam and the training pitches of modern-day Barcelona, the whole hubbub rising up to form a chaotic and vital symphony.

AUSTRIA

Austria's enthusiastic adoption of football in the first three decades of the 20th century turned the country into continental Europe's first major football nation and the professional league that was inaugurated there in 1924 was the first to be established outside Britain.

Austria's *Wunderteam* were the pre-eminent national side of the early 1930s, but the country's football fans have not had a great deal to cheer about since a third-place finish at the 1954 World Cup.

Eiergoalie – eggs goalie

They're fussy about their eggs in Austria. A poor goalkeeper is known as an *Eiergoalie* and if he fumbles a shot into his own net it will go down as an *Eiertor* ('eggs goal'). Not to be confused with an *Eigentor* ('own goal').

See also: *pudrunäpp* (Estonia), *imuri* (Finland), *kova kaleci* (Turkey)

Gurkerl – gherkin

When a player succeeds in prodding the ball between an opponent's legs, it's known in Austria as a *Gurkerl*.

See also: *caneta* (Brazil), *huacha* (Peru), *salad* (Jamaica), *jesle* (Czech Republic), *nutmeg* (England), *klobbi* (Iceland), *panna* (Netherlands), *cueca* (Portugal), *bayda* (Morocco), *yalli* (Senegal), *shibobo* (South Africa), *deya* (Zimbabwe), *lawd daak* (Thailand)

Holzgeschnitzter – wooden carving

A large, clumsy player with no agility might be dubbed a *Holzgeschnitzter*. There's a long history of wood carving in the Austrian Tyrol, where carved Nativity scenes are a central aspect of traditional Christmas decorations.

See also: *caballo* (Costa Rica), *armario* (Spain), *kitasa* (Tanzania), *samaam al amaan* (Saudi Arabia)

Jausengegner – snack opponent

Another food-related term, a *Jausengegner* is a rival team liable to be polished off without much difficulty. To beat an opponent comfortably is to have them *im Reindl* ('in a saucepan').

Primgeiger – first violin

Reflecting the cultured approach to football on which Austria has long prided itself, the stand-out player in a team has traditionally been known as the *Primgeiger* or 'first violin'.

See also: *craque* (Brazil)

Scheiberlspiel

Before *tiki-taka*, before Total Football, before Brazil 1970, before Hungary's Magnificent Magyars, there was *Scheiberlspiel*, the mesmerisingly fluid playing style of Austria's *Wunderteam* of the early 1930s. *Spiel* means 'game' and *Scheiberl* is believed to derive from *schieben*, which means 'to push'. The word they form denoted a supple, synchronised playing style in which short passes were rapidly pushed between teammates. Under the tutelage of pioneering coach Hugo Meisl, Austria developed a graceful but devastatingly effective mode of play that turned them into the dominant team of the time. Their emblematic player was Matthias Sindelar, nicknamed *Der Papierene* ('The Paperman') because of his slender frame, whose technical dexterity and cerebral movement foreshadowed the false nines of the modern game. A 5-0 thrashing of Scotland in May 1931 served as Austria's bugle call. They put 11 unanswered goals past Germany over two meetings in Berlin (6-0) and Vienna (5-0), as well as inflicting crushing defeats upon Switzerland (8-1), Hungary (8-2), Belgium (6-1) and France (4-0). Meisl's men narrowly lost 4-3 to England at Stamford Bridge in December 1932, but *The Times* said they had been the more impressive side and declared them 'a fine team'. Sadly, they had passed their peak by the time of the 1934 World Cup in Italy, their progress ended by a 1-0 semi-final loss to the hosts in Milan. They were beaten again by Italy in the final of the 1936 Olympics and *Anschluss* with Germany meant that there was no Austrian team at the 1938 World Cup in France. Sindelar died of carbon monoxide poisoning in January 1939 at the age of 36, although rumours abounded that he had paid the price for refusing to play for the unified Germany team.

See also: *Hollandse school* (Netherlands), *passovotchka* (Russia), *tiki-taka* (Spain)

BELGIUM

Flemish (a form of Dutch) and French are Belgium's principal languages, while German is also spoken by a minority in the country.

The national team's most durable period of success occurred during the 1980s. Belgium reached the final of the 1980 European Championship, losing 2-1 to West Germany, before a team including goalkeeper Jean-Marie Pfaff, captain Jan Ceulemans and a 20-year-old Enzo Scifo reached the semi-finals of the 1986 World Cup.

Bosman – *free transfer*

As he established himself in the Standard Liège squad in the mid-1980s, Belgian youth international Jean-Marc Bosman probably dreamed of making football history. He could never have envisaged how that would eventually come to pass. After his contract at RFC Liège (his second club) expired in 1990 and the Belgian side refused an offer for his services from French second-tier outfit Dunkerque, Bosman hired lawyers to sue RFC Liège, the Royal Belgian Football Association and UEFA for restraint of trade. The case dragged on for five years before the European Court of Justice delivered a landmark judgement in December 1995, finding in favour of Bosman and ruling that all out-of-contract players in the European Union should be allowed to move clubs on free transfers. (The court also ruled that European leagues could no longer impose quotas on foreign players who came from EU countries.) Edgar Davids became the first high-profile *Bosman* when he left Ajax for Milan in 1996, the ruling serving to expedite the break-up of Louis van Gaal's great Ajax team of the mid-1990s. While Bosman's name is now cited less frequently in the context of free transfers, his place in football history is secure.

buffelstoot – *buffalo push*

A brutish header, the kind you might expect to be scored by Marouane Fellaini or Christian Benteke. Stéphane Demol scored a fondly remembered *buffelstoot* to put Belgium ahead in extra time of their 4-3 victory over the USSR in the last 16 at the 1986 World Cup.

een bal op het hoofd schilderen – *to paint a ball on the head*

Used to describe a very precise high cross that perfectly sets up an attacking player for a headed attempt at goal.

pisballetje – *pee shot*

Belgians are not squeamish about the urinary process, as anyone who's been to Brussels and contemplated the *Manneken Pis* statue of a little boy having a wee will know. In football, a dribbly attempt that doesn't find its target is known as a *pisballetje*. An alternative is *gekraakt schot* (literally a 'cracked shot').

schuiver – *slider*

A hard, low shot struck from long distance, liable to leave the goalkeeper forlornly reclining on his side as the ball flashes into one of the bottom corners.

BOSNIA AND HERZEGOVINA

Established in 1995 after the break-up of the former Yugoslavia, the Bosnia and Herzegovina national team have to date played at only one major tournament, going out in the group phase at the 2014 World Cup.

Totemic former Manchester City striker Edin Džeko is the first player from the former Yugoslavia to have scored over 50 international goals.

bubamara – *ladybird*
Nickname for the old black and white Adidas Telstar ball, which was used at the 1970 World Cup. Ladybirds are considered lucky in Bosnia. When former Yugoslavia winger Predrag Pašić decided to set up a football school in Sarajevo at the height of the Balkan conflict, he called it 'Bubamara'. Thousands of children have since passed through the school, with scores going on to become professional footballers.

See also: *gorduchinha* (Brazil), *la pecosa* (Colombia), *la bendita* (Ecuador)

dimije – *Turkish trousers*
Dimije are traditional Turkish trousers made from billowy fabric. They're gathered in at the ankles and hang low between the legs. If you succeed in nutmegging an opponent in Bosnia, you might suggest that they wear *dimije* next time. Another Bosnian term for a nutmeg is *suknjica* ('skirt').

See also: *sotana* (Argentina), *kupite mu pregaču* (Croatia), *foul thawb* (Qatar)

fildžan – *very small coffee cup*
Another Turkish loanword (the legacy of the Ottoman conquest of the Balkans), this is used to refer to skill in a confined space. Turkish coffee is very strong and is therefore served in a tiny cup known as a *fildžan*. When a tightly marked player succeeds in wriggling past a pair of opponents, you might say: '*Provoza ih u fildžanu*', which means: 'He beat them in a very small coffee cup.'

poslati ga po burek – *to send someone for a pie*
Food-related metaphors are used in several different languages when a defender is sent staggering in the wrong direction by an attacker's sleight of foot, with bread, hot dogs and coffee among the alimentary items the discombobulated player is imagined to have gone to fetch. In Bosnia the items said to be on their

imaginary shopping list are either *burek*, a traditional Bosnian pie, or *ćevapi*, which are meat rolls.

See also: *llevar a alguien a la escuelita* (Panama), *da go pratya za bira* (Bulgaria), *kohvile saatma* (Estonia), *het bos ingestuurd* (Netherlands), *sendt opp i pølsebua* (Norway), *att köpa korv* (Sweden), *pazara göndermek* (Turkey), *kupelekwa shopping* (Kenya)

BULGARIA

For football fans of a certain age, mention of Bulgaria inevitably calls to mind the celebrated collection of -ovs and -evs that shook up the world at the 1994 World Cup in the United States. A team led by the irrepressible Hristo Stoichkov dramatically eliminated France in qualifying, beat Argentina in the group phase and accounted for Mexico and Germany in the knockout rounds before their adventure was brought to an end by Italy in the last four.

brodiram (Бродирам) – *to embroider*
In Bulgaria, where embroidery forms an integral part of the national costume, to deliver a stellar performance is to *brodiram* a match. On a similar theme, a player who passes the ball with great accuracy will be said to *pas po konets* or 'pass the ball along a thread'.

da biya nyakogo kato tupan na svatba (да бия някого като тъпан на сватба) – *to beat someone like a wedding drum*
Traditional Bulgarian weddings are big, boisterous affairs soundtracked from start to finish by the pounding of double-sided *tapan* drums. To give a team a thrashing is to beat them 'like a wedding drum'.

da go pratya za bira (да го пратя за бира) – *to send someone for a beer*
When a player is taken out of the game by an opponent's trick in Bulgaria, he's described as having gone to fetch a beer.

See also: *llevar a alguien a la escuelita* (Panama), *poslati ga po burek* (Bosnia and Herzegovina), *kohvile saatma* (Estonia), *het bos ingestuurd* (Netherlands), *sendt opp i pølsebua* (Norway), *att köpa korv* (Sweden), *pazara göndermek* (Turkey), *kupelekwa shopping* (Kenya)

Gospod e bulgarin (Господ е българин) – *God is Bulgarian*

One of the most celebrated nights in Bulgarian football history occurred in Paris in November 1993 when Bulgaria came from a goal down to stun France 2-1 and qualify for the following year's World Cup. A draw would have been enough to take France through, but with the score 1-1 in the 90th minute David Ginola made the fatal decision to lump a cross into the Bulgarian box from the right. The Bulgarians countered, Luboslav Penev arcing a pass over the top for Emil Kostadinov, who rifled a shot in off the bar to claim his second goal of the game and send Dimitar Penev's side to the United States at the expense of the French. Commentating on the game for Bulgaria's national television channel, the late Nikolay Kolev spontaneously proclaimed, almost in disbelief, '*Gospod e bulgarin!*' ('God is Bulgarian!') The phrase passed into football folklore and is evoked at every triumph by the national team. Bulgaria created another sensation in the tournament itself, eliminating Mexico and Germany (the latter victory courtesy of Yordan Letchkov's flying header) before falling to Italy in the semi-finals.

zaburkvam betona (забърквам бетона) – *to mix concrete*

To tighten up at the back. Concrete is referenced in the context of defensive football in several European countries.

See also: *anti-fútbol* (Argentina), *bunker* (United States), *park the bus* (England), *catenaccio* (Italy)

CROATIA

Known around the world by their unmistakeable red and white chequerboard shirts, Croatia made an immediate impact on the international scene after being recognised by FIFA in 1992 and UEFA in 1993. Following a quarter-final showing on their major tournament bow at Euro 96, Miroslav 'Ćiro' Blažević's team surged to a startling third-place finish at the 1998 World Cup in France, with Davor Šuker's six goals earning him the Golden Boot.

The legacy of stylish playmaking established in the 1990s by Zvonimir Boban and Robert Prosinečki has been carried into the modern era by Luka Modrić.

djelitelj pravde – *dispenser of justice*

A rather grandiose term for the referee. Officiating is an unhealthy obsession in Croatia and Mateo Beusan has been one of the chief beneficiaries. The moustachioed former referee is a familiar face on Croatian TV and his *Oko sokolovo* ('Eye of the Hawk') spot, in which he delivers his verdicts on contentious decisions, has made him a household name.

kupite mu pregaču – *buy him an apron*

A nutmeg in Croatia is known as a *tunel*. If you manage to pull one off against someone, you might slyly advise your victim's teammates to *kupite mu pregaču*.

See also: *sotana* (Argentina), *dimije* (Bosnia and Herzegovina), *foul thawb* (Qatar)

močvara – *swamp*

The word *močvara* refers to the murky state of top-level football in Croatia, where corruption and cronyism have held sway for years, much to the frustration and dismay of the country's passionate fans. A symbolic figure is Zdravko Mamić, widely seen as the most powerful figure in the Croatian game. Formerly the vice-president of the Croatian Football Federation (HNS) and chief executive of Dinamo Zagreb, the country's biggest club, Mamić has been accused of money laundering, tax evasion and making physical threats to journalists and political rivals. Another former HNS vice-president, ex-referee Željko Širić, was sentenced to four years in prison in 2014 after being found guilty of making clubs pay him in order to guarantee 'fair' officiating in their matches, while in 2010 around 20 players and coaches were arrested over a betting scam.

nogomet – *football*

Britain's role in bringing football to the world means that the vast majority of countries use variations of the words 'football' or 'soccer' as their names for it, but that's not the case in Croatia, Bosnia and Slovenia, where it's known as *nogomet*. A linguist called Slavko Rutzner Radmilović is said to have come up with the term he watched students kick a ball around in Zagreb's Mažuranac park in 1893. The word is a portmanteau of *noga* ('foot') and *met* ('target'), the target in question being the goal. With Croatia, Bosnia and Slovenia all part of the Austro-Hungarian empire at the time, the word was adopted in all three countries, but not in neighbouring Serbia, where the sport would become known as *fudbal*.

See also: *vakapipopo* (Paraguay), *calcio* (Italy)

***promašio večeru** – to miss one's dinner*
A colloquial expression used when a player squanders an easy chance. Such a player might be known as a *mrtvac* or 'dead man', which comes from the expression *mrtva šansa* ('dead chance').

***rašlje** – divining rod*
The place where post and bar meet is held to resemble the forked prongs on a divining rod in Croatia. Planting a shot in the top corner is known as *skinuti paučinu* ('to take down the cobwebs').

See also: *onde dorme a coruja* (Brazil), *jep nest* (Trinidad and Tobago), *upper 90* (United States), *postage stamp* (England), *lucarne* (France), *sette* (Italy), *winkelhaak* (Netherlands), *devyatka* (Russia), *donde anidan las arañas* (Spain), *wayn yeskon shaytan* (Algeria), *fil maqass* (Egypt)

CZECH REPUBLIC

Czechoslovakia met with defeat in the finals of the 1934 and 1962 World Cups before triumphing at the 1976 European Championship thanks to Antonín Panenka's immortal penalty.

The Czech Republic's biggest achievement to date came at their first tournament following the 1993 dissolution of Czechoslovakia, when a team containing Pavel Nedvěd and Patrik Berger lost to Oliver Bierhoff's golden goal for Germany at Wembley in the final of Euro 96.

***Angličan** – Englishman*
In a nod to Geoff Hurst's notorious did-it-didn't-it third goal for England in the 1966 World Cup final, a shot that bounces into the net via the woodwork is known in the Czech Republic as an *Angličan*.

See also: *Wembley-Tor* (Germany)

***Česká ulička** – Czech alley*
This is the name given to a ball that cuts through the heart of an opposition defence. It was coined in honour of a pass played by Tomáš Pospíchal during Czechoslovakia's 3-1 loss to Brazil in the 1962 World Cup final in Chile. With 13 minutes on the clock, Pospíchal drifted infield from the right and spotted Josef

Masopust haring into the box from deep. Using the outside of his right foot, the Banik Ostrava midfielder bisected the Brazil defence with a deliciously measured through ball, leaving Masopust with the straightforward task of prodding the ball past goalkeeper Gilmar. Within two minutes Amarildo had equalised and second-half goals by Zito and Vavá allowed Brazil to retain the trophy, but Pospíchal's pinpoint pass would not be forgotten in his homeland. In neighbouring Poland, the same sort of pass is known as a *podanie w uliczkę* ('alley pass').

See also: *caviar* (France), *Zuckerpass* (Germany), *lissepasning* (Norway), *ciasteczko* (Poland), *chọc khe* (Vietnam)

jesle – *crib*

One of the Czech names for a nutmeg, *jesle* (or the diminutive *jesličky*) likens the legs of a nutmegged player to the legs of a wooden crib. An associated term is *housle*, meaning 'violin', which is thought to have been adopted purely because of its phonetic similarity to the word *jesle*.

See also: *caneta* (Brazil), *huacha* (Peru), *salad* (Jamaica), *Gurkerl* (Austria), *nutmeg* (England), *klobbi* (Iceland), *panna* (Netherlands), *cueca* (Portugal), *bayda* (Morocco), *yalli* (Senegal), *shibobo* (South Africa), *deya* (Zimbabwe), *lawd daak* (Thailand)

nabrat na saně – *to take someone on a sleigh ride*

A misleadingly cheery term that describes a player being cleaned out by an opponent's slide tackle. A similar expression exists in Finland: *pulkka*, meaning 'sled'.

See also: *reducer* (England), *Blutgrätsche* (Germany), *to burst someone* (Republic of Ireland), *stop nonsense* (South Africa), *pakka paer pao* (Pakistan), *enbarash* (Saudi Arabia)

panenka – *chipped penalty*

The most iconic penalty in football history might never have been scored had it not been for a training-ground competition over a handful of Czech korun. A talented playmaker for Prague club Bohemians, Antonín Panenka was frustrated by his inability to get the better of goalkeeper Zdeněk Hruška in their end-of-day penalty competitions. Then inspiration struck. '[Hruška] was very good at penalties, defeated me and it cost me quite a lot of money because we had some bets,' Panenka told Karel Häring in *The Blizzard*. 'I thought [about] what I could do to beat him. That was the first idea.' Panenka devised a completely new penalty technique that exploited the goalkeeper's obligation to guess the direction of the taker's shot. He would charge in as if intending to blast the net from its moorings, only to meet the ball with a feathery chip that sent it floating down the middle of the goal in a gentle parabola while the unfortunate goalkeeper plunged to one side. Panenka honed the technique for two years, using it to score several goals for Bohemians, but at the 1976 European Championship in Yugoslavia his teammates urged him not to try it, with roommate Ivo Viktor, the Czech goalkeeper, warning him that he wouldn't be allowed into their room if he did. After Czechoslovakia drew 2-2 with West Germany in the final in Belgrade, Panenka was presented with a chance to make history when Uli Hoeneß became the first player not to score in the penalty shootout, driving the fourth German kick high over the bar. Reckoning that German goalkeeper Sepp Maier was unlikely to have seen many of Bohemians' matches, he put his faith in his training-ground duels with Hruška. As Maier dived to his left, Panenka's shot arced into the middle of the net. Czechoslovakia were European champions for the first time and Panenka became a football immortal, his name referenced every time a player shows the nerve to take their life in their hands from 12 yards. Surprisingly, whereas a chipped penalty is known as a *panenka* the world over, in the Czech Republic it carries a different name. It's called a *vršovický dloubák* ('Vršovice chip'), in honour of the Prague quarter of Vršovice where Bohemians have their stadium and where Panenka first mastered the craft that made his name.

See also: *paradinha* (Brazil), *stutter step* (United States), *cucchiaio* (Italy)

pískat hovna – to whistle shits

If a Czech fan feels his team are being unfairly treated by a referee, he may accuse the official of *píská hovna* ('whistling shits').

See also: *corbeau* (France), *sędzia kalosz* (Poland), *sudyu na milo* (Russia), *referee kayu* (Malaysia)

robinzonáda

Panenka, Johan Cruyff and Cuauhtémoc Blanco have all given their names to moves that you might see on the football pitch, and in parts of Central Europe an Englishman managed to make himself every bit as permanent a part of the sport's patois. On a tour of the region with Southampton in April 1901, Jack Robinson caused jaws to drop by keeping goal with an athleticism that none of the locals had ever witnessed before. As an England international, Robinson's fame preceded him and when Southampton arrived for a match against Slavia Prague, he was persuaded to give a display of his agility before kick-off. Robinson's teammates peppered his goal with shots and in the words of club secretary Ernest Arnfield, 'scarcely a ball passed him'. Local football supporters were used to seeing goalkeepers stretching and reaching to field the ball, but Robinson threw his whole body into spectacular low saves that drew gasps from the crowd. When he had finished showing off his reflexes, spectators streamed onto the pitch and chaired him to the changing rooms. (Austrian journalist Willy Meisl gave an alternative account that Robinson's exhibition took place *after* the game, although he misremembered the year of the tour as 1899.) Southampton played further games in Vienna and Budapest and finished their tour with a record of seven straight wins, having scored 49 goals and conceded only three. By the time the squad left for home, Robinson had become a regional celebrity. Eye-catching saves were known as *robinzonádas* in the Czech Republic, Austria and Hungary until well into the 20th century, and *robinsonada* remains in use today in neighbouring Poland.

DENMARK

Danish students educated in Britain brought football to Denmark in the 1870s and established continental Europe's first football association in 1889. The Danes were quick on the uptake, finishing runners-up at the Olympics in 1908 and 1912. But their greatest moment would not occur until 1992, when Richard Møller Nielsen's fiendishly well-drilled team completed a fairytale victory at the European Championship, having been drafted in at the last minute after civil conflict forced Yugoslavia to withdraw.

Bundesligahår – *mullet*
Germany in the 1980s may have been the football era that fashion forgot, but its legacy lives on across the border in Denmark, where a mullet haircut (short on the sides, long at the back) is known as *Bundesligahår* ('Bundesliga hair'). The hairstyle is also associated with the German top flight in Hungary and the Czech Republic. In some countries it's known as 'ice hockey hair', an expression that lent its name to a 1998 song by Welsh indie band Super Furry Animals.

en Preben Elkjær – a Preben Elkjær

Preben Elkjær was a force of nature, a one-man thunderstorm who helped turn Denmark into one of the most exciting teams of the 1980s, but he was also responsible for perhaps their keenest moment of heartache, to which this expression refers. Sepp Piontek's side had already created shockwaves before they even pitched up at the 1984 European Championship, having eliminated England in qualifying courtesy of a 1-0 victory at Wembley in September 1983. Euro 84 was only their second major tournament (not including the Olympics), but Denmark were no wide-eyed ingénues. They bounced back from an opening loss against hosts France to wallop Yugoslavia 5-0 and then booked a place in the semi-finals with a tumultuous 3-2 win over Belgium in which Elkjær capped a roaring comeback with an ice-cool 84th-minute winner. A 1-1 draw with Spain in the semi-final in Lyon yielded a penalty shootout. After the first eight players to place the ball on the spot had all scored, Elkjær stepped forward . . . and casually side-footed his spot-kick over the bar. Manuel Sarabia made no such mistake with Spain's fifth kick and Denmark were out. Elkjær's misery was captured in a black and white picture that ran on the front page of Denmark's leading tabloid *Ekstra Bladet* the following day: his back to the camera, his right hand forlornly cradling his head, a large rip in his shorts (caused by an earlier collision with Spain goalkeeper Luís Arconada) revealing his backside to the world. The headline was '*FARVELKJAER*', a combination of *farvel* ('farewell') and Elkjær. *En Preben Elkjær* ('a Preben Elkjær') could have referred to so many things. It ended up becoming shorthand for a ballooned penalty.

en rigtig Jesper Olsen – a real Jesper Olsen

For Elkjær in 1984, read Jesper Olsen in 1986. Denmark made a mockery of their so-called 'Group of Death' at the World Cup in Mexico, beating Scotland and West Germany and destroying Uruguay 6-1 to advance to the last 16, where old foes Spain lay in wait. Olsen's 33rd-minute penalty put Denmark 1-0 up in Querétaro, but then calamity struck. After gathering a goal-kick from goalkeeper Lars Høgh, Olsen eased past Julio Salinas in a corridor of shade on the Denmark right and then attempted to play the ball back to Høgh. But he misread Høgh's position and instead delivered the ball straight into the path of Emilio Butragueño, who gleefully gobbled up an equaliser. Butragueño scored three more times in the second half, with Andoni Goikoetxea contributing a penalty, as Denmark capitulated to a 5-1 defeat. A risky pass has been known as *en rigtig Jesper Olsen* ever since in Denmark and the expression is also used in wider society, such as when a politician blunders. It got an airing in March 1999 when Ajax winger Jesper Grønkjær marked his Denmark debut with a *rigtig Jesper Olsen* of his own, his blind back-pass from the halfway line gifting a goal to Filippo Inzaghi in the first minute of a 2-1 loss to Italy in Copenhagen.

kattepote – *cat's paw*

A player with velvet technique, such as Michael Laudrup, might be said to possess a *kattepote*.

papegøje – *parrot*

A shot struck with the outside of the foot is mysteriously known as a 'parrot' in Denmark. If the shot is hit with the toes, giving the player striking the ball no control over where it goes, it might be scornfully dubbed a *tåhyler*, which roughly translates as 'toe howler'.

See also: *de três dedos* (Brazil), *trivela* (Portugal), *shvedka* (Russia), *NASA pass* (Nigeria), *outfoot* (Pakistan)

roligans

From *rolig*, meaning 'calm' or 'peaceful', this is the name given to the Danish national team's hard-drinking but good-natured army of fans. An ironic twist on the English word 'hooligans', it was dreamed up by Danish tabloid *BT* in June 1985 following a 4-2 home win over the Soviet Union in World Cup qualifying.

skovtur – *picnic*

When a goalkeeper comes charging out of his area, he's said in Denmark to have gone for a picnic. From *skov* ('forest) and *tur* ('trip').

See also: *sortie kamikaze* (France), *salir a por uvas* (Spain), *sortie aux fraises* (Switzerland)

ENGLAND

As the country where football as we know it today was invented, England's linguistic influence on the sport extends far beyond its shores. Look across the globe and you'll find sturdy Anglo-Saxon coinages like 'offside' and 'goal' embedded in languages ranging from Japanese to Swahili and everything in between.

England's modern football lexicon is predominantly characterised by a sharp and knowing kind of humour. It's also underpinned by a hardy streak of conservatism. For all the sophistication of the Premier League, football in British English remains a game of passion and physicality, of snubs and spats, route one and Row Z, mind games and the managerial hairdryer.

Slick television coverage and more informed analysis have brought a new level of nuance to the country's appreciation of football in recent times, but in some eternal way it continues to be seen – in Jimmy Greaves's immortal phrase – as a funny old game. While football grips the nation's attention like nothing else, England doesn't feel entirely comfortable taking it seriously.

afters

The confrontation that ensues when a player takes exception to the forcefulness or timing of an opponent's challenge is euphemistically referred to as *afters*. 'Herrera caught Henderson there and there was a little bit of *afters*.' Vocal disagreements might be ironically framed as *pleasantries* or more straightforwardly as *verbals*.

See also: *handbags* (England)

Bambi on ice

A nervous performance by a player – typically an inexperienced defender – calls to English minds the scene in Walt Disney's *Bambi* when Bambi comes a cropper on a frozen pond. Adorable in the film, less so when your centre-back's inability to control a five-yard pass results in your team going 3-0 down.

See also: *bomb scare* (Northern Ireland)

bouncebackability

Grasping for a word to describe his Crystal Palace side's ability to respond to adversity in 2004, manager Iain Dowie ended up inventing a new one: *bouncebackability*. Following a campaign and an online petition, it was added to the *Oxford English Dictionary* in June 2006 (defined as 'the capacity to recover quickly from a setback'), although the venerable book's editors found evidence that it had first been used 45 years previously in the context of American baseball. Dowie had neatly, if inelegantly, plugged a hole in the English language, and his neologism has since come to be used quite widely.

box-to-box

Label applied to a central midfield player who excels at both defensive and attacking tasks. It's a particularly English archetype, players like Duncan Edwards, Bryan Robson and Steven Gerrard having helped to romanticise the notion of the valiant midfielder who tramples every blade of grass in pursuit of victory. In recent years tactical developments have created a more rigid division of labour between defensive and attacking midfield roles, making classic *box-to-box* players something of an endangered species, but the term remains in common use and has been adopted by countries such as Italy and France.

bread and butter

When a team are eliminated from European competition or knocked out of one of the domestic cups, their attention will invariably turn back to the *bread and butter* of the league. The term is also used to describe aimless high balls that make easy work for goalkeepers and centre-backs (also referred to as *meat and drink*).

See also: *keepermat* (Norway)

clean sheet

An expression unique to Britain, a *clean sheet* is obtained (symbolically) by a team or player who go through a match without conceding a goal. It's thought to stem from the time when the Football League obliged teams to fill in score-sheets, prompting managers to ask their players to make sure a 'clean sheet' would be submitted in terms of goals conceded.

See also: *sukhar* (Ukraine)

corridor of uncertainty

This phrase is borrowed from cricket, in which it describes the hazardous zone outside off stump where a batsman attempting a shot runs the risk of nicking the ball to the wicketkeeper or slips. In football it's used to describe a cross (typically a low one) threaded into the space between defenders and goalkeeper. Another cricket-influenced term is *cricket score*, which overlooks the fact that cricket scores tend not to resemble football scorelines much beyond the first over of the day.

doing a Leeds

The Icarus of the Premier League age, Leeds paid the price for overspending in pursuit of success and now exist in a kind of conceptual gibbet cage, grimly incarnating the perils of impatient ambition as a warning to passers-by. A young and enterprising Leeds team managed by David O'Leary reached the Champions League semi-finals in 2000/01, losing over two legs to Valencia. A return to the halcyon days of the Don Revie era seemed to beckon, but the club's entire business model was predicated on qualifying for the Champions League, and when they went two seasons without doing so, the wheels came off. Obliged to slash their wage bill, Leeds began selling players hand over fist and their results nosedived. Three years on from that tie against Valencia they were relegated to the Championship, and within six years they were in League One. *Not doing a Leeds* has since become the go-to phrase for chairmen seeking to reassure fans that they will not gamble their club's livelihood on short-term success.

See also: *leejeu shijeol* (South Korea)

down to the bare bones
In a turn of phrase that conjures up images of Dickensian bleakness, a manager whose squad has been ravaged by injuries and suspensions might complain that he is *down to the bare bones*.

Fergie time
It was one of the defining images of Alex Ferguson's record-breaking 26½-year tenure as Manchester United manager. United would be losing, or perhaps drawing, in the latter stages of a game at Old Trafford and the Scot would storm to the touchline, chewing furiously and jabbing animatedly at his wristwatch every time his team's opponents indulged in anything that might be construed as time-wasting. The fourth official's board would go up to show the amount of injury time to be played, which was always a minute or two more than what the away supporter's gut instinct suggested was appropriate. United would swarm forwards, waves of red shirts crashing against an increasingly frantic sea wall of opposing defenders, until finally the goal arrived in what came to be known as *Fergie time*. A study carried out by Opta in November 2012 found that United, with Ferguson at the helm, had been granted 79 seconds more second-half stoppage time than the average figure when they were losing at home over the previous two and a half seasons – more than any other team in the Premier League (although it's worth noting that statistics show big clubs generally benefit from more added time when they're losing than smaller ones). Ferguson said after retiring in 2013 that tapping his watch

was 'a little trick' he had devised to 'spook the other team' and confessed that he had no idea how much stoppage time should have been forthcoming in any given game.

See also: *Zona Cesarini* (Italy), *jahfali* (Saudi Arabia)

fox in the box

A reasonably direct translation of the French expression *renard des surfaces* ('fox of the boxes'), this phrase was introduced to English in 2001 by Thierry Henry. After Arsenal fell to two Michael Owen goals in the FA Cup final against Liverpool, Henry told French journalists at Cardiff's Millennium Stadium that manager Arsène Wenger needed to buy a *'renard des surfaces'* like Owen to play alongside him. Wenger duly obliged, signing Francis Jeffers from Everton and expressing hope that the 20-year-old Liverpudlian would prove to be 'that fox in the box we have been talking about'. Jeffers, sadly, had left his vulpine wiles at Goodison Park and would score just four league goals for Arsenal before leaving three years later. Another French loanword helped across the Channel by Wenger is *footballistically* (a translation of the equally ungainly French term *footballistiquement*).

ghost goal

Ghost goal is the term applied to a situation where a team are either (a) awarded a goal despite the ball having not clearly crossed the line or (b) not awarded a goal despite the ball having done so. Its use was popularised by José Mourinho, who complained – and continues to complain – that Luis García's decisive goal in Liverpool's Champions League semi-final victory over Chelsea in 2005 didn't cross the line. Replays of the incident were inconclusive. Months earlier, Manchester United goalkeeper Roy Carroll got away with calamitously spilling a 55-yard lob by Tottenham's Pedro Mendes into his own net despite the ball having crossed the line by at least a yard. The most curious *ghost goal* of recent years came in September 2008 when assistant referee Nigel Bannister convinced referee Stuart Attwell to award a goal to Reading against Watford after the ball bounced a couple of yards wide of the right-hand post and didn't even cross the byline before being hooked back into the danger area by a Reading player. The introduction of goal-line technology means that such incidents are increasingly rare.

See also: *Wembley-Tor* (Germany)

goal hanger

Heard more in the playground than the Premier League (although there are exceptions), this is the term for a player who spends the entire game hanging around close to the opponent's goal in the sole hope of getting his name on the score-sheet. A prime English example was Gary Lineker. Sometimes known as a *tap-in merchant*.

See also: *quechón* (Panama), *cherry-picking* (United States), *ficar na mama* (Portugal), *atetɛ nkura* (Ghana), *pettu kedakunnavan* (India)

hairdryer

Coined by former Manchester United striker Mark Hughes, *the hairdryer treatment* refers to the furious close-range bollockings issued by Alex Ferguson during his time as United manager. Ferguson insisted that he was responsible for no more than 'half a dozen' such outbursts while he ruled the roost at Old Trafford, but stories about him blowing his lid were legion. 'There's nothing worse than getting the "hairdryer" from Sir Alex,' Wayne Rooney wrote in his 2012 autobiography, *My Decade in the Premier League*. 'When it happens, the manager stands in the middle of the room and loses it at me. He gets right up in my face and shouts. It feels like I've put my head in front of a BaByliss Turbo Power 2200.' (It might seem strange for Rooney, whose follicular issues are well-known, to be on brand-name terms with such a device, but he has admitted that he needs to have either a hairdryer or a vacuum cleaner roaring beside his bed

David Beckham gets a blast from Sir Alex Ferguson's *hairdryer*

in order to fall asleep.) If they don't reach for the hairdryer, angry managers are also imagined to *throw teacups* during the half-time interval.

handbags

Slightly sexist term used to describe a physical altercation between opposing players or teams during which arms are raised and hands flapped around but no punches thrown.

See also: *afters* (England)

hoof

Long-ball football was once seen as a good, honest tactic in the English game, but in these more enlightened times it has come to be perceived as uncultured. Accordingly, when a centre-back elects not to attempt a risky pass into the feet of a teammate but to larrup the ball upfield with all his might, mocking howls of '*Hoof!*' may be heard from the stands. An alternative is '*Have it!*', as uttered by portly comedian Peter Kay after he interrupts a group keepy-uppy session with an agricultural volleyed clearance in a 2002 John Smith's beer commercial.

See also: *viva il parroco* (Italy)

hospital pass

A pass that leaves a teammate at risk of being painfully clattered by an opponent. The term also exists in rugby union, where the chances of actually ending up in hospital as the result of a bad pass are a good deal higher.

See also: *cemetery pass* (Nigeria)

Keystone Cops

The *Keystone Cops* were a band of comically incompetent policemen who appeared in slapstick silent films produced by the now defunct Keystone Studios in the early 20th century. A hundred years on, their legacy endures through the medium of English football. If a team squander several opportunities to clear the ball before conceding a goal, they might find themselves accused of *Keystone Cops* defending. A panic-stricken defence could also be described as being *at sixes and sevens*, an idiom that can be traced back to the works of Chaucer and Shakespeare, and is believed to derive from a 14th-century dice game called hazard.

See also: *vrouwen en kinderen eerst* (Netherlands), *hawaiifotball* (Norway), *andar aos papéis* (Portugal)

Klinsmann

Derided as a diver following his surprise move from Monaco to Tottenham in 1994 (the legacy of the dying ant routine that helped to get Argentina's Pedro Monzón sent off in the 1990 World Cup final), German striker Jürgen Klinsmann came up with the perfect riposte to his critics. After scoring with a flashing header on his debut in a 4-3 victory at Sheffield Wednesday, he ran towards the touchline before flinging himself to the ground in a mock dive and sliding along on his chest. England was charmed and a celebration beloved of schoolboy footballers was born. The diving celebration, now universally known as a *Klinsmann*, had been the canny suggestion of Klinsmann's new teammate Teddy Sheringham as a ruse to get Britain's tabloid press onside. Klinsmann had considered donning a snorkel and goggles for his introductory press conference, but thought better of it at the last minute and left the props he had brought with him in his backpack.

See also: *Schwalbe* (Germany), *grassrolling* (Iran)

magic sponge

The modern physiotherapist's bag contains a range of sprays, gels and bandages, but the old-fashioned way was to trust in the restorative powers of a freezing cold sponge. When a player is left writhing in apparent agony after a challenge, only to spring to his feet following some fleeting attention from the physio, it's ironically heralded as the work of the *magic sponge*.

Makélélé role

Claude Makélélé excelled to such an extent as a deep-lying midfielder for Chelsea that the position was re-named after him. A crucial cog in a Real Madrid team that won two league titles and the 2002 Champions League, Makélélé was highly esteemed by his teammates, but when he asked for his salary to be brought into line with those of his *Galáctico* colleagues, Florentino Pérez effectively closed the door in his face. 'We will not miss Makélélé,' the Madrid president proclaimed after the France international left for Chelsea in 2003. 'His technique is average, he lacks the speed and skill to take the ball past opponents and 90 per cent of his distribution either goes backwards or sideways.' If Pérez couldn't see what Makélélé brought to a team, José Mourinho certainly could. Arriving at Chelsea a year after Makélélé, Mourinho immediately realised how the former Nantes man could help him to exploit the tactical inertia in England's top flight. 'If I have a triangle in midfield, Makélélé behind and two others just in front, I will always have an advantage against a pure 4-4-2 where the central midfielders are side by side,' Mourinho later explained. 'That's because I will always have an extra man . . . There is nothing a pure 4-4-2 can do to stop things.' With Makélélé imperiously anchoring a three-man midfield, Chelsea romped to the title by 12 points in Mourinho's first season and cantered home eight points clear the following campaign. Madrid didn't win the league again until 2007, by which time Pérez had resigned.

See also: *cinco* (Argentina), *volante* (Brazil), *pihkatappi* (Finland), *sentinelle* (France), *stofzuiger* (Netherlands), *trinco* (Portugal)

Mickey Mouse Cup

Derisive name for a competition deemed inferior by fans, typically used in reference to the League Cup. When Liverpool's fans celebrated winning the FA Cup, League Cup and UEFA Cup in 2001, Manchester United supporters dismissed it as a *Mickey Mouse Treble*, having seen their own side win an illustrious triple of Premiership, FA Cup and Champions League trophies two seasons earlier. The term was turned back on United's fans in 2017 when Mourinho talked up the fact that he had won three competitions in his first season at Old Trafford despite one of those trophies being the Community Shield (which is generally viewed in England as a glorified friendly). The 'Mickey Mouse' tag has also been applied to supposedly second-rate leagues such as Major League Soccer and the Scottish Premiership.

nutmeg

There's no more sure-fire way to shred an opposing player's authority than with a *nutmeg*. How better to humiliate an opponent than to effectively play the ball right through them and then collect it on the other side? 'You want the ball? Here it is. Oh, you don't want it? OK, I'll have it back.' In English, the word *nutmeg* has often been said to be either rhyming slang for 'leg' or a reference to the nutmegged player's testicles (or 'nuts'), since it's directly beneath their reproductive organs that the ball is played. But in *Football Talk: The Language and Folklore of the World's Greatest Game*, Peter Seddon asserts that it actually refers to a phrase that arose from the nutmeg trade in the 1870s. Unscrupulous American nutmeg traders would dilute their product with wood shavings before shipping it across to England, and people who were duped by the scam were said to have been *nutmegged*. The expression passed into common use and from there it was a short hop to the terraces.

See also: *caneta* (Brazil), *huacha* (Peru), *salad* (Jamaica), *Gurkerl* (Austria), *jesle* (Czech Republic), *klobbi* (Iceland), *panna* (Netherlands), *cueca* (Portugal), *bayda* (Morocco), *yalli* (Senegal), *shibobo* (South Africa), *deya* (Zimbabwe), *lawd daak* (Thailand)

one for the cameras

When a goalkeeper eschews a regulation save for something more spectacular – acrobatically tipping the ball over the crossbar instead of catching it, for example – it'll go down as *one for the cameras*. A keeper deemed to have reacted too slowly when beaten by an effort from an opposing player might be said to have *gone down in instalments*.

park the bus

Originally a Portuguese expression (*estacionar o autocarro*), this describes the tactics of a team who defend deep with every player behind the ball in the hope of grinding out a draw or sneaking a win on the counter-attack. Mourinho introduced the concept to British audiences after his Chelsea side were held to a 0-0 draw by Tottenham at Stamford Bridge in November 2004. 'As we say in Portugal, they brought the bus and they left the bus in front of the goal,' he said. The great irony, of course, is that in the years since, Mourinho has arguably come to embody the concept of 'parking the bus' more than any other manager. In perhaps his signature performance, Internazionale weathered the first-half dismissal of Thiago Motta and a Barcelona onslaught to come away from Camp Nou with a 1-0 defeat in April 2010 that was enough to carry them into the Champions League final. 'People say we parked the bus, but it's not true. We parked the plane, not the bus, and we parked the plane for two reasons,' said Mourinho, whose side won 3-2 on aggregate. 'The first reason, because we had 10 men. The second reason, because we beat them 3-1 [at San Siro], not with the bus, or the boat, or the plane, but by smashing them with incredible attacking football.' Thanks to Mourinho, 'parking the bus' has become such a common term that every remotely defensive performance by one of his teams sends a tidal wave of Mourinho bus driver memes flooding across Twitter.

See also: *anti-fútbol* (Argentina), *bunker* (United States), *zaburkvam betona* (Bulgaria), *catenaccio* (Italy)

postage stamp

A shot or header that flies into the top corner of the goal (strictly speaking, the top-*right* corner) might be said to have hit the *postage stamp*. An alternative term is *top bins*.

See also: *onde dorme a coruja* (Brazil), *jep nest* (Trinidad and Tobago), *upper 90* (United States), *rašlje* (Croatia), *lucarne* (France), *sette* (Italy), *winkelhaak* (Netherlands), *devyatka* (Russia), *donde anidan las arañas* (Spain), *wayn yeskon shaytan* (Algeria), *fil maqass* (Egypt)

prawn sandwich brigade

After a low-key Champions League home game against Dynamo Kyiv in November 2000, Manchester United captain Roy Keane launched a broadside about the lack of atmosphere and pointed his finger squarely at the supporters in Old Trafford's hospitality boxes. 'Away from home our fans are fantastic. I'd call them the hardcore fans,' said the Irishman. 'But at home they have a few drinks and probably the prawn sandwiches and they don't realise what's going on out on the pitch. I don't think some of the people who come to Old Trafford can spell "football", never mind understand it.' Leaving aside the confusing equating of corporate affluence with an inability to spell, Keane's words struck a chord and the expression *prawn sandwich brigade* quickly took root as a derogatory term for corporate match-goers.

See also: *kaaskijkers* (Netherlands), *comepipas* (Spain)

reducer

Worried about the Fancy Dan winger limbering up on the opposite side of the halfway line with the flashy boots and socks pulled up over his knees? A good, early *reducer* should sort him out. The *reducer*, as its name suggests, is a deliberately aggressive, bone-crunching tackle aimed at roughing up a talented opponent and thereby reducing their ability to influence the game. Increasingly rare at professional level because of a tightening up of the rules regarding foul play, it remains a hardy perennial of Britain's Sunday league scene. Also referred to as *letting him know you're there*. *Reducer* is an example of *Ronglish*, the name given to the idiosyncratic patter of former television pundit Ron Atkinson. Until his mainstream broadcasting career was brought to an end by a racism controversy in 2004, Big Ron played a big part in shaping the language of English football via his role as a colour commentator for ITV. Terms either coined or popularised by him include *lollipop* (a stepover), *spotter's badge* (awarded to a player for a fine piece of vision), *early doors* (the early stages of a match) and *eyebrows* (a headed flick-on).

See also: *nabrat na sane* (Czech Republic), *Blutgrätsche* (Germany), *to burst someone* (Republic of Ireland), *stop nonsense* (South Africa), *pakka paer pao* (Pakistan), *enbarash* (Saudi Arabia)

route one

A cornerstone of the English game, *route one football* is believed to owe its name to a panel show called *Quiz Ball* that ran on the BBC between 1966 and 1972. Two teams of football players from British clubs attempted to work their way down an electronic football pitch by answering a series of general knowledge questions. *Route one* was the quickest path to goal – a single, death-or-glory question that, if answered correctly, would yield a point. The 1980s was the high point of *route one football* (otherwise known as *kick and rush*) in England, with both Watford and Wimbledon rising from the fourth tier to the top flight – and into FA Cup finals – on the back of the tactic. The influence of foreign managers and players in the Premier League era has brought more tactical variety to the English game, making *route one* a contentious term, but managers such as Tony Pulis have shown that *percentage football* can still be effective.

See also: *bakrom* (Norway), *långa bollar på Bengt* (Sweden), *bbeung chuk gu* (South Korea)

Row Z

Imagined back row of seating in a stadium where rudimentary clearances and wayward shots are pictured to have landed. A defender who pays the price for trying to keep the ball on the deck in his defensive third will be witheringly told that he *should have just put it in Row Z*.

Roy of the Rovers stuff

A term for improbable feats and edge-of-the-seat victories, named after the long-running comic strip about heroic striker Roy Race and his fictional team Melchester Rovers, which first appeared in September 1954. Another comic – the *Schoolboys' Own Library* – was name-checked by commentator Barry Davies when Tottenham's Paul Gascoigne scored his memorable 30-yard free-kick against Arsenal in the 1991 FA Cup semi-final at Wembley. 'Oh, I say!' exclaimed Davies in trademark fashion. 'Brilliant! That is *Schoolboys' Own* stuff.'

show pony

A player who plays to the crowd with showy but ineffective tricks is contemptuously known in England as a *show pony* (cf. Cristiano Ronaldo in his early years at Manchester United). The phrase carries an implied comparison with *workhorse*, the name applied to an honest but technically deficient footballer who earns the affections of his team's supporters by running himself into the ground every time he steps onto the pitch (not to be mistaken with a *carthorse*, which is a sardonic term for a large, useless striker). A player or manager perceived to owe their success to one particular tactic might be scornfully branded a *one-trick pony*. The association between ponies and showing off derives from their use as circus acts in the United States during the 19th century.

squeaky bum time

An Alex Ferguson coinage, this refers to the nervous final weeks of a title run-in and brings to mind the sound made by someone shifting around in a plastic seat while watching a tense match. Ferguson's mastery of *mind games* saw him portrayed by the media as a kind of Jedi mind lord, capable of inflicting mental meltdowns upon rival managers (Kevin Keegan, Rafael Benítez) with a single skilfully placed barb. His first use of the phrase *squeaky bum time* occurred during the closing weeks of the 2002/03 campaign, when United chased down Arsenal's eight-point lead to regain the title lost to Arsène Wenger's side the previous season.

starfish

Peter Schmeichel joined Manchester United from Brondby in August 1991 and English football had never seen a goalkeeper like him. The giant Dane's background was in handball and his use of techniques from the sport was revolutionary. Goalkeepers had long been told to make themselves big, but Schmeichel took things to the next level, dynamically tearing from his line, arms spread wide, to constrict the angle as an attacker bore down on goal. His trademark type of save was the *starfish* (or *star jump*), typically witnessed when an opponent took aim from close range and it was impossible for Schmeichel to predict where the ball would go. The Denmark international would leap into the air and fully extend his arms and legs, turning his giant 6ft 3in frame into a huge, bright green barrier. He memorably used the technique to repel an Iván Zamorano header during United's Champions League quarter-final win over Internazionale in March 1999. It has since been adopted by goalkeepers the world over.

St Totteringham's Day

St Totteringham's Day is the day marked by Arsenal's fans when their team can no longer be overtaken by local rivals Tottenham in the league table. The term was invented by an Arsenal fan called Julian Shulman and was first mentioned on the Arseweb blog in March 2002. Arsenal's supporters celebrated *St Totteringham's Day* for 21 successive seasons between 1995 and 2016 before Spurs finally managed to poop the party in 2017.

tekkers

In *Wayne Rooney's Street Striker*, which ran on Sky 1 between 2008 and 2010, the show's titular figure went in search of talented street footballers, judging their performances in challenges that involved dribbling between rolling tyres or controlling footballs thrown from the tops of high-rise buildings. Rooney was assisted by Andy Ansah, a former Football League player, whose description of impressive technique as 'unbelievable tekkers' was turned into a weekly segment on *Soccer AM*. The word *tekkers* is now used approvingly when a player produces an arresting touch in a game, although it doesn't sound quite right leaving the mouth of anyone aged over 25. A similar term is *swaz* (or *swazz*), a favourite expression of Sky pundit Jamie Redknapp, which is used to describe the effect on a swerving shot.

to pick someone's pocket

To dispossess an opponent, typically having crept up on them and caught them unawares: 'Xhaka was dawdling a bit there and Hazard has *picked his pocket.*'

top, top player

To be described as a *top player* might appear, on the surface, to be a pretty unambiguous compliment, but that's not the case in England, where a cloudy but nonetheless crucial distinction exists between a *top player* and a *top, top player*. Put simply, whereas *top player* is generally felt to mean an impressive elite-level performer, *top, top player* is reserved for those who fall into the *world-class* bracket (the precise meaning of which is another debate entirely). Ferguson caused a storm in 2013 when he used his autobiography to assert that Steven Gerrard, the Liverpool captain, was 'not a top, top player'. Gerrard admitted that he had been 'a bit gutted' to learn of Ferguson's opinion. But as the man who once signed Eric Djemba-Djemba and Kléberson in the same transfer window, Ferguson's ability to spot a good midfielder was not exactly beyond reproach.

war chest

In the eyes of Britain's tabloid headline-writers, this is what a manager receives when he's given money to spend on new players in the transfer market.

wet Wednesday night in Stoke

'It's all well and good walking the ball into the net against your Getafes and your Almerías, but could he do it on a wet Wednesday night in Stoke?' Lionel Messi has won just about everything there is to win in the game, broken just about every record there is to break and scored goals so exquisite it's a wonder people don't spontaneously combust when watching them, but unless and until he does it on a squally evening in the Potteries, there will always be an asterisk beside his name. At least that's what you believe if you subscribe to the notion that England's top division remains football's ultimate testing ground. During the Tony Pulis era, Stoke's Britannia Stadium was considered England's most intimidating top-flight ground, its open corners inviting chill winds to whip across the pitch, its home team playing a kind of brutalist football reminiscent of a battle scene from *The Lord of the Rings*. Andy Gray was the first man to describe the Barcelona–Stoke conundrum during Sky's coverage of a game between Manchester City and Everton in December 2010. 'I don't know if Barcelona have ever gone to a place like the Britannia Stadium and suffered the kind of onslaught from Tony Pulis's team of long throws and free-kicks,' he mused, 'or been up to a place like Blackburn and been beaten up by their long balls into the box.' It would certainly have been an interesting experiment, but even amid a howling gale and beneath a barrage of Rory Delap long throws, you suspect that Messi would probably still have found a way to get past Ryan Shawcross.

Lionel Messi sizes up the opposition on a *wet Wednesday night in Stoke*

ESTONIA

Having never graced a major championship, Estonia's only match to date at a global event was a 1-0 first-round loss to the United States at the 1924 Olympic Games.

Estonia's population of around 1.3 million people means national team coaches have only a tiny talent pool from which to choose players, which helps to explain why the Baltic state has seen more of its international footballers pass the 100-cap mark than almost any other European nation.

barankad – *goalless draw*

A *baranka* is a hard, circular biscuit with a hole in the middle. Two *barankad* side by side are imagined to resemble the zeroes in a 0-0 draw.

See also: *oxo* (Brazil), *brilstand* (Netherlands)

kohvile saatma – *to send (someone) for coffee*
When an attacker deceives a defender with a trick. In a complementary expression, when a shot flies well wide or balloons over the crossbar, the phrase employed is *läks piima järele*, which means 'it went to get milk'.

See also: *llevar a alguien a la escuelita* (Panama), *poslati ga po burek* (Bosnia and Herzegovina), *da go pratya za bira* (Bulgaria), *het bos ingestuurd* (Netherlands), *sendt opp i pølsebua* (Norway), *att köpa korv* (Sweden), *pazara göndermek* (Turkey), *kupelekwa shopping* (Kenya)

maasikas – *strawberry*
Staying in the kitchen, a beautiful goal is known as a 'strawberry'. An associated diminutive is *mammu*, meaning 'berry'.

pudrunäpp – *porridge-fingers*
While an Estonian goalkeeper might be grandly described as a *puurilukk* ('cage lock') or *puurivaht* ('cage guard'), a keeper who routinely lets in goals that he ought to keep out is depicted as having hands made of soggy oats.

See also: *Eiergoalie* (Austria), *imuri* (Finland), *kova kaleci* (Turkey)

FINLAND

Finland's national team have been known as *Huuhkajat* (meaning 'Eagle-owls') ever since an eagle-owl temporarily interrupted a Euro 2008 qualifying match between Finland and Belgium in June 2007 by swooping down into Helsinki's Olympic Stadium and alighting on one of the goals. (The owl in question was subsequently christened 'Bubi'.)

Finland have never qualified for a major tournament, although they came within three points of reaching Euro 2008 under Roy Hodgson.

banaanipotku – *banana kick*
One of Finland's greatest players, Kai Pahlman was credited with inventing a type of free-kick known as the *banaanipotku*, which enabled him to impart wild swerve on the ball. The technique brought him many goals and served as the title for a football book that he published in 1969. As well as playing 56 times for Finland and scoring 191 goals in the Finnish top flight between 1956 and 1972

(a tally bettered only by Heikki Suhonen), Pahlman also found time to work as a professional pianist.

See also: *folha seca* (Brazil), *la maledetta* (Italy), *mukaitenshūto* (Japan)

eteenpäin on menty – *we have gone forwards*

Eteenpäin on menty was a catchphrase frequently uttered by Finland national coach Antti Muurinen to defend the progress his side had made in the face of recurring setbacks. Muurinen was in charge of Finland from 2000 to 2005 and despite failing to guide them to a major tournament in three qualifying campaigns, he was always determined to look on the bright side. His quotation became so well known that it's referred to simply as *EOM*, which is now the name of a Finnish football magazine.

imuri – *vacuum cleaner*

A weak goalkeeper is likened to a vacuum cleaner because he can't stop things passing through him. This term has been in use in Finland since the 1960s.

See also: *Eiergoalie* (Austria), *pudrunäpp* (Estonia), *kova kaleci* (Turkey)

littipeukku – *Litti thumb*

Jari Litmanen, Finland's finest footballer, had a habit of showing approval to teammates on the pitch by performing a kind of bashful thumbs-up in which only the tip of his thumb was raised. His nickname was 'Litti' and his distinctive gesture was known as the *littipeukku*. The word and gesture continue to be used in Finland when people wish to express agreement with something, and there's a long-running internet forum dedicated to collating photographs of people who have been caught performing an accidental *littipeukku*.

pihkatappi – *faecal plug*

When a bear hibernates, a large mass of hardened matter called a faecal plug forms in its colon. Made up of faeces, dead intestinal cells and hair, it sits there, gradually increasing in size, until the bear emerges from its lair in the spring and deposits it outside. In Finland, where the forests teem with bears, the word for a faecal plug is *pihkatappi*. In football terms, it's used to describe a defensive midfielder who plugs the gap in front of his team's defence. And you thought left-back was an unglamorous position.

See also: *cinco* (Argentina), *volante* (Brazil), *Makélélé role* (England), *sentinelle* (France), *stofzuiger* (Netherlands), *trinco* (Portugal)

FRANCE

The French have always had a way with words. From the scandalising satires of Molière to the candid incantations of MC Solaar, via the poetry of Rimbaud, the rousing oratory of De Gaulle and the smoke-enwreathed seductions of Serge Gainsbourg, France is a country defined by its determination to define itself. Its footballers – Thuram, Cantona, Gourcuff – are an uncommonly introspective bunch and its national football vocabulary is thick with imagination and lyricism.

Fittingly for a place where every conceivable facet of a person's day-to-day life is covered by some piece of paperwork or other, France has delineated football's technical nuts and bolts in minute detail. And as you would expect from a country where food is a national obsession, culinary metaphors abound.

aile de pigeon – *pigeon's wing*
This refers to when a player extends a bent leg either behind him or to one side – mimicking the shape of a pigeon's wing – and uses the exterior of his foot or his heel to control the ball, flick it on or steer it towards goal. Zlatan Ibrahimović is a master of the craft, as demonstrated by the gloriously adroit taekwondo flick with which he scored for Paris Saint-Germain against Bastia in October 2013.

Zlatan Ibrahimović demonstrates the skill known in French as an *aile de pigeon* ('pigeon's wing')

93

appels croisés – *crossed calls*
When two forward players deliberately cross paths as they call for the ball in an attempt to disorientate the opposition defence.

bijou – *jewel*
Typically used to describe a delightful goal. Can also refer to a particularly refined pass, touch or piece of skill.

but casquette – *hat goal*
A goal that owes directly to an embarrassing goalkeeping mistake is known in France as a *but casquette*. According to French sources, in an English Second Division game between Hull and Southampton in November 1927, Hull scored the game's only goal after the Southampton goalkeeper's cap dropped down over his eyes, temporarily blinding him. It's a charming tale, but there's no record of the goalkeeper identified in the French accounts of the incident, a certain C. Jailin, having ever played for Southampton. Saints' goalkeeper in the game was Tommy Allen, which is a possible corruption of 'Jailin', but contemporary reports on the match absolve him of blame. Hull's goal arrived early in the second half when Southampton defender Michael Keeping (who would go on to manage Real Madrid) inadvertently deflected a powerful cross from Hull inside-forward Jimmy Howieson over Allen and into his own net. The report on the game that appeared in the *Athletic News* said: 'Allen, excusably, was altogether unprepared for such a happening and had no opportunity of saving.' A more likely explanation is that the expression *but casquette* crept into football parlance on the other side of the Channel because of the frequency of episodes in which goalkeeper's caps somehow got in the way. Stories from the 1950s tell of goalkeepers throwing their caps at the ball or flinging them in the faces of opposition strikers in the hope of putting them off, while Racing Club's daredevil keeper René Vignal once made the headlines for rushing out of his box during a game against Marseille and then ostentatiously removing his hat in order to head the ball away. A calamity-prone goalkeeper may be imagined to wear *gants de peau de pêche* or 'peach-skin gloves'.

See also: *frango* (Brazil), *birthuz* (Israel)

café crème – *coffee with cream*
A top-drawer piece of skill – one liable to elicit an approving 'Ooh' from the crowd and leave one, two or even three opponents floundering – is known as a *café crème*.

casser les reins – *break the kidneys*

The NBA has popularised the concept of the 'ankle-breaker' – a sharp change of direction or feint that sends your opponent careening off in the wrong direction, their ankle ligaments creaking. In French football it's the kidneys, curiously, that are destroyed when a full-back is left flat on the turf by a slippery wide player. Other terms used when a defender is beaten all ends up include *mystifier* ('mystify') and *enrhumer*, which means 'to give (someone) a cold'.

caviar

When a player creates a chance for a teammate that simply cannot be missed, it's known as *un caviar*.

See also: *Česká ulička* (Czech Republic), *Zuckerpass* (Germany), *lissepasning* (Norway), *ciasteczko* (Poland), *chọc khe* (Vietnam)

champ de patates – *potato field*

A poor playing surface. A *patate* is a goal scored from distance with a mighty shot.

coaching

French football writing brims with inelegantly appropriated English terms, of which *coaching* is one. It's typically used to refer to a coach's substitutions. A substitute who comes on and scores is described as an example of *bon coaching* ('good coaching'). A substitute who proves ineffective or the withdrawal of a player who was playing well are signs of *mauvais coaching* ('poor coaching').

See also: *magojastro* (India)

coiffeurs – *hairdressers*

A term used to describe reserve players, said to derive from an exchange overheard at Paris's Stade Saint-Ouen in reference to a 1932 match between Racing Club de Paris and Arsenal that had been scheduled to take place on a Monday. According to a report in *Paris Match* magazine, when someone remarked that nobody would turn up to watch, a spectator replied that '*les bouchers et les coiffeurs*' ('butchers and hairdressers') would, Monday traditionally being a day off for members of both professions.

contrôle orienté – *orientated control*
When a player controls the ball and moves it in his intended direction of travel in one motion (a Zinedine Zidane speciality). A poor piece of control will be teasingly described as *contrôle désorienté* ('disorientated control').

corbeau – *raven*
Less than complimentary nickname for a referee, which made more sense when they all used to wear black. *Les Corbeaux* ('The Ravens') is also the nickname of Congolese heavyweights Tout Puissant Mazembe.

See also: *pískat hovna* (Czech Republic), *sędzia kalosz* (Poland), *sudyu na milo* (Russia), *referee kayu* (Malaysia)

faire trembler les filets – *make the nets quiver*
Synonym for scoring a goal. This being France, it could just as easily be a line from an erotic novel about an amorous fisherman.

faire une arconada – *do an Arconada*
The concept of the championship-winning goal is one of football's most evocative, but it's striking to recall how many major tournaments have been decided by blunders rather than brilliance. For every Geoff Hurst hat-trick or David Trezeguet golden goal, there's Roberto Baggio ballooning his penalty into the Pasadena sky or Oliver Kahn shovelling the ball into Ronaldo's path in the 2002 World Cup final. Even Trezeguet had his own fall guy moment, his missed penalty in the 2006 World Cup final effectively deciding the shootout and handing Italy the trophy. It took France 80 years to win a first major honour and while their breakthrough success owed much to the goal-scoring genius of Michel Platini, it was also partly down to the inadvertent generosity of Luis Arconada. Having reached the final of the 1984 European Championship on home soil, France were struggling to break Spain down at Parc des Princes when Spanish centre-back Salva was penalised for bringing down Bernard Lacombe two yards outside the penalty area and slightly to the left of centre in the 57th minute. Platini, already the tournament's top scorer with eight goals, curled the set-piece towards the bottom-right corner. Arconada, positioned on that side of his goal, had a relatively simple save to make, falling forward and a little to the left to gather the ball. But as he landed, the ball squirmed out from beneath him and rolled over the line. Yvon Le Roux's dismissal came too late for Spain to exploit and in the final

minute Jean Tigana freed Bruno Bellone to run through and chip Arconada for France's second goal. The Basque's role in France's moment of glory is recalled to this day. Whenever a goalkeeper commits a similar gaffe, he's said to have 'done an Arconada'.

fermer la boutique – *close the boutique*
When a team decide to defend a lead. The (very) French equivalent of 'shut up shop'.

fessée – *spanking*
Used, as in English, to describe a heavy defeat. Alternatively known as a *gifle* or 'slap'.

Footix
A jaunty blue cockerel with a red crest, Footix was the mascot for the 1998 World Cup in France. The *-ix* suffix in his name reflects the names given to the Gauls in the *Astérix* comic strip. *Footix* gained a second lease of life after the tournament as a pejorative nickname for people who suddenly developed an interest in football when France became world champions.

grand pont – *big bridge*
The French term for a nutmeg is *petit pont* ('little bridge'). Its sister term, *grand pont*, describes the act of knocking the ball past an opponent on one side and running round to collect it on the other. Ibrahimović and Jérémy Ménez have both used it to elude goalkeepers before scoring in recent years – the former for PSG against Saint-Étienne in April 2015, the latter for Milan against Parma in September 2014 – with Ménez adding an outrageous back-heeled finish (or *talonnade*) for good measure.

See also: *drible de vaca* (Brazil)

jeu à la nantaise
The name used to describe the attractive playing style associated with FC Nantes and, in particular, Jean-Claude 'Coco' Suaudeau, who twice turned the west-coast club into the most spectacular team in the land. As a player at Nantes in the 1960s, Suaudeau played under José Arribas, who's credited with laying the foundations for the *jeu à la nantaise*, a playing philosophy based around quick, one-touch passing, intelligent movement and powerful counter-attacks.

Suaudeau won two Ligue 1 titles under Arribas before becoming academy director and, later, first-team coach. His 1982/83 Nantes team, spearheaded by prolific Yugoslav striker Vahid Halilhodžić, streaked to the Ligue 1 title and are considered one of the greatest club sides France has produced. After being dismissed in 1988, Suaudeau returned to the helm in 1991 and built another fine team around home-grown players such as Christian Karembeu, Nicolas Ouédec and Patrice Loko. A more athletic side than the 1983 vintage, they lost just once over the course of the 1994/95 campaign and surged to the title by 10 points, setting a Ligue 1 record of 32 matches without defeat. Despite losing Karembeu and Loko, the club reached the Champions League semi-finals the following season, going down 4-3 on aggregate to eventual winners Juventus. Suaudeau was succeeded in 1997 by Raynald Denoueix, who had replaced him as academy director. Denoueix employed the same principles to lead Nantes to two Coupe de France successes and the 2001 Ligue 1 crown.

joli – *pretty*

A favoured exclamation of co-commentators, the cry of *'Oh, joli!'* will often go up when a player embarrasses an opponent with an extravagant piece of skill. *'Oh la la!'* is another, the number of *'la'*s rising in direct proportion to the quality of the goal or magnificence of the skill.

langue de bois – *wooden language*

Term used to describe any vague platitude trotted out by a player or coach. *'L'important, c'est les trois points.'*

lucarne – *dormer*

In France, a strike that flashes into the top corner is said to have entered the *lucarne* or 'dormer' – a gabled window projecting out from a sloping roof. A particularly well-placed effort will end up *en pleine lucarne* ('right in the top corner'). A shot into one of the bottom corners finds the *soupirail* ('basement window').

See also: *onde dorme a coruja* (Brazil), *jep nest* (Trinidad and Tobago), *upper 90* (United States), *rašlje* (Croatia), *postage stamp* (England), *sette* (Italy), *winkelhaak* (Netherlands), *devyatka* (Russia), *donde anidan las arañas* (Spain), *wayn yeskon shaytan* (Algeria), *fil maqass* (Egypt)

mouiller le maillot – *wet the jersey*

An expression (and not a particularly attractive one) used to describe physical effort by a player or team. As Marseille's notoriously demanding supporters are fond of chanting: '*Mouille le maillot ou casse toi!*' ('Wet the jersey or sod off!')

neuf et demi – *nine and a half*

Employed to describe a player, perhaps like Wayne Rooney, who's not quite a number nine, but not really a number 10 either.

See also: *schaduwspits* (Netherlands)

papinade

As demonstrated by the YouTube video that shows Mark Hughes hammering a shot into the top-left corner with startling crispness during a Manchester City training session a few years back, some players never lose the ability to time a volley. The Welshman accumulated armfuls of sugar-sweet volleys during his playing career, but few players are more synonymous with the art of meeting the airborne ball on the full than Jean-Pierre Papin. The Marseille great scored over 300 goals in his club career, as well as 30 in 54 games for France (a better scoring rate than any French international apart from Platini and Just Fontaine), but what set him apart was less his strike rate, more what his goals were liable to do to the onlooker's heart rate. He specialised in scorching right-foot volleys, struck with the laces from impossible angles and invariably lashed high into the net past goalkeepers who knew what was coming but could do nothing about it. Even when his form deserted him, his ability to strike a flying ball did not. He scored only three league goals for Bayern Munich during a disappointing two-season stint in Bavaria, but one of those, a textbook-entry scissors kick against KFC Uerdingen in August 1995, is remembered as one of the most impressive goals in Bundesliga history. Struck by the awesome power of two Papin volleys that he witnessed – against Racing Club Paris in December 1986 and Niort in May 1988 – the *Provençal* sports journalist Alain Pécheral coined the term *papinade*. 'It came out spontaneously, in a manner just as sudden as the technique itself,' Pécheral later explained. These days it's used to describe any thumping volley, further enshrining France's most explosive striker in his country's cultural history.

See also: *huguinas* (Spain)

pépite – *nugget*

France has long been a gold mine for young players and never more so than in recent years, with Paul Pogba, Raphaël Varane, Ousmane Dembélé and Kylian Mbappé among the gems to have been chiselled from the rockface. Appropriately, precocious French talents are known as *pépites*.

petit filet – *little net*

The side-netting. Unlike in Britain, the French distinguish between the two sides of the side-netting, using *petit filet* ('little net') and *petit filet extérieur* ('exterior little net').

petit poucet – *little thumb*

The name given to unfancied teams, typically amateur or semi-professional sides in the Coupe de France. It comes from a particularly grisly French fairytale in which *le Petit Poucet* (known as Hop-o'-My-Thumb in English versions of the story) saves the lives of his six brothers by tricking an ogre into murdering his own daughters as they sleep.

See also: *Cenerentola* (Italy)

pichenette – *flick*

Find the gap, draw the keeper, wait for him to go down, dink. Nothing beats a neatly dinked finish, which in French is known as a *pichenette*.

See also: *chute por cobertura* (Brazil), *cherpak* (Russia), *vaselina* (Spain)

pieds carrés – *square feet*

In an insult/term of endearment that recalls the famous 'Blame It on the Boogie' chant invented by Liverpool fans in honour of their Malian dangerman Djimi Traoré (chorus: 'He just can't/He just can't/He just can't control his feet!'), players who struggle to pass the ball from A to B are said in France to have *pieds carrés*.

See also: *tronco* (Argentina), *perna de pau* (Brazil), *duffer* (Republic of Ireland), *derevo* (Russia), *drvo* (Serbia), *tuercebotas* (Spain)

porteur d'eau – *water-carrier*

Dropped by France coach Aimé Jacquet after his infamous kung fu kick on an abusive Crystal Palace fan in January 1995, Eric Cantona never regained his place in the national side and saw his captain's armband taken on by Didier

Deschamps. Cantona delivered a dismissive assessment of Deschamps's ability after Manchester United played the midfielder's Juventus in September 1996, saying he would 'always be a water-carrier' and that players like him could be found 'on every street corner'. Deschamps skippered France to World Cup glory in 1998 and would later retort: 'I don't know if you find players who've won two Champions Leagues on every street corner.' Deschamps may have beaten Cantona 2-0 in terms of Champions League titles, but the former Old Trafford favourite's taunt has taken root as a means of describing an unspectacular midfield organiser.

poteaux carrés – *square posts*

With seven league titles and four Coupes de France in 12 years behind them (plus another Ligue 1 crown on the way), Saint-Étienne approached the 1976 European Cup final against Bayern Munich in Glasgow intending to cement their legacy as the greatest French club side there had ever been. Shortly before half-time, with the score 0-0, Saint-Étienne struck the bar twice in the space of five minutes, first through a 25-yard drive from Dominique Bathenay and then a close-range Jacques Santini header. Commentating on the game on TF1, Pierre Cangioni observed: 'There's a little problem that I wanted to raise, which is that the posts, contrary to what you find elsewhere these days, are square.' Bayern's Franz Roth scored the game's only goal from a free-kick in the 57th minute and Saint-Étienne have been ruing Hampden Park's *poteaux carrés* ever since. The club's lamentations were given extra credence in 2006 when a ballistics study commissioned by *So Foot* magazine showed that had the Hampden crossbar been round and not square, both Bathenay and Santini's efforts would have kissed the woodwork and gone in. Hampden's square posts made their final appearance in a 1987 friendly between Brazil and France after FIFA decided that all goal frames should be uniformly cylindrical. The frame currently resides in the Saint-Étienne museum, having been purchased by the club in October 2013 at a cost of €20,000.

See also: *Bayern-Dusel* (Germany)

roulette

Perfected by – among others – Zinedine Zidane and Diego Maradona, the *roulette* (sometimes known as a *roulette marseillaise* in France) is a dainty piece of skill used by a player to circumnavigate an opponent moving in to attempt a tackle. In one fluid motion, the player performs a drag-back with his lead foot, twirls away from his opponent and then performs a drag-back with the other foot to bring the ball into his direction of travel. In both Spain and Italy it's known as a *verónica*, a bull-fighting term that describes a matador planting his feet in the sand of the bullring and drawing the bull tightly past him by sweeping his cape around himself.

France great Zinedine Zidane leaves an opponent in a spin with a *roulette* turn

sentinelle
Name given to the midfield player who sits just in front of the back four. Also known as a *numéro six*.

See also: *cinco* (Argentina), *volante* (Brazil), *Makélélé role* (England), *pihkatappi* (Finland), *stofzuiger* (Netherlands), *trinco* (Portugal)

sortie kamikaze – *kamikaze sortie*
Term used to describe a goalkeeper rushing from his area to confront an opposition forward, the most infamous example being Toni Schumacher's sickening assault on France's Patrick Battiston in the semi-finals of the 1982 World Cup in Seville. Battiston was knocked unconscious, lost two teeth and suffered three cracked ribs. Dutch referee Charles Corver awarded a goal-kick

and Schumacher went on to save two penalties as West Germany won in a shootout, before losing to Italy in the final.

See also: *skovtur* (Denmark), *salir a por uvas* (Spain), *sortie aux fraises* (Switzerland)

tricoter – *to knit*
When an attacking player buys himself time on the ball with a series of feints.

troisième poteau – *third post*
Whereas in English we refer to the 'near post' and 'far post' when describing the relative positions of the uprights, in France – as in many other countries – they use *premier poteau* ('first post') and *deuxième poteau* ('second post'). *Troisième poteau* refers to an imagined spot roughly a goal's width beyond the far post, where an attacker might ghost in to meet a deep cross. Alternatively, it's where a player's shot might end up when an attempted curler fails to curl.

tueur – *killer*
Used to describe clinical finishing. A striker struggling for goals might be heard to say that he needs to be *plus tueur* ('more killer') in front of goal.

ventre mou – *soft belly*
In France, mid-table teams sit in the *ventre mou* of the league standings. In Spain they refer to the *zona templada* ('temperate zone').

Zlataner – *to Zlatan*
When Qatar's sovereign wealth fund went looking for a figurehead following its 2011 acquisition of PSG, it could scarcely have made a better choice than Zlatan Ibrahimović. Here was a player with a bigger trophy collection than the club he had just joined, a natural haughtiness to rival even the snootiest Parisian waiter and, crucially, a playing style that allied elegance and individual skill with a showman's panache. When 'Ibra' deftly brought down a high ball, disdainfully dispatched a penalty or left an opponent trailing with a wiggle of the hips, the purrs from Parc des Princes could be heard from Sacré-Cœur. He didn't speak French, but he didn't need to – his cocky English soundbites were instantly comprehensible to young football fans raised on Hollywood films, American TV shows and gangster rap and seemed tailor-made for rapid dissemination on social media. It didn't take long for the people behind *Les Guignols de l'Info* ('The News Puppets'), the satirical puppetry show seen as France's answer to *Spitting Image*, to notice the colossal ego in their midst. In

his first appearance on the Canal+ programme, Ibrahimović was depicted as the voice of *FIFA 13*, informing a befuddled teenage gamer who had chosen to play as PSG that he would be playing as 'Zlatan' because 'PSG is Zlatan'. He continued: 'Which opponent do you want to Zlatan?' 'OM,' came the reply. 'Bravo, you have Zlataned Marseille 2-0.' 'But I've not even played!' protested the gamer. 'No need to play,' replied Ibrahimović. 'With Zlatan you're sure to win.' Embarrassingly, PSG had been beaten to the title by Montpellier in 2012, the first season after the Qatar takeover, but the *Guignols* sketch was to prove prescient. PSG won the following four Ligue 1 titles, with Ibrahimović finishing as top scorer in three of his four seasons at the club, and the verb coined by the *Guignols* took on a life of its own. It was added to the Swedish dictionary in 2012 (*zlatanera*, meaning 'to dominate') and Nike ran a 'Dare to Zlatan' advertising campaign in 2014.

GERMANY

Humour and inventiveness proliferate in the language of German football, and there's traditionally been little appetite for the kind of technical hair-splitting found in some Latin countries. But a close look at the evolution of the country's vocabulary reveals the story of Germany's belated arrival at footballing maturity.

As in England, football in Germany was long seen as a game of force and spirit. Like the English, the Germans couldn't see the point in fussing over the sport's finer details, although in their case it was largely because they won everything anyway. Things changed around the last turn of the century with the sudden realisation that, for all their success, Germany was getting left behind tactically. The renaissance that followed, culminating in victory at the 2014 World Cup, was language-led. A massive drive to improve coaching standards created a new, sophisticated linguistic landscape that would liberate German football from the tactical straitjacket that had previously constrained it.

Before Germany could travel the route to glory again, someone had to update the directions.

Abstiegsgespenst – *relegation ghost*
Said to haunt teams struggling at the wrong end of the table.

Ampelkarte – *traffic light card*

When a German referee shows a second yellow card to a player along with a red card, it's called an *Ampelkarte* because of the way it mimics the procession of colours on a set of traffic lights.

Angstgegner – *anxiety opponent*

German equivalent of 'bogey team'. There aren't many opponents who make Germany anxious, but they've learned by bitter experience to be wary of Italy. The *Azzurri* have ended Germany's hopes at four major tournaments, including semi-final victories at the 1970 and 2006 World Cups (two of the finest contests the competition has ever seen), a semi-final win at Euro 2012 and, most painfully of all, a 3-1 victory in the 1982 World Cup final in Madrid.

Anschlusstreffer – *pre-equaliser*

A coinage brimming with optimism, *Anschlusstreffer* is the name given to the goal scored by a team who are two goals behind, halving the deficit and leaving them one score from levelling the game.

Arschkarte – *arse card*

Red card, known as an *Arschkarte* because the referee keeps it in his back pocket. The term is used in general conversation when someone is befallen by misfortune.

ballverliebt – *in love with the ball*

Used to describe a player who's so attached to the ball he'd rather not share it with any of his teammates.

See also: *morfón* (Argentina), *amarrabola* (Peru), *chupón* (Spain)

Bananenflanke – *banana cross*

The name given to a curling cross, as perfected by the long-serving Hamburg and West Germany right-back Manfred 'Manni' Kaltz. Kaltz formed a particularly effective understanding with Hamburg's bruising striker Horst Hrubesch, whose formidable aerial prowess earned him the superb nickname *Das Kopfball-Ungeheuer* ('The Header Monster'). Hrubesch's most celebrated header was an 88th-minute effort from a Karl-Heinz Rummenigge corner that earned West Germany a 2-1 victory over Belgium in the Euro 1980 final in Rome. Hrubesch was a late pre-tournament replacement for the injured Klaus Fischer and opened the scoring in the final with his first international goal. Many of the 96 goals he scored in his 159 Bundesliga games for Hamburg stemmed from Kaltz's finely calibrated right boot. Asked to explain how their partnership worked, Hrubesch replied: *'Manni Banane, ich Kopf, Tor'* ('Manni banana, I head, goal').

Bauernspitz – *farmer's point*
This term for a toe-poke comes from Bavaria, where the use of the toes to kick the ball is associated with the crudeness of the farmyard.

Bayern-Dusel – *Bayern luck*
Bayern-Dusel is the theory that Bayern Munich benefit from more good luck than other German teams. It originated during the club's golden period of the mid-1970s. While Borussia Mönchengladbach, the era's other great German side, were continually ambushed by fate in their quest for the European Cup, Bayern scaled the continental summit at the third attempt and then stayed there for three years admiring the view. In their first European Cup final in 1974, Bayern fell behind to Atlético Madrid with just six minutes of extra time remaining, only for Hans-Georg Schwarzenbeck's speculative 25-yard shot in the last minute to take the game to a replay that Bayern won 4-0. A year later in Paris, Jimmy Armfield's Leeds had a strong penalty appeal waved away and saw a Peter Lorimer volley incorrectly ruled out for offside, before two late goals gave Bayern a 2-0 victory. In 1976, a talent-stuffed Saint-Étienne team rattled the woodwork twice in Glasgow, but Franz Roth scored the game's only goal. Bayern's players occasionally play up to the idea of *Bayern-Dusel*, but not everybody at the club is prepared to joke about it. When general manager Uli Hoeneß was asked by a reporter from Bayern's in-house television channel whether a late win over Karlsruhe in August 2008 had been the result of *Bayern-Dusel*, Hoeneß tried to sack him on the spot. The hapless interviewer only kept his job because he was employed by an outside production company.

Blutgrätsche – *blood tackle*
A dangerous, studs-up tackle.

See also: *nabrat na sane* (Czech Republic), *reducer* (England), *to burst someone* (Republic of Ireland), *stop nonsense* (South Africa), *pakka paer pao* (Pakistan), *enbarash* (Saudi Arabia)

Bogenlampe – *bow lamp*
Used to describe an arcing shot, the trajectory of which is imagined to resemble the curving stem of a bow lamp.

Chancentod – *death of chances*
Sobriquet for a habitually poor finisher. If a player squanders a succession of presentable opportunities, the observation might be made that *er hat Scheiße am Fuß* ('he has shit on his foot').

Doppelpack – *double-pack*
When a player scores twice in the same game. A *Vierpack* ('four-pack') is when a player scores four times in the same game, such as the four-goal salvo with which Robert Lewandowski, then of Borussia Dortmund, sank Real Madrid in the semi-finals of the Champions League in April 2013. A *Doppelpass* ('double-pass'), meanwhile, is the German name for a one-two.

Elfmeter – *penalty*
Football is paced out in metres in Germany, rather than yards. A penalty kick is known as an *Elfmeter* ('eleven-metre') in reference to the spot's distance from the goal.

Ergebniskosmetik – *result cosmetics*
The effect achieved by a consolation goal.

Fahrstuhlmannschaft – *elevator team*
A team that is continually getting relegated and promoted. The equivalent of the English 'yo-yo team'.

Fallrückzieher – *overhead bicycle kick*
Why use three words when one really long one will do? That, to the untrained eye at least, is how language appears to work in Germany, where imaginative use of compound nouns is something of a national custom. One football example is *Fallrückzieher*, the German term for an overhead bicycle kick, which literally translates as 'falling back execution' (another is *Flugkopfball*, for diving header, which means 'flying head ball'). Germany's *König des Fallrückziehers* ('King of the Overhead Bicycle Kicks') was Klaus Fischer, whose picture-book overhead kick in a November 1977 friendly against Switzerland was voted *Tor des Jahrhunderts* ('Goal of the Century') in a 1999 poll run by television station ARD.

See also: *chilena* (Chile), *chalaca* (Peru), *hjólhestaspyrna* (Iceland), *rovesciata* (Italy), *ngả bàn đèn* (Vietnam)

Fingerspitzengefühl – *finger-tips feeling*

This is a general term used to describe a person's ability to appreciate nuance in a particular situation. It might be mentioned by a commentator when a referee faces a difficult decision about whether or not to send a player off.

Fliegenfänger – *fly-catcher*

A goalkeeper who flaps at crosses is thought to resemble someone forlornly trying to snatch flies from the air.

See also: *lepkevadász* (Hungary)

Fritz-Walter-Wetter – *Fritz Walter weather*

Horrible, rainy weather during matches is named in Germany after former West Germany captain Fritz Walter, who was said to play his best football in the rain. Walter contracted malaria while marching through southern Europe during World War II, which made him hate hot weather. He produced his most abiding performance in the 1954 World Cup final when, aided by driving rain and a bog of a pitch, Germany's semi-professional outsiders stunned tournament favourites Hungary by coming from two goals down to win 3-2 in what became known as *Das Wunder von Bern* ('The Miracle of Bern'). An against-the-odds victory built on guts, physical exertion and iron self-belief, it kickstarted Germany's psychological recovery from the shame of World War II and established the template for pretty much every German football triumph that has come since. A player who doesn't fancy it when the weather turns is known as a *Schönwetterfußballer* ('fair-weather footballer') or a *Warmduscher* ('warm shower', the insult being that they can't abide cold water). Poor weather is also known as *Englisches Wetter* ('English weather'). A week featuring matches on the weekend and in midweek is called an *Englische Woche* ('English week').

Gegenpressing – *counter-pressing*

There's a theory in Germany that the national team's triumph at the 2014 World Cup can be traced back to a television appearance made by Ralf Rangnick, then the coach of second-tier SSV Ulm, on 19 December 1998. German football at the time was wedded to three-man defences and man marking, but the bespectacled Rangnick, using a magnetic tactics board to illustrate his points, declared that the future of the game was zonal marking, pressing and flat back fours. He was mocked and accused of being patronising, the tabloid newspapers dubbing him *Der Fußballprofessor* and Germany's new coach Erich Ribbeck complaining that he was treating coaches like a 'bunch of dimwits'. Rangnick, though, was in the vanguard of a group of pioneering coaches that also included Volker Finke of Freiburg and Wolfgang Frank, who had a gangly centre-back called Jürgen Klopp under his orders at Mainz. Jürgen Klinsmann, a Swabian like Rangnick, would adopt many of the principles they were espousing when he became national coach in 2004. Germany's abject group-stage exit at Euro 2000 shone a harsh light on the national team's tactical stagnation and as German football was reconfigured over the decade that followed, it was to Rangnick's tune that it began to dance. Seeking to advance the primitive attitudes towards tactics that had prevailed in Germany for decades, educators at the Deutscher Fußball-Bund (German Football Association) began to introduce more sophisticated concepts to their coaching manuals in the hope of producing a new generation of more tactically enlightened coaches. These terms were lifted directly from the textbooks and popularised via the media by coaches like Rangnick and Klopp, whose ability to overcome initial resistance to what was seen as their highfalutin language enabled a more mature style of tactical conversation to flourish. The most enduring tactical term to emerge from the process was *Gegenpressing*, which describes the actions of a team who react to a loss of possession by aggressively pressing their opponents in order to disorientate them and prevent them mounting a counter-attack. It's most closely associated with the Borussia Dortmund team that won two Bundesliga titles and reached the 2013 Champions League final under Klopp. Other high-end tactical concepts to have emerged in Germany in recent years include *Deckungsschatten* ('shadow marking'), which is the blocking of passing lanes, and the *Geplanter Fehlpass* ('planned foul pass'). The latter is an idea devised by Frank Wormuth, enterprising coach of Germany's Under-20s, which involves deliberately conceding possession in order to be able to press an opponent in a particular area of the pitch. Intentionally giving the ball away feels almost iconoclastic, like an attack on the principles of the game itself, but as Klopp is fond of saying: '*Gegenpressing* is the best playmaker there is.'

Gelbe Wand – *Yellow Wall*

Nickname for Borussia Dortmund's famous *Südtribüne* (South Stand), the precipitous 24,454-capacity tribune at the Westfalenstadion, which turns into a huge, seething yellow froth for Dortmund home games. A particularly intimidating stadium with a crackling atmosphere is known in German as a *Hexenkessel* ('witch's cauldron').

Gurkenpass – *cucumber pass*

They've got a bit of an issue with cucumbers in Germany. An inaccurate pass is known as a *Gurkenpass* ('cucumber pass'), a poor game will be dismissed as *Gegurke*, which roughly translates as 'cucumbering around', and an inept team might be called a *Gurkentruppe* ('cucumber troop'). Uli Stein, West Germany's third-choice goalkeeper, was sent home from the 1986 World Cup in Mexico for calling his team a *Gurkentruppe* and labelling manager Franz Beckenbauer a *Suppenkasper* ('soup buffoon') in reference to the television commercials for soup that Beckenbauer had appeared in during the 1960s. The word *Gurke* ('cucumber') can be traced back to the Middle Greek term *agovros*, which means 'unripe' or 'immature'.

See also: *podanie na zapalenie płuc* (Poland), *vaya pepinazo* (Spain)

Humba

Call-and-response routine involving players and fans, who join together to sing *Humba Täterä*, a well-known pop song released in 1964 by an avuncular singer from Mainz called Ernst Neger. After a victory, a popular player will use a loudhailer to address the fans while his teammates join hands behind him. The song begins with the ringleader commanding the fans to spell out *H-U-M-B-A* ('Give me an H! Give me a U!') before everyone breaks into the song's cheery chorus ('*Humba humba humba, täterä!*') and starts bouncing up and down. The practice began with fans of Mainz in the 1990s and was then picked up by supporters of Werder Bremen, before Lukas Podolski took it mainstream by doing it with the national team during Germany's run to the final at Euro 2008. These days it's a Bundesliga staple.

See also: *Víkingaklappið* (Iceland)

Jokertor – *substitute goal*

A goal (*Tor*) by a substitute (*Joker*). Two players have scored tournament-deciding *Jokertore* for Germany. Oliver Bierhoff's equaliser and Golden Goal winner saw off the Czech Republic in the Euro 96 final and Mario Götze's extra-time chest-and-volley sank Argentina in the deciding game of the 2014 World Cup.

Mario Götze's winning goal for Germany in the 2014 World Cup final was a *Jokertor* ('substitute goal')

Kampfschwein – *battle pig*
Dogged, hard-tackling midfielder. Belgian midfielder Marc Wilmots was known as *Das Kampfschwein* during his time at Schalke. An alternative term is *Wadenbeißer* ('calf-biter'), the calf in question being of the leg rather than baby cow variety.

Kerze – *candle*
An ineffective attempted clearance where the ball is whacked up into the air and comes straight back down.

Kleinklein – *small small*
Passing the ball from player to player without really getting anywhere.

See also: *postbodevoetbal* (Netherlands)

Knipser – *goal-getter*
The first player to be known as a *Knipser* (roughly, 'switcher') was Harry Decheiver, a Dutch striker who was given the nickname by his coach Volker

Finke during a two-year spell at Freiburg in the mid-1990s. Finke said that for Decheiver, scoring goals was as easy as flicking a switch. A player who scores goals at an impressive rate might also be dubbed a *Torjäger* ('goal-hunter'), while a prolific striker will be said to have a good *Torriecher* ('goal-nose').

See also: *cazagoles* (Spain)

Konzessionsentscheidung – *concession decision*
We've all seen it. The referee makes a debatable decision in favour of one team (awarding a dubious penalty, for example), then begins to suspect he's made a mistake and ends up 'evening things up' by making a similarly soft decision in favour of the other team. In Germany this is known as a *Konzessionsentscheidung*.

lupenreiner Hattrick – *flawless hat-trick*
When is a hat-trick not a hat-trick? When it's scored in Germany. A player may score a hat-trick *of sorts* by finding the net three times in one game, but for it to be a *true* hat-trick – a *lupenreiner Hattrick* – all three goals must be scored in the same half without any other player scoring in between. The stem word *lupenrein* literally means 'magnifying-glass pure'. This contrasts with the English definition of a 'perfect hat-trick', which is achieved when a player scores one goal with his right foot, one goal with his left foot and one goal with his head.

Mitspielender Torwart – *joining-in goalkeeper*
An expression that brings to mind an excitable Border Collie trying to join in with a game of catch in the back garden, this is a German term for a sweeper keeper. Also known as a *Torwartlibero* ('libero keeper'). Manuel Neuer, who thinks nothing of sprinting from his box to engage an opposition forward, has been the great German example of recent times.

See also: *vliegende keeper* (Netherlands)

Notbremse – *emergency brake*
When the last defender on a team finds himself with no option but to halt a fleeing forward by foul means, it's likened to yanking the emergency brake on a U-Bahn train.

Pferdekuss – *horse kiss*

In Germany, a dead leg is known as a 'horse kiss'. Former Germany wing-back Christian Ziege thought he'd sustained such an injury while playing for Tottenham in December 2002, only for his leg to swell up to such an extent that he had to undergo emergency surgery to avoid having it amputated. Ziege spent a long time on the sidelines and later joked that he'd been laid low by an *Elefantenkuss* ('elephant kiss').

Reklamierarm – *arm of complaint*

For the Arsenal back four's coordinated offside appeals under George Graham in England, read Neuer's *Reklamierarm* in Germany. No sooner will a shot beat the Bayern Munich and Germany number one than his hand will shoot into the sky and he'll flash a despairing look at the assistant referee, hoping that something, *anything* – offside, a suspicion of handball, a sudden surge of sympathy brought on by his imploring blue-eyed gaze – will move the match officials to rule the goal out. They rarely pay attention to him, but it doesn't stop him trying.

Schlachtenbummler – *travelling fan*

An old-fashioned term used to describe travelling supporters. It literally translates as 'battle rambler' (i.e. someone who rambles from battle to battle).

Schwalbe – *swallow*

Taken from the compound noun *Strafraumschwalbe* ('penalty-box swallow'), this is the name for an act of simulation. An incorrigible diver might be branded a *Schwalbenkönig* ('king of the swallows'). Dives are known as *Schwalben* ('swallows') because of the perceived resemblance between the bird and the body shape a player adopts when looking to deceive the referee. The player's flailing arms are said to resemble the swallow's long, jutting wings and their dramatically splayed legs the bird's bifurcated tale. Another similarity is that swallows are also known to fly low over the ground, although as yet there has not been a documented sighting of one waving an imaginary yellow card.

See also: *Klinsmann* (England), *grassrolling* (Iran)

A German player who takes a dive is said to have committed a *Schwalbe* ('swallow')

Wembley-Tor – *Wembley goal*

The name given to dubious goals, in honour of England's pivotal third effort in their 4-2 victory over West Germany in the 1966 World Cup final. With the score 2-2 in the 11th minute of extra time at Wembley, Geoff Hurst gathered a right-wing cross from Alan Ball, swivelled and thumped in a shot that crashed against the crossbar before bouncing down onto the ground and away. Roger Hunt, following in, immediately turned away in celebration and after consulting Azerbaijani linesman Tofiq Bahramov, Swiss referee Gottfried Dienst awarded the goal. Hurst completed his hat-trick and sealed victory in the final minute, but the issue of whether or not his second goal actually crossed the line remains a matter of debate. In Germany, the term *Wembley-Tor* has come to be used to describe any effort that cannot be said with certainty to have crossed the line. The incident was parodied in a 2006 Adidas TV advert, in which a shot from England midfielder Frank Lampard hit the bar and bounced down into the goalmouth, where it was held by Germany goalkeeper Oliver Kahn. With remarkable irony, Lampard was denied a goal during England's 4-1 loss to Germany at the World Cup in South Africa four years later when a lob that would have made the score 2-2 was not given despite the ball clearly bouncing behind Neuer's goal-line. The Lampard incident prompted FIFA president Sepp Blatter to change his mind about goal-line technology, the subsequent introduction of which has rendered the *Wembley-Tor* a thing of the past at football's highest levels.

See also: *angličan* (Czech Republic), *ghost goal* (England)

Zauberfuss – *magic foot*

A free-kick specialist. A notable *Zauberfuss* to have graced the Bundesliga in recent years was Hakan Çalhanoğlu, who modelled his free-kick technique on Juninho Pernambucano and once beat Dortmund goalkeeper Roman Weidenfeller with a preposterous effort from 45 yards. The Turkey international scored free-kicks at an impressive rate for Karlsruhe, Hamburg and Bayer Leverkusen before taking his enchanted right peg to Milan in 2017.

Zitterpartie – *trembling match*

A taut, knife-edge game is imagined to *zitter* ('tremble') with tension.

Zuckerpass – *sugar pass*

A sweet pass, typically one that carves open an opposition defence.

See also: *Česká ulička* (Czech Republic), *caviar* (France), *lissepasning* (Norway), *ciasteczko* (Poland), *chọc khe* (Vietnam)

Zweikampf – *two-man duel*

Now perceived as something of a linguistic relic from the days before Germany's tactical enlightenment, the *Zweikampf* has long been an archetypal feature of the German game. Before the zonal marking revolution, a football match was viewed as the sum total of a series of one-on-one duels between direct opponents and while the game has since moved on in Germany, these statistics are still collected and discussed. A player's *Zweikampfstärke* ('duel strength') is calculated by dividing the number of *Zweikämpfe* he attempts by the number of *Zweikämpfe* he wins, leaving you with his *Zweikampfquote* ('duel win ratio'). Andreas Christensen, on loan at Borussia Mönchengladbach from Chelsea, was the top *Zweikämpfer* ('dueller') in the 2016/17 season with a *Zweikampfquote* of 67.1 per cent, while Dario Lezcano of Ingolstadt boasted the best *Zweikämpfe pro Spiel* ('duels won per game') average of 27.8. Bixente Lizarazu was famously reluctant to speak German during his time at Bayern, but a phrase he uttered in English in December 2002 captured the German obsession with man-to-man combat. Bayern's football in the early weeks of the season was so seductive that chairman Karl-Heinz Rummenigge described it as *Weißes Ballett* ('White Ballet'), in reference to the team's new all-white strip. But they crashed and burned in the Champions League, limping out in the group phase after failing to win a single game, and Lizarazu said it was time to get back to basics. 'Forget the culture of playing football,' said the Frenchman. 'You have to win *Zweikampf*.' Lizarazu's clunky declaration was immortalised in 2006 when German indie band – and renowned football fans – Sportfreunde Stiller named their fourth album *You Have to Win Zweikampf*.

GREECE

A nation of football obsessives, Greece had precious little to get excited about during the national team's first two major tournament appearances, their combined record across the 1980 European Championship and 1994 World Cup reading: P6 W0 D1 L5 F1 A14.

Then came Euro 2004 – a water-tight defence, Theodoros Zagorakis's exemplary captaincy, Angelos Charisteas's match-winning headers – and the most stunning underdog success in the history of the international game.

eonio talento (αιώνιο ταλέντο) – eternal talent
Elegiac name for a player once tipped for greatness who never delivered on his youthful promise.

metagrafi aerodromiou (μεταγραφή αεροδρομίου) – airport transfer
After a bleak spell at Milan and a short-lived return to Brazil with Cruzeiro, Rivaldo flirted with moves to Bolton and Celtic in the summer of 2004 before finally electing to join Olympiakos, seduced by the prospect of their forthcoming Champions League campaign and charmed by Greece's miraculous victory at Euro 2004. It was one of the biggest transfers in Greek football history and when the 32-year-old Brazilian jetted into Athens airport to complete his move in July, some 4,000 jubilant supporters turned out to greet him. When a transfer succeeds in energising a club's entire fanbase like that, it's known as a *metagrafi aerodromiou*. A player who's attracting a lot of attention from other clubs will be said to have set off *metagrafikes sirines* (μεταγραφικές Σειρήνες), meaning 'transfer sirens'.

palto (παλτό) – coat
Name for a disappointing summer transfer. It rarely gets particularly cold in Greece, with average monthly temperatures only just dipping below 10°C in January and February, so there's little need for heavy winter clothing. A new player who fails to live up to pre-season expectations is likened to a coat: bought in the summer, worn for a month or two, then put in the wardrobe and forgotten about.

periptero *(περίπτερο) – kiosk*
Kiosks are a familiar sight on the pavements of Greece, so when a forward player who stands around in the box waiting for service is described as a *periptero*, the meaning is clear.

prolavoun tin parelasi *(προλάβουν την παρέλαση) – to catch the parade*
There are two annual parades in Greece. One falls on 28 October and marks the date in 1940 when Greece refused to surrender to Italy and the country entered World War II. The other takes place on 25 March, which is when the 1821 Greek Revolution against the Ottoman Empire officially started. If a team make a poor start to the season, speculation will begin to mount as to whether their manager will 'catch the parade'. If he's still around for the second parade, the chances are he'll see the season out. Under-pressure coaches are imagined to be sitting in the *electriki karekla* (ηλεκτρική καρέκλα) or 'electric chair'. A similarly ominous expression is *trizi i karekla* (τρίζει η καρέκλα), meaning 'the [manager's] chair creaks'.

See also: *mangiare il panettone* (Italy)

sporia *(σπόρια) – seeds*
This word is used when a referee is felt to be favouring one team over the other, but only to a marginal degree. The image evoked is of a watermelon being divided up, with the favoured team imagined to be getting one half of the fruit plus the *sporia*. For a perfectly even refereeing performance, you might hear that the referee *mirase to karpuzi sta dyo* (μοίρασε το καρπούζι στα δύο), meaning he 'shared the watermelon in two'. A biased refereeing display could be called a *sfayi* (σφαγή), meaning 'slaughter', or a *herourgio* (χειρουργείο), meaning 'surgery'.

HUNGARY

Hungary's fêted *Aranycsapat* ('Golden Team') stand as an eternal rebuke to the notion that winning is all that matters.

The first truly great post-war football team, Gusztáv Sebes's Magnificent Magyars gave the sport an electric shock with their breathtaking dynamism, sensationally trouncing England 6-3 at Wembley in November 1953. The 1954 World Cup final, which should have been their crowning glory, ended in heartbreak against West Germany in the Bern mud, but Ferenc Puskás, Sándor Kocsis and their teammates had already achieved enough to ensure that they would never be forgotten.

Devecsering

To adopt an anguished pose. It's named after Szilárd Devecseri, who scored a comedy own goal during Hungary's 8-1 annihilation by the Netherlands in an October 2013 World Cup qualifier. With Hungary trailing 5-1 in the second half, Jeremain Lens sent a cross into the box from the Dutch left and in attempting to head the bouncing ball behind for a corner, Devecseri succeeded only in nodding it inside Adam Bogdan's left-hand post. His reaction – sinking to his knees and burying his face in his hands – was despair personified and quickly became an internet meme, with people taking photos of themselves mimicking Devecseri's crestfallen pose in public places and posting them on social media. The Trollfoci ('Troll Football') social media account commemorated the moment by coining the word *Devecsering*.

ennek a labdának szeme volt – *the ball had eyes*

When a player threads a pass through a thicket of opponents and the recipient doesn't even need to break stride, it might be said that *ennek a labdának szeme volt*.

grundfoci – *street football*

The name given to the informal wasteland matches where Hungary's fabled *Aranycsapat* were said to have learned their trade.

kifli – *crescent*

A curling shot is said in Hungary to resemble a *kifli*, a Central European yeast roll that looks a bit like a croissant.

lepkevadász – *butterfly hunter*

Perhaps the most colourful term that exists to describe a feeble goalkeeper. In Hungary, a keeper who keeps coming for crosses and missing is likened to someone unsuccessfully trying to catch butterflies.

See also: *Fliegenfänger* (Germany)

In Hungary, a goalkeeper who flaps at high balls is known as a *lepkevadász* ('butterfly hunter')

meg volt rajzolva – *it was drawn*

When an attacking move unfurls with such devastating precision that every movement appears preordained, it's imagined to have been painted by an artist.

Sándor-szög – *Sándor angle*

Károly Sándor, darting right-winger for Hungary throughout their golden age, used to specialise in scoring goals from narrow angles. A favoured trick of his was to motor to the byline and draw the goalkeeper from his line by shaping to cross the ball before sneakily slipping a shot inside the near post. A goal scored in such a manner might be described as a *Sándor-szög*.

ICELAND

It took Iceland 70 years to reach a major tournament and once they'd achieved that, eliminating England en route to the quarter-finals at Euro 2016, they followed it up by becoming the smallest nation ever to qualify for the World Cup.

The Icelandic word for football is a native coinage: *knattspyrna*, which literally means 'ball-kick'.

hjólhestaspyrna – *overhead bicycle kick*

When bicycles were first introduced to Iceland they were called *hjólhestar* ('horses on wheels'), so the literal translation of *hjólhestaspyrna* (the term that describes an overhead bicycle kick) is something like 'bicycle horse kick'.

See also: *chilena* (Chile), *chalaca* (Peru), *Fallrückzieher* (Germany), *rovesciata* (Italy), *ngả bàn đèn* (Vietnam)

klobbi – *crotchy*

A nutmeg. Iceland is one of several countries where nutmegs are associated with the genital region, which reflects the violating nature of the skill.

See also: *caneta* (Brazil), *huacha* (Peru), *salad* (Jamaica), *Gurkerl* (Austria), *jesle* (Czech Republic), *nutmeg* (England), *panna* (Netherlands), *cueca* (Portugal), *bayda* (Morocco), *yalli* (Senegal), *shibobo* (South Africa), *deya* (Zimbabwe), *lawd daak* (Thailand)

taka þá í bakaríið – *take them to the bakery*

In Britain, when a team are given a thrashing, they're said to have been taken to the cleaners. In Iceland the idiomatic destination is the bakery, which sounds like an altogether nicer place to find yourself when you've just had your backside tanned.

Víkingaklappið – *Viking clap*

It was hosted by France and won by Portugal, but in a way Euro 2016 belonged to Iceland, who squeezed out of their group in death-defying fashion and condemned England to a humiliating exit before falling to the hosts in the last eight. Their communal post-match celebration, the *Víkingaklappið*, came to prominence following their last-gasp 2-1 win over Austria at Stade de France and became one of the defining features of the tournament. Led by luxuriously bearded captain Aron Gunnarsson, Iceland's players would raise their hands in the air and perform one slow clap, which would be copied by their fans and accompanied by an echoing '*Húh!*' The routine would be repeated, the gaps between claps gradually getting shorter and shorter before giving way to a thunderous ovation. It was initially thought to have ancient Viking origins and was compared to the New Zealand rugby team's haka, but more prosaic explanations of its provenance quickly came to light. One story was that fans of Icelandic club Stjarnan had witnessed Motherwell supporters using the chant to kick off their terrace song 'Since I Was Young' during a Europa League qualifier between the teams in July 2014 and decided to copy it. From there, the story went, it was taken on by fans of the national team. But Styrmir Gislason, founder of Iceland's Tolfán (The Twelve) supporters group, provided an alternative explanation. He told Danish newspaper *Jyllands Posten* that his newly formed group was looking for a distinctive chant to adopt in 2007 and came across a YouTube video of Polish handball fans performing the routine. 'It's a variation of something we saw in a Polish handball match,' Gislason said. 'It's not a Viking thing. But it makes us feel like Vikings.'

See also: *Humba* (Germany)

ISRAEL

Geopolitical sensitivities have made the Israeli national team the nomads of international football, the west Asian nation having competed under the banners of the Asian Football Confederation, the Oceania Football Confederation and European governing body UEFA.

Israel won the Asian Cup as hosts in 1964, centre-back Gideon Tish's free-kick securing a decisive victory over South Korea in the final game, and made their one and only World Cup finals appearance in 1970.

birthuz (בירטוז) – Barthez
Fabien Barthez may have ended his career as a world and European champion, as well as a two-time title-winner in England and France, but Israeli followers of English football have not forgotten about the succession of erratic performances that curtailed his time at Manchester United. In the local football terminology, the Frenchman's name is still used as shorthand for a goalkeeping blunder.

See also: *frango* (Brazil), *but casquette* (France)

firfer mishehu (לפרפר מישהו) – to spin someone
This expression will be heard when a nippy attacker leaves his opponents seeing double with a mazy dribble. It comes from the word *forfera*, a version of the *dreidel* spinning toy that Jewish children play with during Hanukkah.

kometz (קומץ) – handful
A word that has come to be used with depressing regularity in Israeli football in recent years in the context of racism and violent behaviour by fans, with

supporters of Beitar Jerusalem (Israel's notorious right-wing club) and Hapoel Tel Aviv (Beitar's left-wing rivals) the chief culprits. Wary of incurring punishments, club owners have invariably dismissed the troublemakers as representing only a *kometz* or 'handful' of supporters and the excuse has been trotted out so commonly that the word has become ingrained in the country's football lexicon.

kunusim (מיסונוק) – cones

Statuesque defenders are likened to the cones a player might dribble between in a training session. A team who defend like a bunch of park players might be described as *shehuna* (הנוכש), meaning 'neighbourhood'.

ITALY

Italians live football with a unique intensity and their attachment to the sport is reflected in their resolve to describe it in their own terms.

While a chipped penalty is known as a *panenka* all around the world, in Italy it's called *il cucchiaio* ('the spoon'). The stepover (*doppio passo*) and the overhead kick (*rovesciata*) have both their own Italian names and their own Italian inventors, while the *rabona* was once considered the handiwork of an Italian, Giovanni 'Cocò' Roccotelli, and known as an *incrociata* ('crossed kick'). Even *calcio*, the Italian word for football, is a native derivation, adopted in the early years of the 20th century as part of a drive to assert Italy, and not England, as the true birthplace of the sport.

Like a car enthusiast carefully dismantling an engine so as to understand how it fits together, Italy has broken football down to its tiniest constituent parts: for every position a sub-position, for every obscure tactical concept a name. But although Italians love football, they love winning even more, and that obsession has helped to create a national dictionary of football in which conspiracy, intrigue and the dead-eyed pursuit of victory shine from every page.

abatino – young priest

No person has done more to give character and meaning to Italian football writing than the journalist, polemicist, novelist and football theorist Gianni Brera, former editor-in-chief of *La Gazzetta dello Sport*. His poetic coinages left the country with a football vernacular that was all its own, and his determination to minutely map the divisions of labour on the pitch bequeathed to the world a wealth of terms for specific positions. Brera also had a flair for devising nicknames, not all of which were entirely complimentary. Unimpressed by the performances of 18-year-old Milan playmaker Gianni Rivera at the 1962 World Cup in Chile, Brera dubbed him *l'Abatino*, meaning 'the Young Priest', in mocking reference to Rivera's slight physique and lack of defensive endeavour. The term became used to describe any thoughtful, willowy midfielder whose excellent vision and passing ability were not matched by his work-rate. Another Brera term was *euclideo* ('Euclidean'), after the Ancient Greek mathematician Euclid, which he used to describe a player who read the game well and moved in logical patterns.

See also: *hankie ball player* (Northern Ireland), *maneken* (Serbia)

autogol alla Niccolai – *Niccolai-style own goal*

Comunardo Niccolai played at centre-back for the Cagliari team who stunned Italian football to win the 1969/70 *scudetto* and turned out for Italy at the 1970 World Cup, but he's chiefly remembered for his own goals. He scored six over the course of his career and many of them arrived at critical moments. If an opposing team were struggling to score against Cagliari, their fans would sing: '*Niccolai, pensaci tu!*' ('Niccolai, make it happen!') His most celebrated *autogol* ('own goal') occurred during a game at Juventus in the March of Cagliari's title-winning campaign when he beat goalkeeper Enrico Albertosi to a cross from Juve's right with a near-post header that flashed into the net. The moment was captured in a classic photograph taken from behind the byline. To the left of the frame, Niccolai is airborne, neck stretched and eyes closed, having just made contact with the ball. Albertosi is leaping to collect the ball in the middle of the picture, palms upturned at waist height to gather it. The ball is a blur behind the goalkeeper's back, hurtling towards the goal. Fortunately for Niccolai, a Gigi Riva brace helped Cagliari to rescue a 2-2 draw. For years afterwards, a memorable own goal would be dubbed an *autogol alla Niccolai*.

bandiera – *flag*

A *bandiera* is an emblematic player, normally a local who rises through the youth ranks at his club and represents them for years. The most celebrated *bandiere* are one-club men such as Paolo Maldini at Milan and Roma's Francesco Totti. The expression has implanted itself in the football language of Japan, where *bandiera* is written バンディエラ. A *gol della bandiera* ('flag goal') is a consolation goal.

bidone – *rubbish bin*

Usually applied to poor (and often foreign) signings, typically ones whose arrivals generate huge levels of expectation. A particularly disappointing acquisition will be known as a *super bidone*. Between 2003 and 2012, the *Catersport* show on Rai Radio 2 ran an annual vote to elect the most disappointing player in Serie A. It was called the *Bidone d'oro* or 'Golden Bin'. Rivaldo, then of Milan, was the inaugural winner in 2003, edging out Al-Saadi Gaddafi (son of Colonel Gaddafi), who was still to make his debut appearance for Perugia and had already failed a drugs test. Volatile Brazilian striker Adriano won it three times.

biscotto – *biscuit*

A *biscotto* is the Italian name for a result that's alleged to have been agreed in advance to benefit both teams. At a tournament, two teams might contrive to produce an outcome that guarantees both will qualify for the next phase. Or on the last day of a league campaign, teams pursuing separate objectives – European qualification and avoiding relegation, for example – might 'settle' for a result that helps both. In Italy, if a team chasing the title face a side with nothing to play for on the final day of the campaign, there will be a widespread expectation that the team whose season is over will not offer too much resistance. When Lazio denied Internazionale the *scudetto* by beating them 4-2 on the last day of the 2001/02 campaign, an emotional Marco Materazzi angrily asked Lazio's players why they were trying so hard, reminding them that his Perugia side had helped the Rome club to win the league two seasons earlier by beating Juventus on the final day. Italy felt that they were victims of a *biscotto* at Euro 2004 when a group-stage draw between Sweden and Denmark sent the Scandinavian neighbours into the knockout phase and condemned the *Azzurri* to an early exit. Football's most notorious *biscotto* was played out at the 1982 World Cup, when West Germany's 1-0 win over Austria took both teams through at the expense of Algeria. It became known as 'The Disgrace of Gijón' and prompted FIFA to rule that all final group-stage games would kick off simultaneously in future. The game was christened *El Anschluss* by the Spanish press and is known in Germany as the *Nichtangriffspakt von Gijón* ('The Gijón Non-Aggression Pact').

See also: *marmelada* (Brazil), *hombre del maletín* (Spain)

calcio – *football*

Uniquely among the game's major nations, Italy has its own name for football – *calcio* – which literally means 'kick'. Introduced to Italy by British sailors in the latter years of the 19th century, the sport was initially known as 'football', but nationalistic resentment towards the British influence created a split that would result in the adoption of a new name. Nationalists took control of the Federazione Italiana Football in 1908 and immediately excluded Milan, Genoa and Torino from the national championship because of their insistence on fielding foreign players. The ban on foreigners was ultimately revoked, but as a compromise *calcio* replaced 'football' as the official name for the game, the Italian federation becoming the Federazione Italiana Giuoco Calcio (Italian Kick Game Federation). A spectacularly violent game called *calcio fiorentino*, which shared a few similarities with modern football, had been played in Florence in the 16th century. Under Benito Mussolini's fascist regime it was resurrected in the 1930s, with elaborately organised matches taking place at Florence's Piazza Della Signoria. Around the same time, theories began to emerge that *calcio fiorentino* was the true antecedent of modern football and that the British had merely warmed it up. It was a fanciful hypothesis, but the name *calcio* nevertheless stuck and games of *calcio fiorentino* continue to take place on an annual basis at Florence's Piazza Santa Croce.

See also: *vakapipopo* (Paraguay), *nogomet* (Croatia)

Calciopoli – *Footballville*

Massive 2006 corruption scandal in which senior officials from several leading clubs were found, via wiretaps, to have influenced the process by which referees were assigned to matches. Juventus paid the heaviest price for their misdemeanours, being stripped of two Serie A titles and demoted to Serie B, while their general manager, Luciano Moggi, was banned from the game for life (the scandal is sometimes known as *Moggiopoli*). Fiorentina, Milan, Lazio, Reggina, Siena and second-tier Arezzo all received points deductions. The revelation that people like Moggi had been in near constant communication with referee selectors confirmed long-held fears about *sudditanza psicologica* ('psychological subjections'), a term used since the 1960s to describe the subtle psychological pressure that encourages referees to favour big clubs. The scandal meant that Italy went into the 2006 World Cup under a cloud, but just as in 1982, when the *Azzurri* shrugged off the effects of the *Totonero* ('Black Betting') match-fixing affair to triumph in Spain, Marcello Lippi's side overcame the odds to prevail. The word *Calciopoli* derives from *Tangentopoli* ('Bribesville'), the name given to the system of corruption in Italian politics that was laid bare by the *Mani pulite* ('Clean Hands') judicial investigation of the early 1990s.

See also: *dogovornyak* (Russia), *dyvnyy match* (Ukraine), *heishao* (China), *jual game* (Malaysia)

cassanata

Cassanata was a term coined in November 2002 by Fabio Capello, then coach of Roma, to describe the perennially exasperating behaviour of mischievous forward Antonio Cassano. Despite his lavish gifts, the Bari native was more closely associated with scrapes and mishaps than goals and trophies, his career a long succession of spats with coaches, training-ground tantrums, off-pitch misdemeanours and on-pitch meltdowns, punctuated by fleeting moments of brilliance.

catenaccio

The *catenaccio* playing system, which revolutionised football in the middle of the 20th century, was devised by an Austrian working in Switzerland called Karl Rappan, but it was in Italy that it found its spiritual home. Rappan's system, introduced during his time as player–coach at Servette in the early 1930s, involved bringing an extra defender into his team at the expense of a forward and positioning him behind the defence in what would come to be known as the sweeper position. Previously, when opposition forwards broke free of their markers they had a clear run on goal. Now, there was an extra line of defence to contend with. Under Rappan's orders, the Swiss national team enjoyed success with the strategy, eliminating Germany at the 1938 World Cup and beating England in a pre-tournament friendly. In Switzerland the defensive configuration was called the *verrou*, a French word meaning 'bolt', and when it crossed the Alps to Italy it became *catenaccio*, which means roughly the same thing. Gipo Viani is credited as having been the first coach to use the system in Italy. He claimed (employing a not insignificant amount of poetic licence) that the idea came to him as he watched fishermen using reserve nets to catch fish that had eluded their main nets on the docks in Salerno, whose team he coached. The first great Italian coach of *catenaccio* was Nereo Rocco, who tested out the system with Triestina and Padova before using it to great success with Milan, leading the club to the 1961/62 *scudetto* and the following season's European Cup. But the high priest of *catenaccio* was Helenio Herrera, known as *Il Mago* ('The Magician'). The game's first superstar manager, Herrera arrived at Internazionale from Barcelona in 1960 and would use *catenaccio* tactics to turn the team into the greatest side on the continent, winning three league titles and two European Cups between 1962 and 1966. It was during the age of *la Grande Inter* ('the Great Inter') that *catenaccio* came to be seen less as a mere playing style and more as an over-arching football philosophy based on rock-solid defensive football and cynical gamesmanship. As an approach, it found an enthusiastic and eloquent adherent in Gianni Brera, who believed that an inherent physical inferiority in Italian footballers left the country with no choice but to pursue alternative paths to victory. (It was Brera, a close friend of Rocco's, who coined the word *libero*, meaning 'free one', for the sweeper position.) *Catenaccio*'s stranglehold on the Italian game would not be broken until the arrival in the late 1980s of Arrigo Sacchi's great Milan side, whose aggressive pressing and zonal marking tactics exposed the flaws in the old system. But even today, the word continues to hold meaning as a byword for the steely pragmatism that has long sat at the heart of the Italian game.

See also: *anti-fútbol* (Argentina), *bunker* (United States), *zaburkvam betona* (Bulgaria), *park the bus* (England)

cenerentola – *Cinderella*
Italian equivalent of the English 'minnow'. Used to denote a rank outsider.

See also: *petit poucet* (France)

coast-to-coast
English-language expression, borrowed from basketball, for a solo goal scored by a player who runs from inside his own half. George Weah scored the ultimate *coast-to-coast* for Milan against Verona on the opening weekend of the 1996/97 season. With Milan 2-1 up late in the match, the Liberian striker gathered Alessandro Manetti's overhit corner kick in his own box and set off on a storming run down the centre of the San Siro pitch. A pirouette enabled him to ride a challenge by Stefano Fattori on halfway and he took Eugenio Corini out of the game by slipping the ball past him and collecting it on the other side before steering a shot into the bottom-left corner.

cucchiaio – *spoon*
Known as a *panenka* everywhere else in the world, in Italy a penalty that's lobbed gently down the middle of the goal is called *il cucchiaio*. Francesco Totti scored a famous *cucchiaio* past Edwin van der Sar during a semi-final shootout against the Netherlands at Euro 2000, telling his teammates with a grin: *'Mo' je*

faccio er cucchiaio' ('Now I'll do him a spoon' in the Romanesco dialect) before dinking the ball into the net as Van der Sar plunged to his right. Andrea Pirlo scored past England's Joe Hart in the same manner in the Euro 2012 quarter-finals, explaining afterwards that the Manchester City goalkeeper's frantic goal-line mugging had made his mind up for him. Italy prevailed in both shootouts.

See also: *paradinha* (Brazil), *stutter step* (United States), *panenka* (Czech Republic)

da del 'tu' al pallone – *calling the ball 'tu'*
When a player is completely at ease with the ball, it's imagined that they use the familiar *tu* ('you') to address it, rather than the more formal *lei*.

fare la gavetta – *to do the mess tin*
Regardless of the standing they attained during their playing days, coaches in Italy are expected to get their hands dirty in lower-league football before earning the right to have a crack at one of the top jobs. It's known as *fare la gavetta*, a reference to the metal dishes that young soldiers eat their meals from in the army, and it's seen as a valuable rite of passage. Marcello Lippi coached Pontedera, Siena, Pistoiese, Carrarese, Cesena, Lucchese and Atalanta before getting a shot at the big time with Napoli in 1993. Carlo Ancelotti began his coaching career with Serie B side Reggiana, while Antonio Conte was sacked and then reinstated in his first season as a coach with second-tier Arezzo.

francobollatore – *postage stamp player*
Italian football has long been famed for the quality of its man marking. A player who sticks so tightly to an opponent that they scarcely have space to breathe – such as Claudio Gentile's infamously aggressive shadowing of Diego Maradona at the 1982 World Cup – might earn the label *francobollatore*. Giovanni Trapattoni was a renowned *francobollatore* during his playing days.

funambolo – *tightrope-walker*
The go-to term for an extravagantly gifted creative player capable of changing a game in an instant is *fantasista* ('imagination player'), but if he's a real virtuoso, he might colloquially be known as a *funambolo*.

garellate
Claudio Garella had such an unorthodox goalkeeping style that it was given its own name. He was blessed with bravery and an incredible spring, but nothing he did came from the goalkeeping manual. He rarely caught the ball, opting

instead to parry it or punch it away, and he was as likely to use his feet or his chest to block shots as his hands. During his time at Lazio he was christened 'Paparella' by the club's fans, a pun on the Italian word *papera* – the equivalent of the English 'howler' – and his gaffes were known as *garellate*. (*Papera* literally means 'duck'. Its usage in the context of gaffe-prone goalkeepers is said to stem from a remark made by Italy coach Umberto Meazza following a calamitous debut performance by Vittorio Faroppa in a 4-3 loss against France in March 1912. Commenting on Faroppa's wretched display, Meazza said: 'Vittorio was stood in goal with his big, clumsy feet, looking like a duck.') By 1981 Garella had spent three years playing in Serie B for Sampdoria, his top-level career seemingly over, when a move to Verona changed his life. Verona won promotion to the top tier in Garella's first season and he was a mainstay in the team that pulled off an incredible upset victory in the 1984/85 *scudetto*. By that stage, the success of his homespun approach to goalkeeping had turned *garellate* into an altogether more fondly used term. His feats with Verona earned him a move to Napoli, where he won a second Serie A title and the Coppa Italia alongside Maradona in 1987. 'Garella is the best goalkeeper in the world,' said Juventus owner Gianni Agnelli. 'Just not with his hands.'

See also: *grandelletje* (Netherlands)

gol alla Del Piero

From time to time a player becomes so closely tied to a particular kind of finish that it starts to be seen as a personal calling card: the Romário toe-poke, the Messi dink, the Thierry Henry side-footer into the bottom-right corner. During his Juventus glory years, Alessandro Del Piero became particularly adept at scoring a certain type of goal: cutting inside from the left and then using his right instep to bend a shot inside the far post. One such strike, in a 3-1 win against Borussia Dortmund in September 1995, helped to establish the association, a 20-year-old Del Piero galloping down the left flank and easing away from Jürgen Kohler before whipping a glorious shot into the top-right corner. A similar finish might today be described as a *gol alla Del Piero*. Eleven years later, Del Piero's goal on the same Westfalenstadion pitch – a cool first-time shot past Jens Lehmann from Alberto Gilardino's reverse pass – sealed Italy's 2-0 win over Germany in the World Cup semi-finals.

gol alla Meazza

One of the first great playboy footballers, Inter idol Giuseppe Meazza was renowned for the delight he took in humiliating opposition players. A natural showman with slicked-back hair, Meazza was able to beat players with ease and the expression *gol alla Meazza* was born to describe a goal in which he had succeeded in leaving a trail of opponents in his wake before scoring. He was also famed for his *gol a invito* ('invitation goal'), which would see him stop and provocatively 'invite' the goalkeeper from his line before rounding him and finishing into an empty net. This was how he scored one of his most famous goals for Italy against Austria's *Wunderteam* in February 1931, dribbling from the halfway line and then outfoxing goalkeeper Rodolphe Hiden before tapping the ball home.

gollonzo – *comedy goal*
The opposite of a *golazo*, a *gollonzo* is a goal scored in farcical circumstances, usually after a defensive mix-up. The word was coined by Marco Santin, Carlo Taranto and Giorgio Gherarducci, the trio of pundits known as Gialappa's Band, on their *Mai dire Gol!* ('Never Say Goal!') TV show.

la maledetta – *the damned one*
Dreamed up by Sky Italia commentator Fabio Caressa, this is the name for a free-kick that flies over the wall before dipping viciously. The most well-known player to have mastered the technique in recent years is Andrea Pirlo, who modelled his free-kick style on Lyon great Juninho Pernambucano. In his 2013 autobiography *Penso quindi gioco* (*I Think, Therefore I Play*), Pirlo described avidly watching DVDs of Juninho's free-kicks and spending hours trying to replicate his method on the Milanello training pitches before his 'Eureka moment' occurred one day while he was sitting on the toilet. 'The magic formula was all about how the ball was struck, not where,' Pirlo wrote. 'Only three of Juninho's toes came into contact with the leather, not his whole foot as you might expect.' The technique involves hitting across and through the ball with the outside of the foot, which – if done correctly – gives it a non-spinning 'knuckleball' trajectory (technically known as the Magnus effect) that makes it impossible for goalkeepers to anticipate how the ball will move. Having mastered Juninho's technique, Pirlo made it look as easy as sipping a cup of coffee.

See also: *folha seca* (Brazil), *banaanipotku* (Finland), *mukaitenshūto* (Japan)

mangia-allenatori – *coach-eater*

A club president with a reputation for sacking coaches, such as Maurizio Zamparini, who has gone through coaches like most people go through bin bags during his spells as owner of Venezia and Palermo. The word is a compression of *mangia* ('eat') and *allenatori* ('coaches').

mangiare il panettone – *to eat the panettone*

When an Italian coach finds himself struggling during the first half of the season, speculation will mount as to whether he will still be around to *mangiare il panettone* when it goes round at Christmastime. The expression caught on after being employed in relation to Arrigo Sacchi's early struggles at Milan following his appointment in July 1987. The phrase *trema la panchina* ('the bench trembles') is applied when a coach is under pressure.

See also: *prolavoun tin parelasi* (Greece)

melina – *little apple*

Nobody shuts a game down like the Italians, who are the masters of killing tempo. The process of drawing the sting from a game is known as *addormentare la partita*, which means 'putting the game to sleep'. Techniques involve taking set-pieces in slow motion, reacting to every instance of contact with an opponent like it's an electric shock and carrying out substitutions at a pace more akin to a funeral procession. A slightly less nakedly cynical tactic is *melina* (literally, 'little apple'), another Gianni Brera term, which describes the process of aimlessly passing the ball around at the back to use up time. It was supposedly the name of a game that students in Bologna used to play in the early 20th century when they would pinch each other's hats and throw them between each other. Associated phrases include *anticalcio* ('anti-football') and *fare legna* ('to do wood'), which means to play defensively.

See also: *fazer cera* (Brazil)

minestra riscaldata – *reheated soup*

A quirk of Italian football is the frequency with which coaches return to clubs that have previously sacked them, which sometimes happens multiple times within the same season. When a club decide to give a second (or third, or fourth, or fifth) chance to a former coach it's known as 'reheated soup'.

mister

The legacy of pioneering Englishmen such as William Garbutt, seen as the father of Italian coaching, *il mister* remains the name given to coaches in Italy. Garbutt joined Genoa in 1912 as the first recognised head coach in Italy, introducing modern training techniques and negotiating Italian football's first transfers. The English imprint on the Italian game was deepened thanks to the work of men like Herbert Burgess and Bob Spottiswood, who respectively took up the reins at Milan and Inter in the 1920s. Fred Pentland and Jack Greenwell flew the flag of St George in Spain, where coaches are also referred to as *misters*.

moviola – *slow-motion replay*

When the slow-motion replay landed in Italy in the 1960s, it could not have asked for a more receptive audience. Italian football had long whirred with paranoia and conspiracy theories – now, here was a means of dissecting the game in even more forensic detail. Journalists who specialised in breaking down the *moviola*, such as Heron Vitaletti and Carlo Sassi, became known as *moviolisti*. Sassi presided over the technology's breakthrough moment in October 1967 when he used slow-motion footage from the Milan derby to prove that a late equaliser awarded to Gianni Rivera had not actually crossed the line. The *moviola* has since become a central component of Italian football coverage and played a particularly prominent role in the weekly Rai show *Il processo del lunedì* ('The Monday Trial'), which pored over contentious incidents from the weekend's matches between 1980 and 2016.

oriundi – *players of Italian ancestry*

Foreign-born players of Italian extraction, chiefly from South America, began moving to Italy after the Italian federation banned clubs from fielding foreign players in 1926. They were known as *rimpatriati* ('repatriated') or *oriundi*, meaning 'natives', which became the default term. *Oriundi* have featured in three of Italy's four World Cup triumphs: Anfilogino Guarisi (Brazil) and the Argentinian quartet of Attilio Demaría, Enrique Guaita, Luis Monti and Raimundo Orsi in 1934; Miguel Andreolo (Uruguay) in 1938; and Mauro Camoranesi (Argentina) in 2006. South America supplied some of Serie A's most iconic stars of the 1950s and 1960s, such as Juventus's audacious Argentinian forward Omar Sívori and the Milan pair of Brazilian striker José Altafini and Uruguayan inside-forward

Juan Alberto Schiaffino. But neither Sívori nor Altafini nor Schiaffino managed to bring success to the national team during their brief spells as Italy internationals and when Camoranesi pulled on an *azzurro* shirt for the first time in 2003, he was the first *oriundo* to have done so for 40 years.

pretattica – *pre-tactics*

The Italian equivalent of 'mind games', *pretattica* is a euphemism for the psychological sniping that accompanies the build-up to a big match. In a striking example of the lengths to which Italian teams will go in order to gain an advantage, in 2013 Genoa youth-team coach Luca De Prà was caught spying on a Sampdoria training session from a wooded area overlooking their Bogliasco training ground on the eve of the city derby. A photograph published on Sampdoria's website showed De Prà – grandson of Genoa goalkeeping great Giovanni De Prà – sitting sheepishly at the foot of a tree dressed in full camouflage gear. Sampdoria likened him to Rambo and jokily reassured fans that 'no blood was shed' during his capture. Genoa, who suspended him, said that it had been a 'personal initiative'. The term *calcio parlato* ('spoken football') refers to the general chatter that surrounds the sport (transfer talk, controversies etc.).

quarto d'ora granata – *claret quarter of an hour*

Il Grande Torino ('The Great Torino'), the legendary Torino team tragically wiped out by the 1949 Superga air disaster, were famed for devastating periods of attacking play known as the *quarto d'ora granata*, in reference to the club's blood-red strip. The charge would be heralded by fanatical Torino fan Oreste Bolmida, a local stationmaster, who would blow a bugle that he brought to every match at Stadio Filadelfia. Valentino Mazzola, the team's great star, would supposedly roll up his sleeves at that point and urge his teammates to attack, triggering an avalanche of goals. The legend was born in the spring of 1946 when Torino reeled off an extraordinary succession of goal-scoring salvos, including a 7-0 victory at Roma on 28 April in which they scored six times in the first 18 minutes. Bolmida's call to arms was credited with inspiring two famous home wins in May 1948: a 10-0 victory over Alessandria – a record winning margin in Serie A – and a 4-3 success against Lazio in which Torino fought back from 3-0 down. Bolmida's bugle, known as *la Tromba del Filadelfia* ('the Filadelfia Trumpet'), now resides in the club museum.

regista – *director*

As in film director. The *regista* is a central midfielder who directs his team's play and can typically be found sitting in front of the defence. He will sometimes be paired with a more defensively minded midfielder, known as a *mediano* ('half-back'). Playing further forward is the *trequartista* ('three-quarter player'), so named because he operates about three quarters of the way up the pitch in the number 10 position.

See also: *shireitō* (Japan)

risultato all'inglese – *English result*

For reasons that are not entirely clear, a 2-0 win with a goal in each half is occasionally described in Italy as a *risultato all'inglese*. One hypothesis is that it refers to the knack that England acquired for winning games in that fashion during the 1960s. Both their group-stage victories over Mexico and France at the 1966 World Cup were 2-0 wins with goals scored either side of half-time, a pattern that was repeated that year in wins over Denmark and Northern Ireland. The same formula brought England success in a third-place play-off against the Soviet Union at the 1968 European Championship, which was hosted by Italy. The expression is generally felt to reflect the fact that the English top flight has traditionally been more high-scoring than its Italian equivalent, where victories must be squeezed like blood from a stone. *Arbitraggio all'inglese* ('English refereeing') describes a referee who lets the game flow and is prepared to tolerate a certain level of physicality. The *media inglese* ('English average') refers to the theory – supposedly developed in England during the 1930s – that in the days when wins were worth two points, a team targeting the championship should aim to win all their home games and draw all their away games. A team's results over the course of a season could therefore be mapped against the *media inglese* to assess their progress.

ritiro – *retreat*

Introduced to Italy by Helenio Herrera during his time as Inter coach, the *ritiro* is an eve-of-game get-together where players are shut off from the outside world and made to observe strict curfews. If a team have been playing particularly badly, the pre-match *ritiro* may last for an entire week and if they are under heavy pressure, they may also observe a *silenzio stampa* ('press blackout'). This phrase was born during the 1982 World Cup, when Italy's players stopped speaking to the media after taking exception to press reports that questioned their bonuses and suggested that striker Paolo Rossi and wing-back Antonio Cabrini were lovers. A siege mentality having taken hold, Italy battled their way past defending champions Argentina and favourites Brazil in the second group stage before seeing off Poland and West Germany to secure the trophy, with Rossi finishing as top scorer.

See also: *sbory* (Russia)

rovesciata – *overhead bicycle kick*

In Italy, the *rovesciata* (literally a 'reverse kick') is associated not with an attacking player but a defender. Carlo Parola introduced the technique to Italian audiences while playing for Juventus in the 1940s and was credited in his homeland as its inventor. Parola would generally employ the manoeuvre to clear the ball downfield and was so adept at pulling it off that he became known as 'Signor Rovesciata'. One particular *rovesciata*, performed during a game against Fiorentina in January 1950, achieved emblematic status. It was captured by photographer Corrado Banchi and ended up being turned into the image that adorns Panini sticker albums in Italy. Parola is shown side-on to the camera, some three feet off the ground, in a textbook scissors kick pose: arms outstretched for balance, left foot hanging beneath him, right foot fully extended, the ball already flying down the pitch as a startled opponent takes evasive action nearby.

See also: *chilena* (Chile), *chalaca* (Peru), *Fallrückzieher* (Germany), *hjólhestaspyrna* (Iceland), *ngả bàn đèn* (Vietnam)

sciabolata morbida – *smooth sabre cut*

A curling cross played into the box from a deep position. Coined by commentator Sandro Piccinini.

scudetto – *little shield*

Small crest bearing the colours of the Italian flag, worn by the defending Serie A champions. Introduced in 1924, when it was initially a patch that was sewn onto the champions' shirts, with Genoa the first team to wear it. The word *scudetto* has come to be used as an alternative term for the title itself.

sette – *seven*

The top-right corner of the goal in Italy is known as *il sette* because of the resemblance between the number and the angle of post and bar. A shot into one of the goal's bottom corners may be said to have found the *angolino* or 'little corner'.

See also: *onde dorme a coruja* (Brazil), *jep nest* (Trinidad and Tobago), *upper 90* (United States), *rašlje* (Croatia), *postage stamp* (England), *lucarne* (France), *winkelhaak* (Netherlands), *devyatka* (Russia), *donde anidan las arañas* (Spain), *wayn yeskon shaytan* (Algeria), *fil maqass* (Egypt)

staffetta – relay

Staffetta is a tactic for managing two players who it's felt cannot play on the same team at the same time (think Frank Lampard and Steven Gerrard – if you weren't already). The original *staffetta* occurred during the 1970 World Cup, when Italy coach Ferruccio Valcareggi decided that he couldn't fit his two playmakers, Gianni Rivera and Sandro Mazzola, into the team. His solution was to start with Mazzola and bring Rivera on at half-time. The mid-match baton handover worked as Italy disposed of Mexico and West Germany in the quarter-finals and semi-finals, but Valcareggi abandoned the tactic in the final as the *Azzurri* were outclassed 4-1 by Brazil. Mazzola played the whole game and by the time Rivera came on, as an 84th-minute replacement for Roberto Boninsegna, Italy were already beaten.

ultràs

Organised hardcore fans. The first *ultrà* fan group in Italy was thought to be Milan's *Fossa dei Leoni* ('Lions' Den'), set up in 1968, and by the mid-1970s every major club in the country had at least one. Over time, their names began to reflect the influence of English fandom and hooliganism. Inter had the *Inter Boys*, Juventus the *Fighters*, Roma and Parma the *Boys*, Bologna the *Mods*. Many groups had overt political leanings. *Ultràs* were meticulously organised, fanatical and violent, taking control of the terraces by laying claim to a *curva* ('curve'), the name given to the stands behind the goals, and marking out their territory with vicious attacks on rival fans. Like Argentina's *barra bravas*, they grew to exert a huge influence over the lives of their clubs, menacing players and club officials, selling tickets and counterfeit merchandise and staging elaborate pre-match displays involving gigantic banners, pyrotechnics and coordinated chanting. *Ultràs* have been known to organise mass boycotts of matches, invade training grounds and even block transfers. In 2004, a group of Roma *ultràs* caused the derby against Lazio to be abandoned four minutes into the second half after false rumours spread that a boy had been killed by a police car outside the ground. *Ultrà* culture has spread throughout Europe, principally taking root in the Balkans, southern France and the Iberian peninsula.

See also: *barra bravas* (Argentina), *torcedores* (Brazil), *fanaty* (Russia)

velo – *veil*
A dummy. As pulled off, with characteristic nonchalance, by Andrea Pirlo in the build-up to Claudio Marchisio's goal against England at the 2014 World Cup.

viva il parroco – *long live the parson*
'*Viva il parroco!*' is the cry when the ball is hoofed into the air in uncultured fashion in an Italian football match. It dates from a time when the local parson would take part in kickabouts at Catholic community centres (*oratori*), which were breeding grounds for many future Italy internationals. A more colloquial translation would be: 'Go on parson!' An inelegant high clearance might also be called a *campanile* ('bell tower').

See also: *hoof* (England)

Zona Cesarini – *Cesarini Zone*
Renato Cesarini was one of the original *oriundi*. Born in Italy in 1906, he moved to Argentina with his family when he was a few months old, but returned to the land of his birth in 1929 when he was signed by Juventus. Cesarini's time in Turin was a triumph as he contributed to five successive Serie A titles, but his most lasting contribution to Italian football was a linguistic one. He was renowned for scoring late goals and famously netted a last-minute winner to earn Italy a 3-2 victory over Hungary in a December 1931 match in Turin. When a goal is scored late in a game, it's said to have been scored in the *Zona Cesarini*. The expression has passed into common parlance to describe something accomplished at the last minute.

See also: *Fergie time* (England), *jahfali* (Saudi Arabia)

MONTENEGRO

Though Montenegro have never appeared at a major tournament, Montenegrin footballers have. Players such as Dejan Savićević and Predrag Mijatović played for Yugoslavia at the 1998 World Cup and Euro 2000, while Dragoslav Jevrić kept goal for Serbia and Montenegro at the 2006 World Cup (and would have been joined in the squad by Mirko Vucinić but for injury).

An independent team since breaking away from Serbia in 2007, Montenegro are one of the world's youngest international sides.

*mala leđa (*мала леђа*) – little back*

Every football culture has a term that serves to warn a teammate in possession of the ball about an approaching opponent, but the Montenegrin system is a little more sophisticated than the average. The word *leđa* ('back') is used when an adversary has closed in from behind and appears to be on the point of stealing possession, but when the opposing player is only just starting to approach and the player on the ball still has a bit of time to assess their options, the warning is softened to *mala leđa*.

See also: *ladrón* (Argentina), *polícia* (Portugal), *house* (Republic of Ireland), *gorísh* (Russia), *yau gwai* (China)

NETHERLANDS

If there was a World Cup for talking a good game, the Dutch would win it at a canter.

While they have lost all three of the finals they have contested, the shimmering football that they unleashed upon the world at the 1974 tournament instilled a belief that to lose with style was nobler than to win with stealth.

The pain of defeat against West Germany in 1974 melded with pride and euphoria over Holland's stunning arrival on the world stage. The loss to hosts Argentina in the 1978 final brought heartbreak and when Marco van Basten swept the team to glory at the European Championship 10 years later, the nation exulted. But when Bert van Marwijk's grimly attritional side fell to Spain in the final of the 2010 World Cup, disappointment was subsumed by a peculiar kind of relief. Clobbering a path to glory is not the Dutch way.

Where other countries quibble about the finer points of tactics and systems, Dutch footballers and coaches talk about the game in a way that suggests some kind of higher calling. It's there in the enigmatic *Cruijffiaans* ('Cruyff-speak') of Johan Cruyff, in the haughty arrogance of Louis van Gaal, in the earnest introspections of Dennis Bergkamp. When Cruyff said, 'Football should always be played beautifully,' he summed up Dutch football's ethos. Sure, winning is nice. But the Dutch are in the perfection business.

avondvoetballer – evening footballer

A player who plays better when the floodlights are on. The endlessly quotable Co Adriaanse coined the term during his time as AZ Alkmaar coach to describe

Barry van Galen after the midfielder produced a below-par display in a lunchtime game against Roda JC.

brilstand – *glasses score*
A 0-0 draw, so named because of the resemblance between the scoreline and a pair of glasses.

See also: *oxo* (Brazil), *barankad* (Estonia)

chocoladebeen – *chocolate leg*
In the Netherlands, a player who plays a pass or attempts a shot using his weaker foot will be said to have used his *chocoladebeen*. Expect to hear it on the rare occasions when Arjen Robben allows the ball to make contact with his right foot.

Dutch winger Arjen Robben takes a swing using his weaker foot or *chocoladebeen* ('chocolate leg')

Cruyff turn
Arguably the most influential figure in modern football history, Johan Cruyff (spelt 'Cruijff' in the Netherlands) gifted the game a move so simple and yet so devastating that it's difficult, if not impossible, to imagine the sport without it. Cruyff unveiled his *Cruyff turn* to the world during an otherwise unremarkable 0-0 draw against Sweden at the 1974 World Cup. Finding his route blocked by Swedish right-back Jan Olsson, Cruyff made as if to play the ball infield,

only to drag the ball behind his standing leg with his right foot and race off towards the byline, leaving the bewildered Olsson looking like someone had just driven off in his car. 'I played 18 years in top football and 17 times for Sweden, but that moment against Cruyff was the proudest moment of my career,' Olsson said. 'I thought I'd win the ball for sure, but he tricked me. I was not humiliated. I had no chance. Cruyff was a genius.' However, if it seemed inconceivable that a trick so straightforward could never have been performed before, that's because it was. Pelé was baffling defenders by flicking the ball behind his standing leg when Cruyff was still in short trousers and a British Movietone film from 1960 shows Barcelona striker Eulogio Martínez pulling off a succession of textbook Cruyff turns during a European Cup match against Wolves at Molineux. While it's entirely fitting that Cruyff should have succeeded in stamping his name upon the game, his widely accepted position as the inventor of the move owes much to the fact that the 1974 World Cup was beamed into more homes than any tournament that had ever been played before. Interestingly, while Cruyff is synonymous with his famous turn all over the world, it doesn't have anything like the same resonance in his homeland, where weekly exposure to his extraordinary gifts dulled the impact of his moment of magic against Sweden.

de dood of de gladiolen – *death or gladioli*
A phrase beloved of Louis van Gaal, this effectively means 'death or glory' and is cited when a team face a match against a weaker opponent where defeat would expose them to ridicule. The expression was popularised by Dutch road cyclist Gerrie Knetemann in reference to the custom of presenting riders with flowers for winning races. It seems to have derived from stories about gladiators in Roman amphitheatres being garlanded with gladioli if they won their contests.

een Beb Bakhuys – *a Beb Bakhuys*
A diving header, named in honour of a famous goal scored against Belgium by Beb Bakhuys in March 1934 on his return to international action for the Netherlands after four years playing in his native Dutch East Indies. Bakhuys's goal was evoked when Robin van Persie scored his memorable leaping header against Spain at the 2014 World Cup. A diving header is also known as a *snoekduik* or 'pike dive'.

See also: *palomita* (Argentina), *gol de peixinho* (Brazil)

engeltje op de lat – *little angel on the bar*

When a team are under severe pressure and their goal is leading a charmed life, they may offer up a prayer of thanks to the *engeltje op de lat* for keeping their opponents at bay.

FC Bal op het Dak – *FC Ball on the Roof*

Picturesque name for a generic amateur team.

See also: *gärdsgårdsserie* (Sweden)

grandelletje

Guadeloupean goalkeeper Franck Grandel joined FC Utrecht from French club Troyes in 2005 and made such a disastrous start to life in Dutch football that the word *grandelletje* was coined to describe his unfortunate habit of shovelling the ball into his own net. It soon became a catch-all term for embarrassing goalkeeping errors. Grandel's endeavours in the Dutch top flight earned him an international call-up from Guadeloupe and he was named Best Goalkeeper at the 2007 CONCACAF Gold Cup in the United States after the islanders made a shock run to the semi-finals. But at Utrecht they had seen enough, one fan even advertising him for sale on eBay (reserve price: €99.95), and he was released when his contract expired in 2008.

See also: *garellate* (Italy)

het bos ingestuurd – *sent into the forest*

A player thrown off balance by an opponent's trickery is imagined in Holland to have been banished to the forest.

See also: *llevar a alguien a la escuelita* (Panama), *poslati ga po burek* (Bosnia and Herzegovina), *da go pratya za bira* (Bulgaria), *kohvile saatma* (Estonia), *sendt opp i pølsebua* (Norway), *att köpa korv* (Sweden), *pazara göndermek* (Turkey), *kupelekwa shopping* (Kenya)

Hollandse school – *Dutch school*

To appreciate the dumbfounding impact that Total Football had on the game, it suffices to watch the highlights of the Netherlands' opening match against Uruguay at the 1974 World Cup. No sooner has a Uruguay player received the ball than he is swamped by orange shirts – two, three, four – snapping at his heels and forcing him into an error. Play the ball backwards or sideways and the orange hordes set upon the next man. Go forwards and it's no use either, for Holland's players flood down the pitch like a cavalry charge, catching armfuls of Uruguay players offside at a time. It's less an offside trap, more an offside dungeon. When Holland have the ball they tear towards goal at terrifying speed, midfielders overlapping wingers, full-backs overlapping midfielders, Cruyff gliding through Uruguayan waters with the ease of the biggest shark in the sea. Two Johnny Rep goals earn Holland victory and by the end of the game Uruguay in their desperation have resorted to ugly, cynical fouls. Anything to stop the onslaught. Anything to catch their breath. After the tournament, the media christened the Dutch approach *totaalvoetbal* ('Total Football'), but in the Netherlands it became known as *de Hollandse school* – a nod to the great Dutch painters of the Renaissance. The players' ability to interchange positions and press in unison seemed almost supernatural, but their understanding was the fruit of an organic process that had started nine years earlier when Rinus Michels was appointed coach of Ajax. As Michels's thinking evolved over the course of his tenure, convincing him of the fundamental need to move up and down the pitch as one, he encouraged his players to take ownership of the way that they played by discussing and debating tactics and team strategy. With Cruyff taking the lead in those discussions, Ajax became a kind of football co-operative, every player fully conversant with not just his own role in the team, but – crucially – everyone else's as well. The players themselves say the switching of positions started to happen almost instinctively. Over time, they learned to find each other with their eyes closed. After leading Ajax to the European Cup in 1971, Michels left for Barcelona, to be replaced by the Romanian Ştefan Kovács, who built on his predecessor's work to deliver two more European Cups. Cruyff, too, left for Barcelona, in 1973, but he, Michels and the rest of the Ajax boys were reunited in 1974 when Michels was appointed national coach. The non-Ajax members of the squad – among them Feyenoord pair Wim Jansen and Wim van Hanegem and the Anderlecht winger Rob Rensenbrink – quickly assimilated the team's bewitching style and Holland took the tournament by storm. Though they would ultimately lose to hosts West Germany in the final, they had created something immortal.

See also: *Scheiberlspiel* (Austria), *passovotchka* (Russia), *tiki-taka* (Spain)

hup Holland, hup – go Holland, go

'*Hup Holland, hup!*' is both a song sung by supporters of the Dutch national team and a general expression of encouragement. It was written in 1950 by Jan de Cler, an employee of radio station KRO. Not being a football fan, De Cler steered clear of specialist terminology, instead imagining Holland as the lion on the Royal Dutch Football Association's crest. De Cler urged Holland's players not to let the lion stand around in his *'hempie'* ('undershirt') and *'pantoffels'* ('slippers'), because he *'durft de hele wereld aan'* ('dares [to take] the whole world on').

kaaskijkers – *cheese-watchers*
Exasperated by the lack of atmosphere at home games during his time as coach of AZ, Co Adriaanse likened the club's subdued supporters to people who watch the slow ripening of cheese (a pointed reference to the city of Alkmaar's reputation for cheese production). While at AZ, Adriaanse also invented the term *scorebordjournalistiek* ('scoreboard journalism'), which he used to describe reporters who based their conclusions on a game purely on the final result, rather than taking into account what happened in the match.

See also: *prawn sandwich brigade* (England), *comepipas* (Spain)

krijt aan de schoenen – *chalk on the boots*
They like their wide men wide in the Netherlands, where 4-3-3 has been the formation *de rigueur* ever since Michels and Cruyff's vision of *totaalvoetbal* began to take shape at Ajax in the early 1970s. Wingers instructed to hug the touchline will be expected to get *krijt aan de schoenen*, a literal equivalent of the English phrase 'chalk on the boots'.

linkerrijtje en rechterrijtje – *left row and right row*
The top and bottom halves of the Eredivisie table are usually displayed alongside each other on TV. Players from mid-table teams will talk about wanting to secure a place in the *linkerrijtje* and stay out of the *rechterrijtje*.

See also: *horyshche* (Ukraine)

panna – *gate*
A nutmeg in Holland is known as a *panna*, a word meaning 'gate' taken from the Sranan Tongo language of Suriname, the former Dutch colony in South America. Several of Holland's greatest players were either born in Suriname or have Surinamese roots – Ruud Gullit, Frank Rijkaard, Edgar Davids, Clarence Seedorf, Patrick Kluivert – and some of Suriname's language has seeped into the Dutch football vernacular. Surinamese footballers who moved to the Netherlands brought with them a playful attitude to the sport, reflecting the

influence of their southern neighbours Brazil. They placed high importance on individual trickery and as their influence began to be felt in *straatvoetbal* ('street football') matches in the multicultural working-class suburbs of Rotterdam and Amsterdam – melting pots of Dutch, Surinamese, Moroccan and Turkish football cultures – so the *panna* came to be treasured as the ultimate expression of superiority over an opponent. In the early 2000s, fiercely competitive and intensely technical urban cage matches spawned a new football variant, known as 'Panna': one-on-one contests on customised courts in which the first player to be nutmegged lost. Thanks to the spread of freestyle football, *panna* has become one of the most widely understood names for a nutmeg around the world. Another freestyle word borrowed from Sranan Tongo is *akka*, meaning 'hook', which describes an aerial skill move.

See also: *caneta* (Brazil), *huacha* (Peru), *salad* (Jamaica), *Gurkerl* (Austria), *jesle* (Czech Republic), *nutmeg* (England), *klobbi* (Iceland), *cueca* (Portugal), *bayda* (Morocco), *yalli* (Senegal), *shibobo* (South Africa), *deya* (Zimbabwe), *lawd daak* (Thailand)

patatgeneratie – *French fries generation*
This phrase was dreamed up by Bobby Haarms, the former Ajax assistant coach and scout, but it's often attributed to Leo Beenhakker. Beenhakker had a richly talented group of young players under his orders at Ajax in the late 1980s – the De Boer twins, Aron Winter, Richard Witschge, Dennis Bergkamp, Bryan Roy – but he described them as the *patatgeneratie* because he feared that they were spoilt and lacked motivation. '[It was] because of their comfort,' Beenhakker would later explain. 'I've often blamed myself over that. But perhaps I've also made a contribution to the journey they all went on.'

postbodevoetbal – *postman football*
When a player spends his time shuttling between his teammates and playing very short passes, he's dismissively said to be playing *postbodevoetbal*. Adriaanse calls aimless passing football *woonerfvoetbal* ('residential zone football'), in reference to residential areas in Dutch cities where motorised traffic is not allowed to exceed walking pace.

See also: *Kleinklein* (Germany)

schaduwspits – *shadow striker*
Evocative name for a player such as Bergkamp who plays in support of a main striker, roving around the pitch like his shadow.

See also: *neuf et demi* (France)

stofzuiger – *vacuum cleaner*
A *stofzuiger* is a midfield player renowned for his ability to hoover up danger. The term was first used to describe Willy van der Kerkhof, whose nickname was 'De Stofzuiger'. A more recent example is Edgar 'De Pitbull' Davids.

See also: *cinco* (Argentina), *volante* (Brazil), *Makélélé role* (England), *pihkatappi* (Finland), *sentinelle* (France), *trinco* (Portugal)

vliegende keeper – *flying keeper*
Dutch football has played a pioneering role in the development of the sweeper keeper, who in Holland is known as a *vliegende keeper*. Heinz Stuy, Ajax's goalkeeper in their first three European Cup wins, was allowed to get away with fumbling the occasional high cross because he was so effective at coming out of his area to police the space behind his defence. When fitness concerns (and an awkward relationship with Cruyff) prevented Jan van Beveren from playing at the 1974 World Cup, Cruyff persuaded Michels to pick 34-year-old FC Amsterdam veteran Jan Jongbloed – who had won his only previous cap in 1962 – because of his ability on the ball. Ajax were not unduly inconvenienced by the introduction of the back-pass rule in 1992, meanwhile, because unlike many of his contemporaries, their young goalkeeper, Edwin van der Sar, was perfectly at ease with the ball at his feet. By the time Van der Sar retired in 2011, sweeper keepers like Manuel Neuer, Víctor Valdés and Hugo Lloris had all established themselves, but it had taken the best part of 20 years for the rest of the goalkeeping fraternity to catch up with him.

See also: *Mitspielender Torwart* (Germany)

vrouwen en kinderen eerst – *women and children first*
When a team are frantically trying to clear the ball inside their own penalty area, the situation may be amusingly described as 'women and children first'. A comparable, nonsensical term, coined by the flamboyant former Willem II, Sparta Rotterdam and Vitesse Arnhem coach Bert Jacobs, is *hotseknotsbegoniavoetbal* (roughly, 'hotchpotch begonia football'), which

refers to the kind of desperate, long-ball football that's often witnessed in the latter stages of a tight game.

See also: *Keystone Cops* (England), *hawaiifotball* (Norway), *andar aos papéis* (Portugal)

winkelhaak – *try square*
A *winkelhaak* is a kind of ruler used by metalworkers and carpenters to measure right angles. In Dutch football parlance, it refers to the top corners of the goal. An alternative term is *kruising*, meaning 'crossing'.

See also: *onde dorme a coruja* (Brazil), *jep nest* (Trinidad and Tobago), *upper 90* (United States), *rašlje* (Croatia), *postage stamp* (England), *lucarne* (France), *sette* (Italy), *devyatka* (Russia), *donde anidan las arañas* (Spain), *wayn yeskon shaytan* (Algeria), *fil maqass* (Egypt)

zondagsschot – *Sunday shot*
When the big centre-back ambles across the halfway line, glances up and lets fly with a speculative 35-yarder that somehow manages to lodge itself in the top corner, it's known as a *zondagsschot*. Van Gaal left British journalists a little baffled when he employed the term after Swansea beat Manchester United in February 2015 thanks to a long-range Jonjo Shelvey shot that flicked into the net off Bafétimbi Gomis. The expression also exists in German (*Sonntagsschuss*).

zwembadaffaire – *swimming pool affair*
Holland's preparations for the 1974 World Cup final were disturbed when German tabloid *Bild* published an incendiary story, headlined '*Cruyff, Sekt, nackte Mädchen und ein kühles Bad*' ('Cruyff, champagne, naked girls and a cool bath'), about unnamed Dutch players carousing with naked women in their hotel pool on the eve of their semi-final victory over Brazil. There were suggestions that the incident had been a set-up orchestrated by *Bild*, but Cruyff was said to have spent the day before the final protesting his innocence on the phone to his furious wife, Danny, which was held up in some parts as an explanation for the way he had faded out of the game. The truth of what happened has never been fully revealed and the story has been used both to illustrate the Dutch squad's free-spirited nature and to emphasise the lack of discipline in their camp.

NORTHERN IRELAND

Representing the smallest country in the United Kingdom, Northern Ireland have punched well above their weight at international level, reaching the quarter-finals of the World Cup in 1958 and making it to the second round of the tournament in 1982.

The nation's greatest player, the tormented genius George Best, never played at a major tournament, but won the Ballon d'Or in 1968 after inspiring Manchester United to glory in the European Cup at the age of 22.

barstool

A *barstool* is a disparaging name for a Northern Irish football fan who prefers to watch televised English Premier League games rather than support a local club.

big baddin'

If a manager in the Northern Irish Premiership wants to have the option of playing a long-ball game, he will look to secure the services of a *big baddin'*, a tall, lumbering centre-forward who can be relied upon for the occasional flick-on. If the player's approach to nutrition leaves a little to be desired, he may be described as a *puddin'*.

See also: *bombardir-taran* (Russia)

bomb scare

In a darkly humorous nod to the climate of tension that existed in Northern Ireland during the 30 years of the Troubles, a disaster-prone defender is known as a *bomb scare*.

See also: *Bambi on ice* (England)

hankie ball player

Hankie ball players are midfielders blessed with vision and technical ability, but likely to be castigated for their reluctance to get stuck in.

See also: *abatino* (Italy), *maneken* (Serbia)

NORWAY

Norway's golden age occurred in the 1990s, when a team of rare obduracy coached by Egil Olsen qualified for successive World Cups (1994 and 1998).

Three of the players from that era, Ronny Johnsen, Henning Berg and Ole Gunnar Solskjær, were members of the Manchester United squad that won a Treble of Premier League, FA Cup and Champions League trophies in 1999, while John Arne Riise, who won the first of his record 110 caps in 2000, lifted the European Cup with Liverpool in 2005.

bakrom – *back-room*

FIFA didn't publish its first world rankings until August 1993, but by October the list already had a very familiar look to it: 1. Brazil; 2. Norway; 3. Italy; 4. Germ– hang on, sorry, Norway? The Norwegians had gone 55 years without playing at a major tournament, but under the no-nonsense stewardship of Egil Olsen, they were a team transformed. Over the previous 13 months they had beaten England, the Netherlands, Poland and Turkey in World Cup qualifying and seen off the United States in a friendly and they were weeks away from securing a place at USA 94. Olsen was nicknamed 'Drillo' because of his dribbling skills as a player, but as a coach he was an über-pragmatist. Taking his cue from the statistical analysis carried out in England by statistician Charles Reep and FA coaching director Charles Hughes, Olsen turned Norway into one of the most direct international teams in the game's history. His obsession was the *bakrom*, the space behind the opposition's defence, which was to be targeted at every available opportunity. His formation of choice was a 4-5-1 in which a midfield of scurriers supported loping lone striker Jostein Flo. The team's key tactic was the *flo-pasning* ('Flo pass'), which involved the full-backs pelting high balls towards Flo, who would isolate himself against a shorter opposition full-back and then nod the ball down for the midfield runners to attack. Olsen demanded that his players be *best uten ball* ('the best without the ball'). The phrase was originally used to describe Øyvind Leonhardsen, who played for Rosenborg under Nils Arne Eggen, another coach who favoured direct, attacking football. Leonhardsen became the prototype for a kind of fast-breaking attacking midfielder known in Norway as an *indreløper* ('inner runner') and in 1994 he joined Wimbledon, who were no strangers to putting it in the mixer themselves. To describe his philosophy, Olsen invented the term *gjennombruddshissig*, an essentially untranslatable word comprising *gjennombrudd* ('breakthrough') and *hissig*, which usually means 'aggressive'. Many sneered at Olsen's approach, but by the time he stepped down in 1998, he had taken Norway to two successive World Cups. They have not been to one since.

See also: *route one* (England), *långa bollar på Bengt* (Sweden), *bbeung chuk gu* (South Korea)

hawaiifotball
Chaotic, disorganised football.

See also: *Keystone Cops* (England), *vrouwen en kinderen eerst* (Netherlands), *andar aos papéis* (Portugal)

keepermat – keeper food
A weak shot, floaty cross or gently descending high ball are all examples of what Norwegians call *keepermat*, which any goalkeeper worth his salt will gobble up without a second invitation.

See also: *bread and butter* (England)

lissepasning – shoelace pass
A pass played with such accuracy that it hits the receiving player's shoelaces.

See also: *Česká ulička* (Czech Republic), *caviar* (France), *Zuckerpass* (Germany), *ciasteczko* (Poland), *chọc khe* (Vietnam)

makrellfotball – mackerel football
The great IK Start team of the late 1970s played with such slick coordination that they were said to move like a shoal of fish. The team's core players, such as Svein 'Matta' Mathisen, Trond Pedersen and Preben Jørgensen, had come through the youth ranks together and their slickly synchronised attacking football inspired the team to championship glory in 1978 and 1980. They know a thing or two about fish in Start's home city of Kristiansand, where Norway dips its toes in the Skagerrak, the strait that links the North Sea and the Baltic Sea, which helps to explain why IK Start's flashing football came to be known as *makrellfotball*.

potet – potato
A player who can slot into any position is likened to a potato, which is considered one of the most versatile elements of Scandinavian cuisine.

sendt opp i pølsebua – *sent to the sausage stand*
The Norwegian take on the player-being-bamboozled-by-an-opponent trope imagines the befuddled defender being dispatched to buy hot dogs.

See also: *llevar a alguien a la escuelita* (Panama), *poslati ga po burek* (Bosnia and Herzegovina), *da go pratya za bira* (Bulgaria), *kohvile saatma* (Estonia), *het bos ingestuurd* (Netherlands), *att köpa korv* (Sweden), *pazara göndermek* (Turkey), *kupelekwa shopping* (Kenya)

POLAND

The flowering of two towering talents catapulted Poland to third-place finishes at the World Cups of 1974 and 1982: the former success founded upon the seven goals of tournament top scorer Grzegorz Lato, the latter driven by the all-action displays of Zbigniew Boniek, who had signed for Juventus shortly before the competition.

Rangy goal machine Robert Lewandowski is their modern heir and became in October 2017 the first player to amass a half-century of goals in a Poland shirt.

ciasteczko – *little cookie*
A *ciasteczko* is a pass that creates a gilt-edged chance for a teammate.

See also: *Česká ulička* (Czech Republic), *caviar* (France), *Zuckerpass* (Germany), *lissepasning* (Norway), *chọc khe* (Vietnam)

farbowane lisy – *dyed foxes*
Farbowane lisy is the name given to foreign-born players who have played for Poland at international level. Nigerian striker Emmanuel Olisadebe and Brazilian midfielder Roger Guerreiro were controversially fast-tracked for Polish citizenship after playing club football in the country. Other 'dyed foxes' included the French-born pair Damien Perquis and Ludovic Obraniak, who have Polish roots, and Sebastian Boenisch and Eugen Polanski, who were born in Poland but brought up in Germany. Assimilation proved problematic for all of the players. Olisadebe, in particular, was subjected to some horrendous racial abuse, but secured a place in the country's affections by scoring eight goals in 10 games to help Poland qualify for the 2002 World Cup. Obraniak was once challenged to sing the Polish national anthem at a press conference and before Euro 2012,

which Poland co-hosted with Ukraine, former national team goalkeeper Jan Tomaszewski declared that he would not support a team full of 'Germans and Frenchmen'. Former Poland coach Franciszek Smuda first used the expression to describe the players of Polish, Turkish, Brazilian and Ghanaian extraction who played for Germany at the 2010 World Cup. Smuda's Poland squad at Euro 2012 contained four *farbowane lisy*, but their numbers have dwindled since.

See also: *UB40s* (Jamaica), *mujannisoon* (Qatar)

grecque

The *grecque*, as it's known in Poland, is a terrace routine whereby fans put their arms around each other and jump up and down while facing away from the pitch. It was adopted by Manchester City supporters after they witnessed fans of Polish side Lech Poznań doing it during a Europa League game in October 2010 and has become known in England as the *Poznań*.

karny z kapelusza – *penalty out of a hat*

When the referee conjures up a penalty out of thin air, it will be described as a *karny z kapelusza*.

Obrona Częstochowy – *The Defence of Częstochowa*

In the winter of 1655, a Swedish army bolstered by German mercenaries attempted to capture the Jasna Góra monastery in the southern Polish city of Częstochowa, only to be rebuffed by a small band of monks and local volunteers. It was turned into a silent film in 1913 called *Obrona Częstochowy* and the film's title is evoked during a football match when all 10 outfield players in a team are desperately defending the edge of their own penalty area.

See also: *táctica del murciélago* (Ecuador), *ući golmanu u krilo* (Serbia), *mball camp yi* (Senegal)

podanie na zapalenie płuc – *pneumonia pass*

A poor pass that fails to find its intended target. To play a teammate into trouble is to *wsadzić na konia*, which means 'to put (someone) on a horse'.

See also: *Gurkenpass* (Germany)

sędzia kalosz – *welly referee*

This is an old insult that used to be slung at referees in Poland. It dates back to an ice hockey match between Poland and Czechoslovakia in 1931, during which a Polish dignitary articulated his frustrations with the referee by removing one of his boots and throwing it at him.

See also: *pískat hovna* (Czech Republic), *corbeau* (France), *sudyu na milo* (Russia), *referee kayu* (Malaysia)

trzy punkty na nodze – *three points on the leg*
A player who finds himself with an opportunity to score the winning goal in a game is said to have *trzy punkty na nodze*. His team's supporters will pray that he doesn't *strzelić panu Bogu w okno* ('shoot in God's window'), which means to send the ball sailing over the crossbar.

PORTUGAL

Although Portugal and Brazil share a language and a cultural heritage, football evolved separately in the two countries and they have different names for the positions on the pitch. A goalkeeper is a *goleiro* in Brazil, for example, but a *guarda-redes* ('net-guard') in Portugal, while a centre-back is a *central* in Portugal but a *zagueiro* ('back') in Brazil.

Nevertheless, though Brazil may have become the official home of *o jogo bonito*, skilful play is appreciated just as much in the mother country Portugal.

andar aos papéis – *walking on papers*
In Portugal, when a dangerous cross comes into the box and the goalkeeper makes a complete hash of his attempt to deal with it, he will be described as *andar aos papéis*. In day-to-day speech it's used to indicate a state of general confusion.

See also: *Keystone Cops* (England), *vrouwen en kinderen eerst* (Netherlands), *hawaiifotball* (Norway)

banho de bola – *shower of balls*
When a team have completely wiped the floor with their opponents, bettering them in every single department, they are said to have given them a *banho de bola* ('shower of balls'). (Strictly speaking, *bola* means 'ball', but 'shower of ball' would sound a bit weird.)

brinca na areia – *plays in the sand*

Said of players who have excellent skills, but no end product. The original *brinca-na-areia* was Joaquim Dinis, an Angola-born left-winger who played for Sporting Lisbon and Porto and won 14 caps for Portugal in the early 1970s. Rangy and quick, Dinis had an easy, natural sidestep and could beat players for fun, but he sometimes gave the impression that he had as much of an idea about where the ball was going as anybody else. Dinis upstaged Eusébio at the 1972 Brazil Independence Cup (staged to commemorate the 150th anniversary of the Brazilian Declaration of Independence) by scoring five goals as Portugal reached the final, where they lost to an 89th-minute Jairzinho goal against Brazil.

chicotada psicológica – *psychological whip*

If a coach in Portugal pays for his team's poor form by getting sacked, the club president will be said to have given his players a *chicotada psicológica*. The hope is that the shock of seeing the coach bundled through the exit door will bring the team to their senses and the popularity of the tactic means that Portugal has some of the most trigger-happy club presidents in European football. During the 2016/17 season, 13 of the 18 clubs in the Portuguese top flight changed coaches at least once in the space of just seven months.

cueca – *undies*

What the Portuguese call a nutmeg. Saucy bunch.

See also: *caneta* (Brazil), *huacha* (Peru), *salad* (Jamaica), *Gurkerl* (Austria), *jesle* (Czech Republic), *nutmeg* (England), *klobbi* (Iceland), *panna* (Netherlands), *bayda* (Morocco), *yalli* (Senegal), *shibobo* (South Africa), *deya* (Zimbabwe), *lawd daak* (Thailand)

ficar na mama – *stay at the teat*

Describes a striker who's reluctant to leave the penalty area for fear of missing out on a scoring chance. If a player ends a goal drought, they are said to have *parou o jejum* ('stopped fasting').

See also: *quechón* (Panama), *cherry-picking* (United States), *goal hanger* (England), *atetɛ nkura* (Ghana), *pettu kedakunnavan* (India)

nó cego – *blind knot*

Going one-on-one with a tricky forward exposes a defender to the risk of being tied into a *nó cego*. If a player is left in a spin by an elusive opponent, it might be remarked that he *precisa duma bússola* ('needs a compass').

polícia – *police*
Without wishing to cast any aspersions about the national character of the Portuguese, it's interesting to note that whereas in Brazil the word called out when a teammate has an opponent sneaking up on them is *ladrão* (meaning 'thief'), in Portugal the equivalent expression is *polícia*.

See also: *ladrón* (Argentina), *mala leđa* (Montenegro), *house* (Republic of Ireland), *gorísh* (Russia), *yau gwai* (China)

pontapé de moinho – *windmill kick*
A close cousin of the overhead bicycle kick, the *pontapé de moinho* is an acrobatic volley performed in mid-air, but with the player side-on to the goal rather than facing away from it. The nearest English equivalent is 'scissors kick'.

pôr a carne toda no assador – *put all the meat on the barbecue*
A coach will *pôr a carne toda no assador* when he throws on all his attacking players in a game and goes for broke. The expression was invented by well-travelled former Porto, Braga and Vitória Guimarães coach Quinito. It was given a new slant by Benfica coach Jorge Jesus in March 2013. Asked how he would handle a fixture schedule that included matches in the league, the Taça de Portugal and the Europa League, Jesus replied: 'Remembering my friend Quinito, we're going to put all the meat on the barbecue and then see.' Sadly for Jesus, the coals proved a little too hot. Benfica were pipped to the league title by Porto, lost 2-1 to Vitória in the Taça de Portugal final and succumbed to an injury-time Branislav Ivanović header against Chelsea in the final of the Europa League.

trinco – *latch*
In Portugal, a holding midfielder is known as a 'latch' because of the way that they secure the vulnerable area in front of their team's defence.

See also: *cinco* (Argentina), *volante* (Brazil), *Makélélé role* (England), *pihkatappi* (Finland), *sentinelle* (France), *stofzuiger* (Netherlands)

trivela
As with many of football's most successful technical innovations, it instinctively feels like the *trivela* belongs to Brazil, where successive generations of players have mastered the art of playing the ball with the outside of the foot (specifically, *de três dedos* or 'with three toes'). Yet over the past decade, the technique has become synonymous with Portuguese winger Ricardo Quaresma, whose right foot is so dextrous as to have furnished him with a shooting and crossing range not dissimilar

to that of a two-footed player. Quaresma's speciality is to cut infield from the right flank and use the outside of his right foot either to bend a cross into the box or whip a devilish shot towards the back post. It brought him his first Portugal goal in a Euro 2008 qualifier against Belgium in Lisbon in March 2007. After gathering a pass from Cristiano Ronaldo, he drove past Belgium left-back Peter Van der Heyden and then, from the right-hand apex of the area, used the outside of his right foot to curl a sublime shot inside the left-hand post, leaving goalkeeper Stijn Stijnen rooted to the spot in apparent disbelief. Quaresma belongs to a tradition of skilled *trivela* practitioners to have graced the Portuguese championship. Serbian winger Ljubinko Drulović was well known for his use of the skill during his 11 years with Gil Vicente, Porto and Benfica. Drulović strongly favoured his left foot and was inspired by Maradona to develop the *trivela* technique so that he would be able to strike the ball in the manner of a right-footed player using their instep. Brazilian right-back Heitor, who played in Portugal for Vitória Guimarães, Nacional and Marítimo, was another player who excelled with the 'wrong' side of his foot. Famous Brazilians to have upheld the tradition include Roberto Rivellino, Branco and Roberto Carlos, while Franz Beckenbauer, Peru great Teófilo Cubillas and Jay-Jay Okocha are among the players to have used the *trivela* to score from free-kicks.

See also: *de três dedos* (Brazil), *papegøje* (Denmark), *shvedka* (Russia), *NASA pass* (Nigeria), *outfoot* (Pakistan)

REPUBLIC OF IRELAND

It took an English World Cup hero to turn the Republic of Ireland into an international force, Jack Charlton steering the 'Boys in Green' to the 1988 European Championship and the knockout rounds of the next two World Cups.

Ireland's achievements at international level – and the country's ability to produce world-class players such as Liam Brady and Roy Keane – are rendered all the more impressive by the fact that Irish football must fight for space with vastly popular native sports like hurling and Gaelic football.

banger
That kid who turns up for an Under-13s match sporting a day's growth of stubble, neck tattoo and arms hairier than a baboon's? In Ireland he's known as a *banger*, which in junior football circles is the name for a non-registered player (or *ringer*) who's clearly over the age limit.

duffer

A big, hopeless player is known as a *duffer* in Ireland, which – ironically – is also the nickname of Damien Duff, one of the most talented footballers the country has known. A selfish player is a *glorier*, while a goal hanger is a *hatcher*.

See also: *tronco* (Argentina), *perna de pau* (Brazil), *pieds carrés* (France), *derevo* (Russia), *drvo* (Serbia), *tuercebotas* (Spain)

house

The equivalent of 'man on', this is an abbreviation of the Irish expression *watch your house*, which basically means 'watch your back'. *Watch Your House for Ireland* was the title of the Ireland squad's official song for the 1994 World Cup. Along with the obligatory uilleann pipes, the song's chorus incorporated a chant that Ireland's fans had directed at the BBC cameras during their 1-0 win over England at Euro 88: 'What's the score? / Up one-nil / Are you watching Jimmy Hill?' It went straight to the top of the Irish charts.

See also: *ladrón* (Argentina), *mala leđa* (Montenegro), *polícia* (Portugal), *gorísh* (Russia), *yau gwai* (China)

McGeady spin

One ingenious piece of trickery has turned Irish winger Aiden McGeady into something of a global reference in the domain of skilful play. A well-watched YouTube clip shows him pulling off his trademark move during a game between Celtic and Aberdeen in October 2004. Having run onto a pass from John Hartson, McGeady finds himself facing the left-hand touchline with his back to the play. As Aberdeen midfielder Steve Tosh approaches from behind, McGeady performs a Cruyff turn directly into Tosh's path, but then flicks the ball down the touchline with the outside of his left foot, leaving his opponent comically flatfooted as he scampers away. McGeady performed the trick so readily that it was soon included as a skill move in the *FIFA* video game series, where it's known as the *McGeady spin*. He may have failed to hit the heights since leaving Celtic in 2010, but thanks to YouTube, *FIFA* and – above all – his own ingenuity, McGeady has made a mark on the game.

to burst someone

To tackle an opponent aggressively without necessarily paying too much attention to where the ball is. As Roy Keane wrote of his notorious foul on Alf-Inge Håland in 2001: 'The ball was there (I think).'

See also: *nabrat na sane* (Czech Republic), *reducer* (England), *Blutgrätsche* (Germany), *stop nonsense* (South Africa), *pakka paer pao* (Pakistan), *enbarash* (Saudi Arabia)

ROMANIA

One of only four European teams (along with Belgium, France and Yugoslavia) to have participated in the first World Cup in 1930, Romania enjoyed their finest hour at the 1994 tournament in the United States when the great Gheorghe Hagi led his countrymen to the quarter-finals.

At club level, Romania became only the eighth country to have produced a European club champion (notably beating France to the punch) and the first from Eastern Europe when Steaua Bucharest defeated Barcelona on penalties in the 1986 European Cup final in Seville.

boabe – beans

Colloquial term for goals.

chirurgul – surgeon

When a player goes around the pitch drawing blood from his opponents with precisely placed kicks and blows, he's likened to a surgeon. Dan Alexa, a former defensive midfielder/hatchet man with Dinamo Bucharest and the Romania national team, was so renowned for putting opponents in hospital that he became known as 'Chirurgul'.

See also: *patas con sangre* (Chile)

creierul – brains

Having gifted the magnificent Gheorghe Hagi to the world, it's no surprise that Romania has several terms for playmakers. A team's chief string-puller could be described as the *creierul* of the team, the *coordonator* ('co-ordinator') or the *decar* or *zece*, both of which mean 'ten'. Hagi was known as 'the Maradona of the Carpathians' around the world and as *Comandante* ('Commander') during his richly successful five-year spell with Galatasaray. In Romania they call him simply *Regele* or 'the King'.

See also: *çilingir* (Turkey)

rezultat decis la masa verde – *green-table decision*
When a match has had to be abandoned or a team are found to have fielded an ineligible player and the result needs to be decided by committee, it's known in Romania as a *rezultat decis la masa verde*.

RUSSIA

Traces of nostalgia for the Soviet Union can still be found in Russia and where football is concerned, at least, things really were better before the Iron Curtain fell.

The Soviet Union won the inaugural European Championship in 1960 and reached three other finals, while a fourth-place finish at the 1966 World Cup came amid a run of four successive runs to the quarter-finals or beyond. After Russia began competing as a solitary nation in 1992, they went out in the group phase at seven of their first eight major tournaments. As Russia have faded as a force on the pitch, so the country's off-pitch problems – chiefly corruption, fan violence and racism – have taken on increasing prominence.

The language of Russian football reflects widely held suspicions regarding the honesty of players, referees and the sport's authorities, but also contains elements of wit, fragments of folklore and an appreciation of the game's subtler features. While the murkiness of the Russian game is well documented, there is light amid the shadows.

balaból (балабол) – *chatterbox*
A *balaból* in Russian folklore is a person who talks too much. The word might be used by a Russian football fan to complain about a garrulous commentator or a manager who's a little too fond of the sound of his own voice.

bombardir-taran (бомбардир-таран*) – battering-ram striker*
This is a term for a big, unwieldy centre-forward, the kind of player whose stock-in-trade is flick-ons, lay-offs and crashing back-post headers. One Russian example is Artem Dzyuba, whose large, angular frame and crude technique have turned him into a kind of football folk hero.

See also: *big baddin'* (Northern Ireland)

cherpak (черпак) *– ladle*
A delicate chip or lob. Moustachioed Spartak Moscow great Fyodor Cherenkov was renowned for his ability to beat the goalkeeper with a delicate *cherpak* and in more recent times, Andrey Arshavin has excelled in the field. An alternative term is *parashyut* (парашют), meaning 'parachute'.

See also: *chute por cobertura* (Brazil), *pichenette* (France), *vaselina* (Spain)

derevo (дерево) *– tree*
A technically inadequate player, typically one who's tall and doesn't move around very much, is imagined in Russia to have literally taken root on the pitch. The Berezutski twins, Aleksei and Vasili, were both saddled with this description during the early years of their careers.

See also: *tronco* (Argentina), *perna de pau* (Brazil), *pieds carrés* (France), *duffer* (Republic of Ireland), *drvo* (Serbia), *tuercebotas* (Spain)

devyatka (девятка) *– nine*
There's a Russian training exercise designed to improve shooting accuracy that divides the goal into three evenly sized squares and then sub-divides the two squares either side of the central square into nine further squares. Each sub-square is numbered from one to nine, with '1' occupying the bottom square nearest the centre of the goal and '9' the square in the top corner. Accordingly, to score into the top corner is known as hitting the *devyatka*.

See also: *onde dorme a coruja* (Brazil), *jep nest* (Trinidad and Tobago), *upper 90* (United States), *rašlje* (Croatia), *postage stamp* (England), *lucarne* (France), *sette* (Italy), *winkelhaak* (Netherlands), *donde anidan las arañas* (Spain), *wayn yeskon shaytan* (Algeria), *fil maqass* (Egypt)

In a nod to a Russian shooting drill, to hit the top corner is to find the *devyatka* ('nine')

dogovornyak (договорняк) – *agreed match*

Dogovornyak describes the practice, long believed to be endemic in Russian football, whereby a team agree to throw a particular match and are then 'rewarded' with a victory over the same opponents either later the same season or the following campaign. The practice is protected by a code of omerta, but Evgeny Lovchev, who played for Spartak Moscow and the Soviet Union in the 1970s, is on record as saying that 'whole series of matches were fixed' during his playing days. Countless games have fallen under suspicion over the years since and the Football Union of Russia's slippery president Vitaly Mutko has said that there are only four or five honest teams in the entire country. A succession of committees set up by Mutko to investigate corruption have all proved equally toothless, and although the Russian parliament has stiffened punishments for match-fixing, actual sanctions have been few and far between. While match-fixing is principally thought to take the form of clubs 'trading' thrown matches, the discovery of suspicious betting patterns around allegedly fixed games in recent seasons has shown that there's money to be made from the practice as well. In a notorious second-tier match in 2010, FK Nizhny Novgorod striker Dmitry Aydov was gifted an 84th-minute equaliser against city rivals Volga when opposition defender Dmitri Polyanin inexplicably ran away from the ball instead of trying to clear it. Another goal would have taken Nizhny up, but – muddying the conspiracy theories – the game finished 2-2 and Volga were promoted instead. While the full extent of match-fixing in Russian football is not and may never be known, fears about it have poisoned the game to such a degree that results that would be cherished as memorable upsets in other countries tend to be greeted with a collective raised eyebrow.

See also: *Calciopoli* (Italy), *dyvnyy match* (Ukraine), *heishao* (China), *jual game* (Malaysia)

fanaty (фанаты) – *fanatics*
Fanaty were hardcore Russian fans whose emergence could be traced back to the Moscow football scene of the early 1970s. They owed their moniker to the vast distances that they were obliged to travel as they criss-crossed the Soviet Union in support of their teams, often deliberately choosing the most convoluted train routes – involving multiple changes – in order to keep costs as low as possible. In the late 1980s and 1990s, hooligan elements emerged from within the *fanaty* groups, taking as models England's hooligan firms and Italy's *ultràs*. While they may not have infiltrated the clubs that they followed to the same extent as their equivalents in Italy, their reputation for violence against fans of other teams was frightening. The word *fanaty* has lost its association with violent football fans over the intervening years and might now be used to describe music lovers or fans of a particular TV show, but Russia's football hooligans remain. The English boot boys of the 1970s and 1980s continue to provide an anachronistic reference point, inspiring both the brutal pitched battles that Russian supporters from rival clubs engage in and the vicious attacks that they carried out on England fans in Marseille during Euro 2016.

See also: *barra bravas* (Argentina), *torcedores* (Brazil), *ultràs* (Italy)

glor (глор) – *glory-hunter*
A supporter who switches allegiance to the most successful team of the moment is called a *glor*, while a fan who comes to a game and doesn't get involved in the chanting is dismissively known as a *kuz'mích* (кузьмич). Played by actor Viktor

Bychkov, Kuzmich was a peace-loving forest ranger who first appeared in the 1995 comedy *Osobennosti natsionalnoy okhoty* (*Peculiarities of the National Hunt*), which became Russia's first national comedy franchise.

See also: *chaquetero* (Spain)

gorchichnik (горчичник) – *yellow card*

Gorchichniki are poultices made from clay or paste and mixed with mustard powder. The process produces yellow, rectangular-shaped plasters resembling slices of cheese that are sold in packets of 10 or 20. A mainstay of Soviet medicine, *gorchichnik* has come to be used as a synonym for a yellow card.

See also: *slice of cheese* (Australia)

gorísh (горишь) – *you're burning*

The phrase used to warn a teammate in possession of the ball that an opponent is approaching.

See also: *ladrón* (Argentina), *mala leđa* (Montenegro), *polícia* (Portugal), *house* (Republic of Ireland), *yau gwai* (China)

lazaret (лазарет) – *lazaretto*

When a player is injured, he's said to be in the 'lazaretto', which is the name given to quarantine stations for maritime travellers.

na vtorom etazhe (на втором этаже) – *on the second floor*

This term refers to the aerial side of the game. If a team have been conceding a lot of headed goals from set-pieces, for example, they might be said to have problems 'on the second floor'.

passovotchka (пассовочка)

Eight years before the trauma of England's seismic 6-3 defeat at home to Hungary's *Aranycsapat* ('Golden Team'), the game's inventors were given a warning that should have set the alarm bells ringing long before Ferenc Puskás, Nándor Hidekguti and Sándor Kocsis trotted out of the tunnel at Wembley. In 1945, Dynamo Moscow toured Britain and caused a sensation, their razor-sharp attacking football enchanting seasoned observers as they fought a gripping 3-3 draw with Chelsea, edged Arsenal 4-3 in a fog-bound thriller at White Hart Lane, annihilated third-tier Cardiff 10-1 and drew 2-2 with Rangers. Dynamo's style of play was known as *passovotchka* and was the brainchild of trailblazing coach Boris Arkadiev. Russian football had been slow to respond to the emergence of the W-M formation in European football and it wasn't until a visiting Basque XI reeled off a series of one-sided wins during a tour of the Soviet Union in 1937 that the country's leading clubs realised the extent to which they had been left behind. Uniquely for a coach of the time, Arkadiev actively drilled his players on tactics, hammering home the importance of movement and encouraging the players in his front five to switch positions in order to disorientate their opponents. Their bewitching interplay carried them to a Soviet title triumph in 1940 and after the war they repeated the feat under Arkadiev's successor, Mikhail Yakushin. Dynamo's style was christened 'organised disorder' by an admiring Russian media and the British press were similarly smitten. 'I have never seen football like it,' wrote Davie Meiklejohn, the former Rangers captain, in the *Daily Record*. 'They simply wandered here and there at will, but the most remarkable feature of it all, they never got in each other's way.' Dynamo's approach prefigured both the strategy with which Hungary would so confound England in 1953 and the dizzying universality of Holland's Total Football in the 1970s.

See also: *Scheiberlspiel* (Austria), *Hollandse school* (Netherlands), *tiki-taka* (Spain)

pas Streltsova (пас Стрельцова) – *Streltsov pass*

One of the most stylish and skilful players to have come out of Russia, Eduard Streltsov embedded his name in his country's football glossary via his mastery of the back-heeled pass, which became known as a *pas Streltsova*. A shining star with Torpedo Moscow and the Soviet Union, Streltsov was forced to abandon his career in 1958, at the age of 20, when he was thrown into the forced labour camps of the Gulag after being convicted of rape in dubious circumstances. (A renowned playboy, Streltsov was said to have fallen foul of Communist Party officials. He also had the misfortune of playing for Torpedo rather than Dynamo, the police club, or CSKA Moscow, the army club.) Freed five years into a 12-year sentence, he returned to action for Torpedo and the national team, finishing his career with a tally of 25 goals from 38 international appearances.

See also: *madjer* (Algeria)

pushka strashnaya (пушка страшная) – *scary cannon*

This slightly naff term describes a shot that's struck powerfully from distance. It briefly became a cult phrase after being blurted out by commentator Georgy

Cherdantsev during Russia's quarter-final win over Holland at Euro 2008 to describe a meaty strike by defender Denis Kolodin. More generally, *pushka* ('cannon') is used to describe any forcefully hit shot.

See also: *pombo sem asa* (Brazil), *evrogol* (Serbia), *intercontinental ballistic missile* (Nigeria), *bballaejul katteun shoot* (South Korea)

sbory (сбор) – training camp

A Russian tradition with strong militaristic overtones, *sbory* are intense pre-season training camps that can last for up to two months at a time. They are often loathed by players, who find themselves isolated from their friends and families in secluded hotels, typically overseas or in the warmer resorts of the Russian south. Once in place, they are put through gruelling fitness regimes and obliged to observe strict diets and curfews. Boredom abounds and while players return for the start of the season primed for action (if they've not been completely run into the ground), they're invariably sick of the sight of their teammates.

See also: *ritiro* (Italy)

shvedka (шведка) – Swede

A pass or shot played with the outside of the foot is known in Russia as a *shvedka*, which is the feminine form of the word 'Swede'. It's thought to have come into use after the 1958 World Cup in Sweden, where Brazilian players such as Didi demonstrated their mastery of the technique.

See also: *de três dedos* (Brazil), *papegøje* (Denmark), *trivela* (Portugal), *NASA pass* (Nigeria), *outfoot* (Pakistan)

stenochka (стеночка) – little wall

A *stenochka* is a one-two and the word is particularly associated with the great Spartak Moscow team coached by Konstantin Beskov from 1977 to 1988. They won the Soviet Top League in 1979 and 1987 and their dashing interplay made them a neutral's favourite. Another diminutive is *schyochka* (щечка) or 'little cheek', which refers to the inside of the foot.

sudyu na milo (судью на мыло) – ref on soap

Popular in Soviet times, this sinister chant was aimed at referees who were felt to be treating a team unfairly. It refers to the old Soviet practice of culling stray dogs and using their fat to make soap. A biased referee is said to *posadit' na svistok* (посадить на свисток), which literally means 'imprison on the whistle'. The expression will be heard when an official appears to be clamping down on a team's every transgression, no matter how minor, and is sometimes perceived as an indication of *dogovornyak*. A dodgy penalty might be described as a *leviy penalty* (левый пенальти) or 'left penalty', *leviy* being the word for something that is inauthentic or of poor quality.

See also: *pískat hovna* (Czech Republic), *corbeau* (France), *sędzia kalosz* (Poland), *referee kayu* (Malaysia)

sukhoi list (сухой лист) – *dry leaf*
Whereas the Portuguese term *folha seca* ('dry leaf') describes a dipping free-kick, in Russia the same phrase refers to a goal scored direct from a corner kick. Grigory Fedotov, the great CSKA striker of the 1940s, was said to have pioneered the technique and Valeriy Lobanovskyi, future emblematic coach of Dynamo Kyiv, was also famed for his ability to find the net from the corner arc.

See also: *gol olímpico* (Argentina)

zvyozdnaya bolezn' (звёздная болезнь) – *star sickness*
The term *zvyozdnaya bolezn'* was used in the 1970s to describe the crude and boorish behaviour of the leading Soviet players of the time. Despite being notionally amateurs, they received all manner of secret perks and the leniency of the football authorities meant that they were generally free to do as they pleased. Today it's generally evoked whenever a famous person starts getting too big for their boots.

See also: *jogar de salto alto* (Brazil)

SCOTLAND

The world's joint-oldest national team, Scotland took a different approach to the sport from the very beginning, their 0-0 draw with England in the first recorded international in November 1872 noteworthy for the way that the Scots met the head-down-and-dribble approach of their opponents with a more considered passing style. But despite qualifying for eight World Cups – including five in a row between 1974 and 1990 – Scotland are still to make it beyond the first round.

The Old Firm derby between Glasgow foes Rangers and Celtic, first contested in May 1888, is one of the most passionate and compelling club rivalries in the game.

blooter

To strike the ball with extreme force. 'Griffiths absolutely *blootered* that shot and the goalie didn't stand a chance.'

gallus

A *gallus* player is someone who plays the game with a sense of mischief and showmanship. It's a concept embodied by Jim Baxter's legendary display of keepy-uppies in the closing stages of Scotland's 3-2 win over world champions England at Wembley in 1967. Inspired by Denis Law's nonchalant back-heel pass, Baxter flicked the ball into the air and kept it airborne with three touches before scooping a return pass into Law's path. It lasted no more than a few seconds and achieved nothing in a material sense, but it became a monument to Scottish bravado. 'Today I'd be booked for that kind of stuff,' Baxter said in 1999. 'Back then I saw football, always, as a job of entertainment; you were putting on a show for the fans.' Scotland's manager Bobby Brown was irked by Baxter's showboating and felt that the visitors would have come away with a margin of victory that more amply reflected their dominance of the game had the Sunderland left-half shown greater urgency. Law concurred, praising Baxter's overall display but complaining that his indulgences had prevented Scotland from inflicting a 'massacre' that would have fully avenged their 9-3 loss to England on the same pitch six years previously. Nevertheless, the win allowed Scotland's fans to proclaim their team unofficial world champions and Baxter's circus act made him a modern-day folk hero.

heid the ba

Also known as a *ba-heid*, a *heid the ba* ('head the ball') is a fool or someone with an over-inflated sense of self-importance. One of the very earliest football songs, penned in Scotland in the 1880s, explored the negative potential impacts of playing football on someone's intelligence. It was called 'The Dooley Fitba Club' and is thought to have been written by James Currin, a popular Glasgow songwriter. The song became more widely known when it was re-released as *Football Crazy* by folk duo Robin Hall and Jimmie Macgregor in 1960. Its chirpy chorus – 'He's football crazy, he's football mad / The football it has robbed him o' / The wee bit o' sense he had' – helped to further underscore the links between football and idiocy.

his jaiket's oan a shoogly nail

When speculation begins to swirl that an under-performing manager is at risk of the sack, his *jaiket* ('jacket') will be said to be hanging *oan a shoogly nail* ('on a wonky nail').

stramash

A word that succeeded in inveigling its way into football parlance south of the border, a *stramash* describes an almighty goalmouth scramble or a set-to involving several players. Venerable STV sports presenter Arthur Montford popularised the expression and it was also associated with the warm burr of late BBC rugby commentator Bill McLaren.

tanner ba' player

The *tanner ba'* was an under-sized football made from rubber that could be bought for a *tanner* (sixpence) in post-war Scotland. When young boys dribbled down alleyways beside Glasgow tenement blocks or jostled for possession on wastegrounds in central-belt industrial towns, the *tanner ba'* was inevitably the ball they were chasing. Its small size obliged players to hone their close control and the intensely physical nature of street football matches taught them how to survive on their wits. It was amid the swiping feet and swinging elbows of such games that the *tanner ba' player* was born, a short, will-o'-the-wisp footballer blessed with a gossamer touch, embodied by the great Celtic winger 'Jinky' Jimmy Johnstone. With Scottish football having slithered into the doldrums over recent decades, the *tanner ba' player* exists today in rose-tinted nostalgia as a reminder of a time when Scotland's players ranked among the best in the world.

See also: *potrero* (Argentina), *kora sharab* (Egypt), *sakora park* (Ghana)

SERBIA

Nicknamed *Orlovi* (Орлови), meaning 'The Eagles', Serbia have competed as a separate nation since 2006 and have qualified for two World Cups during that time.

Many of the finest players to have played for Yugoslavia were from Serbia, among them Blagoje 'Moša' Marjanović, prolific pin-up of the team that reached the semi-finals at the 1930 World Cup, and Dragan Džajić, Red Star Belgrade's luminous left-wing virtuoso of the 1960s and 1970s.

drvo (дрво) – *wood*

A player with very poor technique. From the expression *lopta se odbija od njega kao od drva* ('the ball bounces off him like wood').

See also: *tronco* (Argentina), *perna de pau* (Brazil), *pieds carrés* (France), *duffer* (Republic of Ireland), *derevo* (Russia), *tuercebotas* (Spain)

evrogol (еврогол) – *Euro goal*

Impressive long-range goal. Takes its name from *Eurogol,* a highlights programme showing eye-catching strikes from across Europe that was broadcast on Italian TV channel Rai 2 between 1977 and 1994. The word carries the same meaning in Italy.

See also: *pombo sem asa* (Brazil), *pushka strashnaya* (Russia), *intercontinental ballistic missile* (Nigeria), *bballaejul katteun shoot* (South Korea)

maneken (манекен) – *model*

A player who doesn't make any effort or get stuck in will be derisively dubbed a *maneken* in Serbia, the implication being that he'd be better off flouncing up and down a catwalk.

See also: *abatino* (Italy), *hankie ball player* (Northern Ireland)

otresti ga kao slinu (отрести га као слину) – *to shake someone off like saliva*

Not that saliva has ever seemed a particularly easy thing to shake off (just ask Rudi Völler), but in Serbia, this is the metaphor that's used when a player dominates another in a physical duel.

ući golmanu u krilo (ући голману у крило) – *to fall into the goalkeeper's lap*

Few things in football shred a supporter's nerves more quickly than the sight of their team's defence dropping deeper and deeper and deeper as they desperately try to cling on to a narrow lead. In Serbia, when a team find themselves penned inside their own penalty area, they're imagined to be sitting in the goalkeeper's lap.

See also: *táctica del murciélago* (Ecuador), *Obrona Częstochowy* (Poland), *mball camp yi* (Senegal)

zmaj (змај) – *dragon*
Zmaj is the name given to a speedy player such as one-time Serbia winger Miloš Krasić whose pace allows them to sidestep opponents with ease.

SLOVAKIA

Formerly part of Czechoslovakia, Slovakia began playing under their own flag in 1994. They achieved their most impressive result to date at the 2010 World Cup in South Africa, when a team captained by spiky-haired Napoli midfielder Marek Hamšík knocked defending champions Italy out of the competition in the group phase before losing to eventual finalists the Netherlands in the last 16.

dostať kopačky – *to get the football boots*
To get dumped. *Kopačky* comes from the word *kopať*, meaning 'to kick', so the idea is that when a couple break up, the person who gets rejected is literally kicked away. They don't really go in for conscious uncoupling in Slovakia.

hypnotizovať loptu – *to hypnotise the ball*
A player who can pluck a ball from the sky with ease or make difficult pieces of control look routine is credited with the ability to 'hypnotise the ball'.

rozhodca začal hrať mariáš – *the referee started playing mariáš*
In the English-speaking world, a punctilious match official might be said to be dishing out cards 'like it was Christmas'. In Slovakia, the referee is imagined to be playing *mariáš*, which is one of the country's most popular card games.

SLOVENIA

Along with Croatia, Slovenia was one of the first republics to declare independence from Yugoslavia and the country's football team played their first official match against Estonia in June 1992. Slovenia made their maiden major tournament appearance at Euro 2000, blowing a 3-0 lead to draw 3-3 with 10-man Yugoslavia in their opening match. They have since played at two World Cups (2002 and 2010).

cariniti žogo – *keeping the ball in customs*
Footballers at all levels of the game like to think they know precisely how to time a pass, but when a player exasperates his teammates by constantly ignoring their cries for the ball, he's said to be 'keeping the ball in customs'.

ne zadene Olimpijskega bazena – *couldn't hit an Olympic swimming pool*
A novel take on the couldn't-hit-a-cow's-arse-with-a-banjo idiom, this is the phrase that will be uttered in exasperation when a Slovenian striker is having an off day in front of goal.

See also: *fallar más que una escopeta de feria* (Spain)

petarda – *firecracker*
Pet is the Slovenian word for 'five', so when a team score five goals in a game, it's known as a *petarda*.

SPAIN

Spain's football vocabulary articulates a morass of contrasts. It's a country where creativity has flourished in the club game, but where the national playing style was long held to be a frantic amalgam of intensity and brute force known as *la furia roja* ('the red fury'). While the country had always produced skilful footballers, it was only when the churning tide of physicality that threatened to submerge the sport in the early years of the new millennium finally receded

– drawn back by the lunar pull of football's evolutionary cycle – that the polished pebbles of Spain's technical artistry finally caught the sunlight.

The language of Spanish football is also, inevitably, the language of Barcelona and Real Madrid, ideological foes locked in an eternal face-off across the Ebro basin, whose rivalry dominates to such an extent that everything else in the Spanish game is swept to the margins. A journey through Spanish football-speak takes us to the bedroom, the bathroom and the dinner table, to the farmyard and the bullring, outer space and the gates of Hell, but we always, always wind up back at the Bernabéu and Camp Nou.

abrir la lata – *to open the can*
When the pressure that builds up before a game is released by the scoring of the first goal, it's equated with pulling the ring-pull on a canned drink.

amarrategui
Amarrategui is a play on words used to describe a defensive coach. It's formed of *amarrar* (meaning 'to hold') and the suffix *-egui* in honour of the former Racing Santander, Celta Vigo and Espanyol coach José María Maguregui. Renowned for his safety-first approach, Maguregui was partly responsible for establishing the notion that Basque coaches are dour and defensive, with Javier Clemente perhaps the most eminent example. A quarrelsome and potty-mouthed chain-smoker, Clemente espoused tough, physical football and regularly employed a tactic known as the *bloque*, which involved plonking two defensive midfielders in front of the back four (when in charge of Spain, he once paired Miguel Ángel Nadal and Fernando Hierro, two centre-backs, in central midfield). One of his catchphrases was *'Patapún y p'arriba!'*, which roughly translates as: 'Bish, bosh, up it goes!'

armario – *wardrobe*
A large, sturdy and uncompromising player. Basically what all Spanish centre-backs looked like before Gerard Piqué came along.

See also: *caballo* (Costa Rica), *Holzgeschnitzter* (Austria), *kitasa* (Tanzania), *samaam al amaan* (Saudi Arabia)

cagómetro – *crapping-yourself-ometer*
Former Barcelona president Joan Laporta called it the *caverna mediática* ('media cave'), while Catalan journalist Carles Torras coined the term *central lechera* ('milk board'). Both expressions describe the Madrid media pack, that influential

collection of pro-Real Madrid news outlets – led by the sports newspapers *AS* and *Marca* – which are only too happy to do the club's bidding, be it fanning the flames of refereeing conspiracies, goading opponents or unsettling transfer targets. One of their number, former *AS* journalist Tomás Guasch, came up with the concept of the *cagómetro* or 'crapping-yourself-ometer', which he would use to measure the extent to which Barcelona were cracking up amid the pressure exerted upon them by Madrid. (It tied in with the peculiar tradition of *el caganer* or 'the crapper', a ceramic figurine of a person defecating that is included in Catalan nativity scenes.) As Barcelona wobbled during the closing weeks of the 2015/16 title race, losing three games in succession, Madrid captain Sergio Ramos was overheard breezily exclaiming '*¡Vuelve el cagómetro!*' ('The crapping-yourself-ometer is back!') during a training session at Valdebebas. Barcelona managed to regain control of their bowel movements, however, and pipped Madrid to the title by a point.

cancerbero – *goalkeeper*
A particularly agile goalkeeper might be compared to a cat in Britain, but in Spain keepers are loftily likened to Cerberus, the monstrous three-headed dog that guards the gates of Hades in Greek mythology.

cantar el alirón – *to sing el alirón*
Cantar el alirón is a metaphor for winning a trophy and refers to a song sung by supporters of Athletic Bilbao: '*¡Alirón! ¡Alirón! ¡Athletic campeon!*' ('*Alirón! Alirón!* Athletic champions!') The Basque account of the song's origins begins in the 19th century with the English phrase 'all iron', which would be chalked on newly dug ore mines in the region if they were found to have high iron content. More iron meant more money for the poorly paid local miners and so 'all iron' – transformed into *alirón* on their tongues – became a sort of victory cry. A more compelling (albeit slightly less romantic) version holds that the song arrived in the Basque Country on New Year's Eve 1913 when a famous cabaret singer called Teresita Zazá performed a number called *El Alirón* at Bilbao's Salón Vizcaya music hall. At the time, Athletic were competing to become the first team to win the newly formed Campeonato Regional del Norte (Northern Regional Championship) and when Zazá invited the audience to sing the song's chorus ('*¡Alirón! ¡Alirón! ¡Pon, pon, pon, pon!*'), they replied: "*¡Alirón! ¡Alirón! ¡Athletic campeon!*" As Athletic stormed to the title over the following months, the song became a fixture at the newly built San Mamés. The Royal Spanish Academy asserted in its 2001

dictionary that the word *alirón* came from the Hispanic-Arabic expression *al'ilan*, which means 'proclamation', only to backtrack in 2014 and declare that its origins were 'unknown'.

cantera – *youth academy*

Literally meaning 'quarry', *cantera* is the Spanish name for a youth academy. An equivalent Catalan term is *planter* ('nursery'). The *cantera* holds special significance for the Basque clubs Athletic Bilbao and Real Sociedad, both of whom traditionally insisted on only fielding local players. La Real relaxed their policy in 1989 in order to sign John Aldridge from Liverpool, but it remains in place at Athletic. Both Barcelona and Real Madrid boast celebrated academies, respectively known as La Masia ('The Farmhouse') and La Fábrica ('The Factory'). Barcelona's period of dominance under Pep Guardiola with a team largely made up of home-grown players was heralded (in Catalonia at least) as a triumph of their *cantera* over Madrid's *cartera* ('wallet'), even if Barça have never been exactly shy about spending money themselves.

cazagoles – *goal-hunter*

Also known as a *chupagoles* ('goal-sucker'), this is a name given to a prolific striker. The top marksman in La Liga each season receives the *Trofeo Pichichi*, which has been awarded since 1953 by *Marca* in honour of Rafael 'Pichichi' Moreno, who scored goals at a blistering rate for Athletic Bilbao in the second decade of the 20th century. He was said to have been given his nickname, which means 'Little Duck' in the Basque language, by his brother, Raimundo, in reference to his thin, feeble frame. The goalkeeping equivalent of the *Pichichi*, presented by *Marca* to the goalkeeper with the best ratio of goals conceded to games played, is the *Trofeo Zamora*, which is named after Ricardo Zamora, the legendary Spanish goalkeeper of the 1920s.

See also: *Knipser* (Germany)

chaquetero – *turncoat*

From the word *chaqueta* (meaning 'jacket' or 'coat'), this term describes fans or players who change their allegiances in order to suit themselves. The most famous *chaquetero* of recent times was Luís Figo, whose shock transfer from Barcelona to Real Madrid in 2000 earned him several lifetimes of opprobrium from the supporters of the club he left.

See also: *glor* (Russia)

Cholismo

A word that's achieved high prominence in both La Liga and the Champions League in recent seasons, *Cholismo* refers to the high-intensity football and win-at-all-costs mentality instilled at Atlético Madrid by Diego 'Cholo' Simeone. Simeone began his playing career at Vélez Sársfield under the orders of Victorio Spinetto, who sowed the seeds of *anti-fútbol* during his time as Vélez coach in the 1940s. Spinetto, who coached Vélez's youth teams until his death in 1990, christened Simeone 'Cholo' (meaning someone with a blend of indigenous and European heritage) because he reminded him of the former Boca Juniors defender Carmelo 'Cholo' Simeone (no relation). Renowned for his ruggedness and tenacity as a player, Simeone carried the same approach into his career as a coach. Hired by Estudiantes in May 2006, he fashioned the most well-drilled and hard-working team in Argentina and led them to their first league title in 23 years. His success with Estudiantes created a template for his time with Atlético, who have consistently punched above their weight amid unprecedentedly fierce competition from Barcelona and Real Madrid, winning La Liga, the Copa del Rey, the Europa League and twice reaching the Champions League final. Rather than a tactical concept, *Cholismo* is almost a code for how to live: aggressive, ultra-committed, in-your-face and relentless. In his trademark black suit, black shirt and black tie, Simeone is as much a protagonist as any of his players, ceaselessly organising, gesticulating and haranguing from the touchline. In the truest *anti-fútbol* traditions, he has few qualms about underhand tactics – once getting a three-game ban for instructing a ball boy to throw a ball onto the pitch in order to disrupt an opposition counter-attack – but at a time when every other club in Spain has wilted in the heat emitted by the duelling fireballs of Barça and Madrid, his success with Atleti has been outstanding.

See also: *anti-fútbol* (Argentina)

chupón – ball-hog

From *chupar*, meaning 'to suck', a *chupón* is a player who doesn't pass the ball. It's also the word for a baby's dummy.

See also: *morfón* (Argentina), *amarrabola* (Peru), *ballverliebt* (Germany)

chutar al muñeco – to kick at the doll

To put a shot straight at the goalkeeper. *Muñeco* is the Spanish term for a table football figurine.

cola de vaca – *cow's tail*

There are 23 minutes on the clock in Barcelona's home game against Real Madrid in January 1994 and the score is 0-0 when Pep Guardiola collects a pass from Guillermo Amor in the inside-left channel. Loitering in the space between Madrid centre-back Rafael Alkorta and right-back Paco Llorente, Romário gestures to Guardiola that he wants a pass into his feet and the future Barça coach obliges. With Alkorta standing off him, Romário takes a touch and then produces an outlandish piece of skill, cradling the ball with his right foot and scooping it past the Basque defender like a hockey player playing a push pass, whirling through 180 degrees as he does so and driving into the box. Alkorta takes one step back towards his own goal, but immediately realises he's beaten and Romário completes the job by stabbing the ball beneath the advancing Francisco Buyo. The move became known as the *cola de vaca* or 'cow's tail' because it brought to mind a cow lazily swishing its tail to swat away flies. Romário had been under a bit of pressure going into the game, having gone five matches without finding the net, but his goal set Barcelona up for a historic 5-0 win that proved the catalyst for Johan Cruyff's team to go on and win a fourth successive La Liga title. Romário finished the season as the top scorer in Spain with 30 goals, the strike against Madrid both the pick of the bunch and one of the highpoints of Barça's 'Dream Team' era.

Romário pulls off the *cola de vaca* ('cow's tail') prior to scoring against Real Madrid

175

comepipas – *seed-eater*

Spectators munching sunflower seeds are a common sight on the sun-drenched terraces of Spain's football stadiums, but to be called a *comepipas* is to be accused of watching your team passively rather than getting on your feet and supporting them properly.

See also: *prawn sandwich brigade* (England), *kaaskijkers* (Netherlands)

croqueta – *croquette*

La croqueta is the piece of skill utilised by a player who rapidly knocks the ball from foot to foot in order to evade an incoming tackle or squeeze through a gap between two opponents, like a cook flipping a croquette from one side of the frying pan to the other. Its patron saint is Michael Laudrup, its most famous modern practitioner Andrés Iniesta.

dar un baño – *to give (someone) a bath*

To beat a team convincingly.

donde anidan las arañas – *where the spiders nest*

Not that you'll find many cobwebs in Spanish goalmouths, but a shot that finds one of the top corners is said to have ended up *donde anidan las arañas*.

See also: *onde dorme a coruja* (Brazil), *jep nest* (Trinidad and Tobago), *upper 90* (United States), *rašlje* (Croatia), *postage stamp* (England), *lucarne* (France), *sette* (Italy), *winkelhaak* (Netherlands), *devyatka* (Russia), *wayn yeskon shaytan* (Algeria), *fil maqass* (Egypt)

entregar la cuchara – *to give up the spoon*

In Spanish football, to 'give up the spoon' means to give in or to accept defeat. It originates from the Great Siege of Malta in 1565, which pitted Spanish troops against the invading armies of the Ottoman Empire, known as Janissaries. The Janissaries wore ornate hats known as *börk* in which they displayed a kind of spoon called a *kaşıklık* that symbolised their comradeship with their fellow soldiers. When Janissaries were killed or captured, the spoons would be kept as trophies by their adversaries, which gave rise to the expression *entregar la cuchara* or 'give up the spoon'. More generally, the word *cuchara* describes a scooped pass or shot.

espaldinha – *little back*

During Barcelona's 3-0 victory over Murcia in October 2003, goalkeeper Víctor Valdés bowled the ball out to Ronaldinho and the Brazilian used his *back* to cushion a pass into the path of Rafa Márquez. The whole of Camp Nou gasped in unison. This was a crowd that had witnessed the gifts of László Kubala, Cruyff and Maradona, Romário, Ronaldo and Rivaldo, but Ronaldinho was something else. A born entertainer, his mouth permanently fixed into a buck-toothed grin, he was the most innovative player of his generation and during his Barcelona years he seemed to make it his mission in life to devise as many ways to dazzle his opponents as possible. There were the *elásticos*, the *pedaladas*, the combinations of *sombreros*, the no-look passes. The back pass was one such party piece and it was named in his honour as the *espaldinha* (from *espalda*, the Spanish word for 'back', and *inha*, a Portuguese diminutive). A year after premiering it against Murcia, he used it to set up a goal for Ludovic Giuly in a game against Osasuna. Though it's since been appropriated by, among others, Cristiano Ronaldo, Zlatan Ibrahimović and Alexis Sánchez, it will always belong to Ronaldinho. *Ganar la espalda*, meanwhile, means 'to win someone's back' and refers to a forward's ability to get in behind his marker.

fallar más que una escopeta de feria – *to misfire more than a fairground shotgun*

Of a goal-shy striker. It might also be said that he *no marca ni a un arco iris* ('couldn't even score through a rainbow').

See also: *ne zadene olimpijskega bazena* (Slovenia)

falso nueve – *false nine*

Before every match that his teams play, Pep Guardiola locks himself away and pores over video footage of his opponents, searching for what he calls the 'flash of inspiration' that will unlock the door to victory. Perhaps his most famous Eureka moment occurred on 1 May 2009, as he sat in his office at Camp Nou preparing for the following day's *Clásico* at Real Madrid, who trailed his side by four points in the title race. Noticing the space that habitually opened up in front of Madrid centre-backs Fabio Cannavaro and Christoph Metzelder, he decided that he was going to get Messi to come off the right wing and replace Samuel Eto'o up front, but in a withdrawn role that would leave Cannavaro and Metzelder with nobody to mark. Despite it being 10 o'clock at night, he summoned Messi to his office and presented him with his masterplan. Messi started the game on the right, but on Guardiola's signal he moved infield. And wreaked havoc. In the signature display of Guardiola's first season, Barcelona swaggered to a majestic 6-2 win in which Messi scored twice and created a goal for Thierry Henry. Metzelder and Cannavaro would later admit that they had been completely baffled by Messi's positioning and had no idea how to handle him. It was not a new tactic – Nándor Hidegkuti was doing the same thing for Hungary in the 1950s, Matthias Sindelar for Austria in the 1930s – but it brought it bang up to date. Playing in that role, Messi would amass an astonishing 173 goals over the following three seasons and before long, false nines were popping up all over Europe.

Galácticos

The *Galácticos* were the galaxy of megastar footballers lured to Real Madrid by club president Florentino Pérez in the early 2000s, and the word came to stand for both the recruitment policy itself and the folly it would ultimately be seen to represent. The first years of the project yielded ominous success. Figo and Zinedine Zidane, brought to the Bernabéu in 2000 and 2001 respectively, combined to deliver Madrid a ninth European Cup in 2002 – a triumph synonymous with Zidane's wonderful volley against Bayer Leverkusen at Hampden Park. After Ronaldo joined the fray, Madrid won the league title in 2003, but then things went south. David Beckham's arrival that summer laid bare the vanity of the strategy – one that seemed to be as much about selling replica shirts as winning trophies – and with a disastrously unbalanced team creaking beneath the weight of so many world-famous players, Madrid foundered, tumbling off the pace in La Liga and losing their way in the Champions League. Pérez resigned in February 2006, only to return in June 2009 with Madrid reeling from their mauling at Barcelona's hands the previous season. Within 10 days of Pérez's return Madrid had broken the world transfer record twice with staggering moves for Kaká and Cristiano Ronaldo, whose arrivals were supplemented by the additions of Karim Benzema and Xabi Alonso. The second wave of *Galácticos* found themselves living in Barça's shadow to begin with, but Ronaldo, Benzema and Alonso would stick around long enough to steer the club back to the pinnacle of world football.

hombre del maletín – briefcase man

When a lowly team pull off an unexpected result against one of Spain's big guns, and particularly when the outcome has a significant impact on the battle to avoid relegation, the question will be asked as to whether the *hombre del maletín* might have made an appearance at the team hotel before the match, the suggestion being that their performance had more to do with briefcases full of banknotes than pure sporting motivation. Cristiano Ronaldo insinuated as much after Real Madrid encountered unanticipated resistance during a must-win game at Celta Vigo in the final week of the 2016/17 title race. The Madrid number seven was caught by TV cameras mimicking the act of lifting a briefcase and goading Celta defender Gustavo Cabral: *'Dinero, tú mucho. . . Maletín!'* ('Money, lots for you . . . Briefcase!') Related scandals are known as *maletinazos*.

See also: *marmelada* (Brazil), *biscotto* (Italy)

huguina

A distinction is sometimes made in football between a player who's a great goalscorer and someone who's a scorer of great goals. Players generally fall into one of the two categories, but very occasionally, they straddle both. Such was the case of Hugo Sánchez. A committed gymnast during his childhood in Mexico City, he brought his prodigious spring to the football pitch and became famed for his ability to score dumbfounding volleys and overhead kicks. Each would be celebrated with a somersault and fist-pump, which he was supposedly taught by his elder sister, Herlinda, who competed for Mexico in the gymnastics at the 1976 Olympics in Montreal. During his 11 relentlessly prolific seasons in Madrid – four with Atlético, seven with Real – Sánchez scored gravity-defying overhead kicks with such frequency that they became known as *huguinas*. The pint-sized number nine netted his most celebrated *huguina* for Real Madrid in a game against Logroñés in April 1988, flinging himself at Martín Vázquez's left-wing cross and hooking a sumptuous left-foot shot into the top-left corner. Sánchez claimed that Vázquez's cross had hung in the air for so long that he even had time to decide which post to aim for, eventually plumping for the far post to make it 'more spectacular'. The goal was baptised *el señor gol* ('the master goal') and Madrid coach Leo Beenhakker said: 'When a player scores a goal like that, play should be suspended and a glass of champagne offered to the 80,000 fans who witnessed it.' A precursor to the *huguina* was the *llagosta* or 'grasshopper', an acrobatic type of volley associated with Pepe Samitier, the Barcelona star of the 1920s, who was known in Catalonia as *l'home llagosta* ('the grasshopper man') because of his remarkable agility.

See also: *papinade* (France)

la furia – *the fury*

La furia española ('the Spanish fury'), alternatively known as *la furia roja* ('the red fury'), was the term used to describe the Spanish national team's characteristically aggressive style of play in the days when their calling cards were bruising centre-backs and thundering challenges rather than diminutive midfielders and dainty passing triangles. The term was born during the 1920 Olympics in Antwerp when Basque midfielder José María Belauste scored a header of such force against Sweden that he took several Swedes into the net with him. A Dutch newspaper, evoking the Spanish army's sacking of Antwerp in 1576, employed the term *la furia española* and it caught on in Spain. *Tiki-taka*, with its emphasis on intricate passing football, definitively sounded the death knell on the *furia* style, but Jorge Valdano believes its demise was ushered in 25 years earlier by his quicksilver former Real Madrid teammate Emilio Butragueño. 'For many years, Spanish football was associated with *la furia*, meaning aggression and directness,' Valdano said. 'There was no beauty to it, but it dominated for decades. Then Emilio came along and was an instant hero despite representing the opposite of the *furia* stuff . . . He changed the way the Bernabéu viewed the game and the legacy has grown.' While it may not accurately describe the team's football anymore, *La Furia Roja* has retained currency as one of the national side's nicknames.

Madridismo

Madridismo describes a set of elevated principles associated with emblematic Real Madrid president Santiago Bernabéu – nobility, hard work, style, humility – which the club aspires to uphold. It's also used more generally as a metaphor for the Madrid 'family' and is most often cited, internally and externally, at times when the mood of the club needs summing up. Naturally, not everyone sees *Madridismo* in quite such a laudatory light as those who are inside the Bernabéu looking out. Reflecting deep-seated suspicions about favourable refereeing and curious strokes of luck, rival fans sing: '*Así, así, así gana el Madrid!*' ('Like this, like this, Madrid win like this!') The chant, dreamed up by fans of Sporting Gijón in 1979, has been appropriated by Madrid's supporters to celebrate statement performances and dramatic last-gasp wins.

manita – *little hand*

Iván Iglesias had just scored the fifth goal of Barcelona's 5-0 win over Real Madrid in January 1994 and Camp Nou was a sea of *blaugrana* flags. Tonny Bruins Slot, Johan Cruyff's assistant, emerged from the dug-out. Wearing a sea-green Kappa anorak and grinning broadly, he raised his right arm and spread open the palm of his hand to show five fingers to Barça's jubilant fans. The *manita* was born. *Marca* would later write: 'That gesture stung more than the

5-0 itself.' Almost 17 years later, in November 2010, Barça were 4-0 up at home to Madrid when Jeffren Suárez emulated Iglesias by coming off the bench to score a late fifth goal. For Gerard Piqué, a player steeped in Barcelona's traditions, the coincidences were too delicious to go unremarked. As he peeled away from the giddy throng of players and coaches celebrating in front of the dug-outs, he turned to face the crowd and held up the five fingers of his right hand. The gesture was reflected back at him all around the stadium. His teammates followed his lead, notably Carles Puyol, Éric Abidal and Víctor Valdés, but it was Piqué's beaming face – and proudly splayed fingers – that were plastered all over the following day's sports papers.

morbo

A fiddly word to translate, *morbo* describes the potent blend of bitterness, needle and intrigue that fuels Spanish football and particularly the rivalry between Barcelona and Real Madrid. It can mean 'disease', but in football terms it's used to describe a kind of dirty thrill, that leering state of glee that can only be brought on by an opponent's misfortune. Riven by regionalism, pulled in multiple directions by separatist movements and still coming to terms with the legacy of Francoism, Spain is a nation divided, and when rival football teams face off, the social, political and historical subtexts that come bubbling to the surface can make for a heady and volatile brew. In Italy, a related term, *gufare*, describes supporting whoever your most hated rivals are playing against.

pañolada – *handkerchief protest*

Spanish football fans wave white handkerchiefs (*pañuelos*) to express disgust when their team have fallen to a heavy defeat or to protest against decisions made by the coach or club president. (If you've made the mistake of coming to the stadium without a white handkerchief, flapping a piece of white paper works just as well.) White handkerchiefs are also waved in bullfighting to encourage the president of the bullring to reward a brave matador with the ears of the bull he has slain. Claiming a part of the bull is known as *tocar pelo* ('to touch hair'), which is used in football as a metaphor for winning a trophy.

pase de la muerte – *death pass*

When a player steams to the byline and then cuts the ball back for a teammate running in, presenting him with a clear sight of goal, it's known as a *pase de la muerte*.

pelopina

Xavi's trademark move is as effective and beguilingly simple as the player himself. Finding his path towards goal blocked by an opposition player, he will turn back to face his own goal, inviting his opponent to pursue him, before shifting the ball sideways and then moving forwards into the space that his adversary – now blindly following him like a dog chasing its own tail – was occupying just a second previously. You could call it 'how to make a defender disappear', but in Spain it's known as a *pelopina* in reference to Xavi's rather unfortunate nickname. During his time at La Masia, Xavi and his youth-team colleague Miguel Ángel would call each other 'pelopo', meaning 'pube head', and to Xavi's misfortune, the nickname stuck. (*Pelopo* is a combination of *pelo*, meaning 'hair', and *polla*, a slang term for the penis.) Fortunately, Xavi would acquire another nickname – 'Maki', short for 'Máquina' ('Machine'), because of his metronomic passing – but his inimitable 360° turn continues to keep his adolescent moniker alive.

píntalo de amarillo – *paint him yellow*

What a player will implore the referee to do when he believes an opponent has committed an offence worthy of a yellow card.

remontada – *comeback*

After Real Madrid lost 3-1 to Internazionale in the first leg of a UEFA Cup semi-final in April 1986, striker Juanito uttered a phrase that would enter Bernabéu folklore. Speaking in approximative Italian, he warned Inter: '*Noventi minuti en el Bernabéu son molto longo*' ('Ninety minutes in the Bernabéu are very long'). Madrid duly won the second leg 5-1 and thanks to Juanito's role in a succession of successful fightbacks, *el espíritu de Juanito* ('the Juanito spirit') has since been invoked whenever they've found themselves with a daunting deficit to overcome. Stirring comebacks – or *remontadas* – became a speciality for the team that Juanito played in. En route to UEFA Cup glory in 1985, they overturned three first-leg deficits against HNK Rijeka, Anderlecht and Inter (coming from 3-0 down against Anderlecht in the third round to win 6-1 at the Bernabéu). Before eliminating Inter in the following season's competition, which they also won, Madrid had bounced back from a crushing 5-1 first-leg loss against Borussia Mönchengladbach to win the second leg 4-0, taking them through on away goals. The spirit of Juanito, who died in a car crash in 1992, was summoned again in 2016 when, after a surprising 2-0 loss away to Wolfsburg in the Champions

League quarter-finals, they hit back to win the second leg 3-0. (*AS* journalist Tomás Roncero claimed to have contacted Juanito using a Ouija board after Madrid lost 2-0 to Atlético in the first leg of a Copa del Rey tie in January 2015. Sadly, the spectre's reported prediction for the return match – a 3-0 win – proved wide of the mark as a 2-2 draw sent Atleti through.) For all Madrid's historical associations with *remontadas*, the most eye-popping comeback of recent years was achieved by Barcelona. Beaten 4-0 by Paris Saint-Germain in the first leg of their Champions League last 16 tie in February 2017, Barça found themselves 5-3 behind on aggregate with two minutes of the return leg remaining at Camp Nou, only for Neymar to score twice and then set up a gobsmacking 95th-minute winner for substitute Sergi Roberto. PSG were so determined never to let the same thing happen again that six months later they paid £200 million to bring Neymar to Paris.

rondo

The *rondo* exercise was introduced at Barcelona by Cruyff when he returned to the club as coach in 1988. It's one of football's most simple training drills – a ball, a circle of players, two men in the middle breathlessly trying to intercept their passes – but for Barcelona it represents the central tenet of their modern on-pitch identity. 'It's all about *rondos*,' Xavi has said. '*Rondo, rondo, rondo.* Every. Single. Day. It's the best exercise there is.'

See also: *pelota jagua* (Paraguay)

salir a por uvas – to go out to collect grapes

This expression is used to describe a goalkeeper who makes an ill-advised advance from his goal-line to collect a cross or a loose ball, only to get nowhere near it. The phrase is employed in general speech when someone gets in a muddle.

See also: *skovtur* (Denmark), *sortie kamikaze* (France), *sortie aux fraises* (Switzerland)

sombrero – hat

Familiar to football fans all over the world, a *sombrero* is when a player outwits an opponent by flicking the ball over their head. Another hat-related term from Spain is *txapeldun*, a Basque word meaning 'champion'. It comes from *txapela*, a broad beret that was presented as a trophy to Basque sportsmen.

See also: *chapéu* (Brazil), *baptiser* (Cameroon), *kanzu* (Kenya), *height* (Nigeria), *deff ko watt* (Senegal), *kanyumba* (Zambia)

tiki-taka

It was the motif of Spanish football's golden age, but the man considered the father of *tiki-taka* doesn't care for it. 'I hate *tiki-taka*. I hate it,' Pep Guardiola told Martí Perarnau in *Pep Confidential*. '*Tiki-taka* means passing the ball for the sake of it, with no clear intention. And it's pointless. Don't believe what people say. Barça didn't do *tiki-taka*! It's completely made up!' Guardiola was trying to draw a distinction between sterile possession football and the kind of rapid attacking interchanges that were the hallmark of his Barcelona team, but he's fighting a losing battle. *Tiki-taka*'s place in the annals has long been secure as the name for the percussive pom-pom-pom of passes that took Spain and Barcelona to the summit of the sport. With Spain, it owed its existence to a process of trial-and-error overseen by Luis Aragonés during qualifying for Euro 2008. Spain started poorly, losing successive games against Northern Ireland and Sweden, but as Aragonés drafted in creative midfielders like Iniesta and David Silva, so the team found an identity. Signs that something special was taking shape could be seen during a 3-1 away win against Denmark in October 2007 when Sergio Ramos scored a goal from right-back after an elaborate move involving 27 passes. When Spain prevailed at Euro 2008, *tiki-taka* was the word on everyone's lips. That same summer, Guardiola was promoted from his role as Barcelona B coach and assiduously began to apply the tactical precepts that he had learned under Cruyff 20 years earlier. Guardiola's football was far more aggressive than that played by Spain – the passing quicker and more incisive, the pressing higher and more urgent – but it retained at its core the same commitment to ball circulation and quick, short passing. The presence of so many talented Spanish players at Barça (the legacy of Cruyff's vision for La Masia) gave Spain a strong Barcelona core that allowed the two teams to progress symbiotically, success for one informing success for the other and inspiring both to unprecedented heights. *Tiki-taka* was also a product of its time. Football's evolution in the first decade of the 21st century – innovations with the offside rule, clampdowns on foul play, a significant improvement in the quality of pitches – created conditions that enabled teams of small, physically unprepossessing players to excel playing fast, technical, high-risk possession football. The term itself means 'clackers' (as in the child's toy) and is believed to have been first mentioned in a football context by Javier Clemente, who employed it pejoratively to talk about possession football with no end product. It was first associated with the national team during the 2006 World Cup when La Sexta's Andrés Montes, commentating on Spain's 3-1 win over Tunisia in Stuttgart, exclaimed: '*Estamos tocando el tiki-taka*' ('We're playing *tiki-taka*'). There were times, particularly during Euro 2012, when *tiki-taka* took on an oppressive monotonousness, revealing itself to be a tactic that, in seeking to deprive the opposition of the ball, was as much about stifling as it was about creating. But at its peak, during Guardiola's first three years at Barcelona, it was the most dazzling coordinated football the game had ever seen.

See also: *Scheiberlspiel* (Austria), *Hollandse school* (Netherlands), *passovotchka* (Russia)

tuercebotas – *twisted boots*
A player with two left feet. An equivalent term is *paquete* ('lump').

See also: *tronco* (Argentina), *perna de pau* (Brazil), *pieds carrés* (France), *duffer* (Republic of Ireland), *derevo* (Russia), *drvo* (Serbia)

vampiros – *vampires*
Imaginative name for drug-testers (based on the fact that they come to take players' blood).

vaselina – *vaseline*
A smooth, dinked finish, as perfected by Messi.

See also: *chute por cobertura* (Brazil), *pichenette* (France), *cherpak* (Russia)

vaya pepinazo – *what a great big cucumber*
Vaya pepinazo (or, more accurately, *¡Vaya pepinazo!*) is an expression shouted out by Spanish football supporters when a player spectacularly propels the ball into the net from prohibitive range.

See also: *Gurkenpass* (Germany)

virus FIFA
When players return to Spanish clubs after picking up injuries in FIFA-mandated international fixtures, they're said to have succumbed to the *virus FIFA*.

SWEDEN

Discounting the 1948 Olympics, Sweden's men's football team have never won a major tournament, but they've come closer than most, losing in the final to

Brazil as hosts of the 1958 World Cup, finishing third at the 1950 and 1994 tournaments, and reaching the semi-finals on home soil at Euro 92.

The team's 21st-century iteration was long synonymous with Zlatan Ibrahimović, who scored a record 62 goals in 116 caps prior to his retirement from international football in 2016.

att köpa korv – *to buy a hot dog*

'First I went left. He did, too. Then I went right and he did, too. Then I went left again and he went to buy a hot dog.' Thus a young Zlatan Ibrahimović explained how he'd left Liverpool defender Stéphane Henchoz seeing stars with an *elástico* during a pre-season friendly with Ajax in 2001, thereby introducing a new phrase to his country's footballing argot. According to Jamie Carragher, when Henchoz was asked what had happened after returning to the changing room, he replied: 'I don't know. I honestly don't know. The ball was there, then it was gone!'

See also: *llevar a alguien a la escuelita* (Panama), *poslati ga po burek* (Bosnia and Herzegovina), *da go pratya za bira* (Bulgaria), *kohvile saatma* (Estonia), *het bos ingestuurd* (Netherlands), *sendt opp i pølsebua* (Norway), *pazara göndermek* (Turkey), *kupelekwa shopping* (Kenya)

In Sweden, to be sent the wrong way by an attacker is *att köpa korv* ('to buy a hot dog')

blåbärslag – *blueberry team*

An inept team might be referred to in Sweden as a *blåbärslag*, which stems from
the colloquial use of the word *blåbär* ('blueberry') to describe an inexperienced
or incompetent person. An English equivalent would be 'newbie'. In an example
of another culinary term, a pass that arrives right at the feet of its intended
recipient is a *smörpassning* ('butter pass').

gärdsgårdsserie – *round-pole fence league*

Gently disparaging name for an amateur league, which refers to a traditional
rural method of fence-building using cylindrical wooden poles.

See also: *FC Bal op het Dak* (Netherlands)

långa bollar på Bengt – *long ball to Bengt*

An expression used to describe the practice of humping high balls towards a
centre-forward, Bengt being a popular male name in Sweden. The phrase was
the name of a pop song released in 1992 by Swedish band Svenne Rubins. The
song's protagonist reminisces about playing for a team whose coach installed
his son, Bengt, up front and instructed the rest of the side to launch long balls
towards him. In later life the protagonist returns to the same pitches, where
he finds that Bengt is now coaching the team and has picked his own son,
Bengt Jnr, at centre-forward. Sweden's dependence on Ibrahimović during
his 15 years in the national team gave rise to the expression *långa bollar
på Zlatan*.

See also: *route one* (England), *bakrom* (Norway), *bbeung chuk gu* (South Korea)

strumprullare – *sock roller*

It's a sensation familiar to schoolyard footballers everywhere. You wind up
for a net-splitting volley, only for the ball to roll down your shin and flop
apologetically off the end of your foot. In Sweden the phenomenon is known as
a *strumprullare*. When you strike the ball with your shin, you're said to have a
träben ('wooden leg').

See also: *cic hosan* (Wales)

SWITZERLAND

As exemplified by the national team's three nicknames – *Schweizer Nati* in German, *La Nati* in French and *Squadra nazionale* in Italian – Switzerland is a country split along linguistic lines, and the emergence of second-generation immigrants of Balkan descent such as Xherdan Shaqiri and Granit Xhaka has only added to the richness of the cultural blend in the Swiss changing room.

Switzerland reached the quarter-finals at three of the first five World Cups (1934, 1938 and, as hosts, 1954), but went 28 years without featuring at the tournament between 1966 and 1994.

sortie aux fraises – *sortie for strawberries*
The Swiss French take on the goalkeeper who comes tearing off his line and gets nowhere near the ball pictures him going out to pick strawberries.

See also: *skovtur* (Denmark), *sortie kamikaze* (France), *salir a por uvas* (Spain)

Stürchel – *stumbler*
From *stürcheln*, the Swiss German word for 'stumble'. Used to describe a striker, typically a lanky one, who seems to be perpetually tripping over his own feet.

Uuschügele – *out-marbled*
From *Chugle*, which means 'marble' but can also be used as a word for the ball. *Uuschügele* describes a dizzying passing combination that cuts an opposition defence to pieces.

veryoungboyse – *to Young Boys*
Bern team Young Boys have become so famous for agonising near-misses over the past 30 years that a verb now exists to describe the phenomenon. *Veryoungboyse* means to allow victory to slip through your fingers and it's used to describe any team who fall short in calamitous circumstances. In two Swiss Cup finals – 1991 and 2009 – Young Boys went 2-0 up against the same team – Sion – but somehow contrived to lose 3-2. The teams also met in the 2006 final, Sion winning on penalties despite being in the second tier at the time. After a 10-year absence from European competition, Young Boys qualified for the UEFA Cup in 2003, only for a team spearheaded by veteran striker Stéphane Chapuisat to go down 5-4 on aggregate to Finnish outsiders MyPa in

the qualifying round. It made them the first Swiss team to be eliminated from a European tournament by a side from Finland. Most traumatic of all was the title run-in of 2010. Propelled by the goals of striker Seydou Doumbia, Young Boys led main rivals Basel by 13 points in early September and appeared certain to claim a first league title since 1986. But as the finishing line loomed into view, they faltered catastrophically. A 5-1 shellacking at Luzern in their penultimate fixture left them facing a last-day showdown at home to Basel. A draw would have been enough for Basel to take the title, so Young Boys needed to win. They lost 2-0.

TURKEY

Turkey is home to some of the most madly committed football supporters on the planet, which turns clashes involving the Istanbul giants Beşiktaş, Fenerbahçe and Galatasaray (to name but three clubs) into spectacular assaults on the senses.

The country's World Cup record is a virtual desert, save for a first-round elimination at the 1954 tournament and a storming surge to the semi-finals in 2002, when a team led by all-time leading scorer Hakan Şükür eliminated Japan, the co-hosts, and Senegal before losing to a Ronaldo toe-poke against eventual champions Brazil.

bal yapmayan arı – *bee without honey*
A player who buzzes around the pitch to no discernible effect. Can also be used to describe a hard-working but ineffective team.

See also: *mbua* (Democratic Republic of Congo)

çilingir – *locksmith*
A *çilingir* is a playmaker who has the ability to unpick even the most tightly locked defence. A player who's technically deficient but throws everything he has into the game is known as a *kazma* or 'pickaxe'. The opposite – a skilful player who shies away from hard work and physical contact – might be labelled a *matmazel* ('mademoiselle').

See also: *creierul* (Romania)

A particularly talented playmaker is referred to as a *çilingir* ('locksmith') in Turkey

hacı – *hadji*

A die-hard fan who goes to all his team's away games is known as a *hacı*, which is the name given to Muslim pilgrims who have completed the Hajj to Mecca.

kova kaleci – *bucket goalie*

A hopeless goalkeeper in Turkey is likened to a bucket because of his unfortunate propensity for taking on water. Hapless Turkey keeper Yaşar Duran acquired the nickname 'Bucket' after shipping eight goals in an 8-0 loss to England in qualifying for the 1986 World Cup. A shellshocked shot-stopper might alternatively be described as an *uçan manda* ('flying buffalo'), an *uçan kova* ('flying bucket') or an *uçan çuval* ('flying sack').

See also: *Eiergoalie* (Austria), *pudrunäpp* (Estonia), *imuri* (Finland)

pazara göndermek – *to send someone to the bazaar*

When a defender comes charging into a challenge, determined to take out both man and ball, only to be left flat on his back by an opponent's change of direction, he's imagined in Turkey to have been dispatched to the nearest bazaar. An alternative term is *belinden su almak* ('to take water from someone's back'), which suggests that the beaten player has unwittingly undergone a medical procedure.

See also: *llevar a alguien a la escuelita* (Panama), *poslati ga po burek* (Bosnia and Herzegovina), *da go pratya za bira* (Bulgaria), *kohvile saatma* (Estonia), *het bos ingestuurd* (Netherlands), *sendt opp i pølsebua* (Norway), *att köpa korv* (Sweden), *kupelekwa shopping* (Kenya)

plakasına tükürmek – *to spit on the number plate*

To 'spit on the number plate' is to beat the away team, the suggestion being that the victorious team have marched out into the stadium car park and fired some phlegm at the visitors' bus.

timsaha yatmak – *doing a crocodile*

Going into the final round of matches in the 2009/10 Süper Lig season, Fenerbahçe led second-place Bursaspor by a point and needed only to match their result to claim the title. Fenerbahçe's 1-1 draw at home to Trabzonspor left things in the balance, but when it was announced over the PA system at Şükrü Saracoğlu Stadium that Bursaspor had conceded a late equaliser in their home game against Beşiktaş, Fener's fans poured onto the pitch in jubilation. Some of them mockingly mimicked Bursa's 'crocodile walk' goal celebration – kneeling down in a line, grasping the ankles of the person in front and marching forwards on their knees. Unfortunately for Fenerbahçe, the announcement was a mistake: Bursa had held on for a 2-1 win, giving them the first league title in their history. Fener's fans reacted furiously, clashing with police, lighting fires in the stadium and rampaging through the streets outside the ground. The phrase *timsaha yatmak* has since been adopted by Turkish football fans to describe a situation where someone has got ahead of themselves.

UKRAINE

The Ukrainian national team have only competed as an independent nation since late 1994, but prior to that the country's football fans already had a representative team to will on in the shape of Dynamo Kyiv.

Dynamo were the most successful team in the Soviet Top League, gate-crashing the hegemony of the Moscow clubs to win 13 titles. Under their revolutionarily scientific coach Valeriy Lobanovskyi they won two European Cup Winners' Cups (1975 and 1986) and reached the European Cup semi-finals on three occasions (1977, 1987 and 1999).

arytmiya (аритмія) – arrhythmia
When a match undergoes a change in pace.

dyvnyy match (дивний матч) – strange match
Just like neighbouring Russia, Ukraine is no stranger to football corruption, with even the great Lobanovskyi falling under suspicion. He was suspected of 'arranging' draws in Dynamo's away matches, having calculated that if his side won all their home games and drew all their away games, it would be impossible to prevent them winning the title. The Soviet football authorities became so concerned about the abundance of drawn matches in the late 1970s that they ruled that teams would only score points for up to eight draws per season (subsequently increased to 10), after which drawn games would yield no points. CSKA Moscow were relegated in 1987 after a 1-1 draw in their penultimate game at home to Zenit Leningrad counted for nothing because they had already filled their 'quota' of drawn games. The point they forfeited would have kept them up. The system remained in place until 1988. Following Lobanovskyi's departure, Dynamo were disqualified from the Champions League in 1995 after Spanish referee Antonio López Nieto alleged that they had tried to bribe him with a payment of $30,000, as well as two fur coats, before their opening group match against Panathinaikos. A similar fate befell Metalist Kharkiv in August 2013 when they were kicked out of the Champions League over a fixed match against Karpaty Lviv that had taken place in 2008. In recent years, the focus has turned to low-interest matches that produce unusual outcomes after huge sums of money are bet on them. The tongue-in-cheek term *dyvnyy match* ('strange

match') has been adopted to describe games where there is clearly more going on than meets the eye.

See also: *Calciopoli* (Italy), *dogovornyak* (Russia), *heishao* (China), *jual game* (Malaysia)

hol v rozdyahal'nyu (гол в роздягальню) – *goal into the dressing room*

A goal scored right at the end of the first half. A goal scored at the beginning of the second half is a *hol z rozdyahal'ni* (гол з роздягальні) or 'goal out of the dressing room'.

See also: *gol de vestuario* (Argentina)

horyshche (горище) – *attic*

The upper half of the league table. The lower half of the table is the *pidval* (підвал), meaning 'basement'.

See also: *linkerrijtje en rechterrijtje* (Netherlands)

sukhar (сухар) – *biscuit*

Clean sheet. A clean sheet with a saved penalty on top is a *sukhar z rodzynkamy* (сухар з родзинками), which means 'biscuit with raisins'.

See also: *clean sheet* (England)

WALES

Quarter-finalists at the 1958 World Cup, Wales had to wait 58 years for their next taste of international football, whereupon a team built around Gareth Bale and Aaron Ramsey produced a colossal surprise by reaching the semi-finals at Euro 2016.

Getting to a major tournament in the first place was an achievement that proved beyond such well-known players as Ian Rush, Mark Hughes and Ryan Giggs.

camsefyll – *offside*

The Welsh term for offside literally translates as 'mis-standing' (i.e. standing in the wrong place).

See also: *na banheira* (Brazil), *milpa* (Costa Rica)

chwip o gôl – *whip of a goal*

When Gareth Bale leaves the net billowing with a scorching long-range effort that causes spectators to catch their breath, it's known in Welsh as a *chwip o gôl*.

cic hosan – *sock kick*

A bad miskick or slice.

See also: *strumprullare* (Sweden)

crymanu – *to curl*

From the word *cryman*, meaning 'scythe', *crymanu* is the verb employed to describe a player expertly bending the ball around the reach of a despairing goalkeeper.

BETWEEN THE LEGS – NUTMEG NAMES

In English it's a 'nutmeg', in many countries it's a 'tunnel', but wherever you go in the world, you can be sure that the archly provocative act of sticking the ball between an opponent's legs will have a name. Here are some of the best ones.

Beinschuss – *leg shot (Germany)*
Reflecting the damage to the psyche that being nutmegged can inflict, Germans equate falling victim to the trick with being shot in the legs.

caño – *pipe (Argentina)*
Alternatively known as a *túnel*, the *caño* was a favoured weapon of Boca Juniors maestro Juan Román Riquelme.

cueca – *undies (Portugal)*
How embarrassing does it feel to be nutmegged? Well in Portugal they reckon it's like being stripped to your underpants.

deya *(Zimbabwe)*
From the Shona word *mateya*, meaning 'rickets' or 'bowlegs', this taunt suggests the nutmegged player would not have been shown up if there wasn't such a huge gap between their legs.

Gurkerl – *gherkin (Austria)*
If you thought finding a gherkin in your cheeseburger was unpleasant, wait until you find one between your legs.

housle – *violin (Czech Republic)*
This term is believed to have come into circulation as a corruption of *jesle*, meaning 'crib' – another name for a nutmeg that likens the nutmegged player's pins to the legs of a wooden crib.

huacha *(Peru)*
The Peruvian name for a nutmeg is thought to come from the English 'washer' – a flat metal disk with a hole in the middle used to tighten screws.

janelinha – *little window (Brazil)*
A diminutive of *janela* ('window'), this is one of several Brazilian names for a nutmeg. The word also serves to describe the gap left in a person's mouth by a missing tooth.

kobri (كوبري) – *bridge (Saudi Arabia)*
Alternatively spelt *kobry*, this is the default name for a nutmeg across the Arab world.

kötény – *apron (Hungary)*
Kötény belongs to a sub-genre of nutmeg words comprising items of clothing that might have prevented the nutmegged player from being hoodwinked. In this case, an apron.

luka – *hatch (Norway)*
The gap between a nutmeg casualty's legs is perceived as a hatch or opening in Norway. Master of the art though he is, it's nothing to do with Luka Modrić.

mrezhichka (мрежичка) – *little net (Bulgaria)*
If you nail someone with a nutmeg in Bulgaria, it's customary to invite them to bring a *mrezhichka* with them next time to help guard against a repeat.

one-kina *(Papua New Guinea)*
In Papua New Guinea, the player on the receiving end of a nutmeg is imagined to resemble the country's one kina coin, which has a hole through its middle.

panna – *gate (Netherlands)*
Panna drifted into Holland's football vernacular courtesy of immigrants from the former Dutch colony of Suriname and came into use around the world via the street football scene.

petit pont – *little bridge (France)*
France's football lexicon contains two methods of beating an opponent with a bridge: a *petit pont* (nutmeg) or a *grand pont* ('big bridge'), which involves prodding the ball past someone on one side and collecting it on the other.

r kka ghi (알까기) – *hatching an egg (South Korea)*
When the ball is played between someone's legs in South Korea, the player on the receiving end is pictured to have popped out an egg.

salad *(Jamaica)*
A curious coinage unique to Jamaica, this expression has been in use since the mid-1960s.

suknjica – *skirt (Bosnia and Herzegovina)*
Fall prey to a nutmeg in Bosnia and – metaphorically at least – you'll find yourself wearing a skirt.

tung haang keoi (通坑渠) – *through the sewage pipes (Hong Kong)*
On the five-a-side pitches of Hong Kong, a nutmegged player's carelessly splayed legs are held to resemble the gaping mouth of a sewage pipe.

xâu kim – *threading the needle (Vietnam)*
In a rare departure from conventional nutmeg lore, the focus in Vietnam is on the skill of the nutmegger rather than the shame of the nutmeggee.

AFRICA

Of the 308 matches that took place over the course of the first 11 World Cups, only 10 involved African teams, but Africa is now a major player in world football, its biggest stars – Milla, Weah, Drogba – among the brightest to have twinkled in the sport's firmament.

A continent of some 1.2 billion people, Africa supports a complex linguistic ecosystem of over 2,000 languages, in which Arabic and native tongues like Swahili, Hausa, Oromo, Amharic, Yoruba, Igbo, Shona and Zulu coexist with colonial languages such as English, French and Portuguese, as well as innumerable local dialects.

No examination of the language of African football can proceed without mention of *muti* ('witchcraft'). A shadowy blend of supernatural beliefs and practices, it springs from the conviction that players and teams can gain an edge over their opponents by performing elaborate mystical rituals prescribed by witch doctors (variously known as *muti men, juju men, gris-gris men* or *sangomas*).

The Confederation of African Football has attempted to chase the witch doctors from the sidelines of the African game, but although traditional practices are felt to be dying out, the recurrence of *muti*-related controversies shows that the *muti men* continue to make their presence felt.

ALGERIA

Known as 'the Greens', 'the Fennecs' or 'the Desert Foxes', the Algerian national team have experienced two purple patches. In the 1980s a team driven by the gifted trio of Lakhdar Belloumi, Rabah Madjer and Salah Assad played at successive World Cups (1982 and 1986) before Madjer skippered them to glory as hosts of the 1990 Africa Cup of Nations.

More recently, two quite different teams made it to the World Cup in 2010 and 2014, the 2014 side losing to eventual champions Germany after extra time in the round of 16.

chemma league – *dipping tobacco league*

Chemma league is a self-deprecating nickname for the Algerian top flight, which plays on a perceived lack of professionalism in the division. High-profile Algerian players such as Rafik Saïfi were often seen playing with dipping tobacco in their mouths and in 2015 USM Alger winger Mokhtar Benmoussa was caught on camera fishing a brown wad of *chemma* from beneath his top lip as he awaited kick-off in the second half of a match in the Coupe d'Algérie. The Algerian second division is sometimes called *Afras 2* after a local cigarette brand.

el ghoraf (الغُراف) – *the jug*

It may be considered the trademark of Ronaldinho and Cristiano Ronaldo by younger generations, but ask an Algerian who invented the *elástico* and they will tell you straight: Salah Assad. A blisteringly quick and ferociously direct left-winger, Assad was one of the stars of the effervescent Algeria team that reached successive World Cups in 1982 and 1986. He claims to have devised the trick commonly known as the *elástico* all by himself while kicking around stones, rag balls and plastic bottles during his childhood in Kabylie, and boasts that whereas players like Rivellino and Ronaldinho could only pull it off from a standing start, he was able to execute it at full pace. It was known as *el ghoraf* in Arabic and *la louche* ('the ladle') in French, and whoever else may have mastered it over the past 20 years, in Algeria its father will always be Assad. His Algeria teammate Lakhdar Belloumi is credited with having invented another technique closely associated with Ronaldinho: the no-look pass.

See also: *elástico* (Brazil), *culebrita* (El Salvador)

madjer

A classy and versatile forward with an eye for the flamboyant, Rabah Madjer announced his arrival on the global stage when he stabbed home the first goal of Algeria's shock 2-1 victory over European champions West Germany at the 1982 World Cup. While the Germans' notorious 1-0 win over Austria in Gijón would bring Algeria's tournament to a premature conclusion nine days later, Madjer's group-stage displays meant that he had at least succeeded in positioning himself squarely in the shop window. A domestic regulation that prevented Algerian footballers aged 28 or under from playing overseas initially denied him the chance to exploit his new status by joining a major European team, but following a long stand-off with the Fédération Algérienne de Football, he was allowed to sign for Racing Club Paris in 1983. From there he would join Porto, in 1985, and it was with the Portuguese giants that he scored the goal that secured his place in European and North African football folklore. Appearing in their first European Cup final against Bayern Munich in Vienna in 1987, Porto were trailing 1-0 in the 77th minute when Brazilian forward Juary gathered a pass from fellow substitute António Frasco and played a square ball across the six-yard box from the right. A deflection on the cross meant that Madjer arrived slightly ahead of the ball, but he adjusted brilliantly, planting his left foot in the turf, allowing the ball to pass between his legs and then guiding it past covering defender Hans-Dieter Flick with a wonderfully deft back-heel. 'I was already running to the near post and I let the ball go between my legs and I hit it with the back of my heel,' he said. 'There was a defender on the line, so if I'd controlled the ball, I'd never have scored.' Three minutes later Madjer returned the compliment by setting up Juary for the winning goal, making Porto the first Portuguese side to lift the European Cup in 25 years. Later that year, Madjer scored an extra-time winner as Porto beat Peñarol of Uruguay in the Tokyo snow to win the Intercontinental Cup and in 1990 he captained Algeria to glory on home soil at the Africa Cup of Nations. Thanks to his Viennese twirl, his legacy lives on in the Francophone world, where back-heeled goals are routinely referred to as *madjers*.

See also: *pas Streltsova* (Russia)

wayn yeskon shaytan (وين يسكن شيطان) – *where Satan lives*

In African qualifying for the 2010 World Cup, Algeria finished dead-level with hated enemies Egypt at the top of Group C, necessitating a one-off play-off match in November 2009 that took place amid a huge police presence in the Sudanese capital Khartoum. The game rekindled memories of the teams' infamous qualifying play-off before the 1990 tournament, which was nicknamed 'the Death Match'. Egypt goalkeeper Essam El-Hadary appeared set to frustrate Algeria, but after keeping them at bay for most of the first half, he was beaten in the 40th minute when centre-back Antar Yahia latched onto Karim Ziani's lofted pass and powered a shot in off the crossbar from a narrow angle on the right. It was the goal that sent Algeria to their first World Cup in 24 years. In a post-match interview filmed in the changing room against a raucous backdrop of celebrating teammates, Yahia said: 'We hit it on the ground, he [El-Hadary] stopped it. We hit it in the air, he stopped it. [So] we hit it where the devil couldn't reach.' The beIN Sports commentator Hafid Derradji has since popularised the use of the phrase *wayn yeskon shaytan* ('where Satan lives') to refer to the top corners of the goal.

See also: *onde dorme a coruja* (Brazil), *jep nest* (Trinidad and Tobago), *upper 90* (United States), *rašlje* (Croatia), *postage stamp* (England), *lucarne* (France), *sette* (Italy), *winkelhaak* (Netherlands), *devyatka* (Russia), *donde anidan las arañas* (Spain), *fil maqass* (Egypt)

BURKINA FASO

Burkina Faso have never played at a World Cup, but they reached the final of the Africa Cup of Nations in 2013, going down 1-0 to Nigeria in Johannesburg.

The team's nickname, *Les Étalons* ('The Stallions'), refers to the steed rode by legendary 12th-century warrior princess Yennenga, who's considered the mother of the country's Mossi people.

pieds nickelés – *leaden feet*
A striker who cannot find the net no matter how many sights of goal he gets is imagined to be playing in leaden boots. The expression comes from a long-running French comic strip called *Les pieds nickelés* that was first published in 1908. It recounts the adventures of three brothers – Croquignol, Filochard and Ribouldingue – who have grand plans but keep slipping back into a life of indolence and crime.

CAMEROON

Heavyweights of African football, Cameroon have appeared at seven World Cups and in 1990 became the first team from Africa to reach the quarter-finals, a side inspired by charismatic 38-year-old striker Roger Milla disposing of Colombia in the last 16 before losing to England.

The only Cameroonian player to have eclipsed Milla's goal-scoring feats was four-time African Player of the Year Samuel Eto'o, who scored 56 goals in 118 international games and helped Cameroon to the third and fourth of their five Africa Cup of Nations crowns (1984, 1988, 2000, 2002 and 2017).

acheter une cigarette – *buy a cigarette*
If a player deceives an opposition goalkeeper – such as when a penalty-taker sends the keeper the wrong way from the spot – he's pictured to have dispatched the custodian to fetch a cigarette.

baptiser – *to baptise*
When a Cameroonian player has the ball lifted over his head by an adversary, he's said to have been 'baptised'. The expression is also found in Ivory Coast.

See also: *chapéu* (Brazil), *sombrero* (Spain), *kanzu* (Kenya), *height* (Nigeria), *deff ko watt* (Senegal), *kanyumba* (Zambia)

dans la sauce – *in the sauce*
The omens didn't look good for Cameroon before the 2017 Africa Cup of Nations in Gabon. No fewer than eight players turned down call-ups, obliging coach Hugo Broos to plug the gaps in his squad as best he could, and a row over bonus payments rumbled on throughout the tournament. Yet as the competition progressed, so Cameroon found strength in adversity and the harmony that developed within Broos's patched-up squad found expression in a song. Cameroonian singer-songwriter Reniss had released her dance track 'La Sauce' months earlier, in May 2016. Influenced by Cameroon's *bikutsi* genre, it had a playful, juddering rhythm and its shouty chorus – *'Dans la sauce! Dans la sauce!'* – made it a massive hit among Cameroon's fans. It became the unofficial soundtrack of the team's tournament, the hashtag #danslasauce climbing further up the trending charts with each improbable victory. A succession of opponents were left *dans la sauce* – Senegal in the quarter-finals, Ghana in the semis – before Cameroon came from 1-0 down to beat Egypt 2-1 in the final, Vincent Aboubakar's unforgettable volleyed winner in the 88th minute completing a triumph as stunning as it was unexpected. Congratulating Broos's squad on their success, Cameroonian president Paul Biya said: 'You have faced the most formidable teams, the most experienced teams, and as you say, you put them in the sauce.'

mboundja – *goal*
Mboundja (alternatively spelt *boundja*) is Cameroon's goal word: to *mboundja* is to score a goal and *'Mboundjaaaaaaaa!'* is what you cry when the ball hits the back of the net.

See also: *laduma* (South Africa), *il y est* (Tunisia)

ntoum – *stake*

A speciality of rugged Cameroonian defenders, the *ntoum* is an uncompromising means of winning possession that involves stepping over the ball into an opponent's path and planting your shoulder into their chest. Its literal meaning is 'stake' or 'pestle'.

DEMOCRATIC REPUBLIC OF CONGO

As Zaire, the Democratic Republic of Congo won two Africa Cups of Nations (1968 and 1974) and became the first team from Sub-Saharan Africa to play at a World Cup in 1974. Their contribution in West Germany was chiefly memorable for a 9-0 thrashing by Yugoslavia and some unconventional defending of a free-kick against Brazil. Mwepu Ilunga, the defender who famously broke from the wall on the referee's whistle to hoof the ball downfield, said that he did so to waste time after the team were threatened with severe punishment by President Mobutu Sese Seko in case of a heavy defeat.

aza na yombo – *to have bad luck*

Applied to a player, coach or team against whom fate appears to have conspired. It might be said of a striker who keeps missing chances or a team who are stuck in a rut of bad results. *Yombo* was the name given to a black hair dye imported from western Africa in the 19th century. The suggestion is that a footballer who has *na yombo* has been touched by some kind of dark misfortune.

joueur ngomba – *mountain player*

A *joueur ngomba* is a player who believes in witchcraft. Specifically, it refers to the clients of a renowned *féticheur* ('shaman') called Mort-Mort (Death-Death), who lives on a hill in Kinshasa (hence 'mountain player') near the city's university. Mort-Mort is believed to have the ear of high-profile players, coaches and club presidents from right across Congolese football and is held to have the ability to change a player or team's fortunes single-handedly.

manque du lait – *lack of milk*

Said of a footballer who's not in good shape and allows himself to be physically dominated in duels with his opponents, the accusation being that he's undernourished. Often shouted by supporters.

mbua – *dog*

A player who gets himself worked up and runs around enthusiastically, but doesn't really achieve anything.

See also: *bal yapmayan arı* (Turkey)

EGYPT

By every measure bar their World Cup record, Egypt are Africa's pre-eminent football nation. The national team have won a record seven Africa Cups of Nations and Egyptian club Al Ahly are the most decorated team in the African Champions League (with Cairo rivals Zamalek not far behind).

Egypt were the first African country to play – and score – at a World Cup, in 1934, but since then they have only qualified for the tournaments of 1990 and 2018.

fil maqass (في المقص) – *in the scissors*

An effort that ends up in the corner of the goal is said in Egypt to have gone *fil maqass*. In Alexandria, the top corner is known as *el tess'inat* (التسعينات), meaning 'the 90s', which refers to the 90° angle formed by post and bar.

See also: *onde dorme a coruja* (Brazil), *jep nest* (Trinidad and Tobago), *upper 90* (United States), *rašlje* (Croatia), *postage stamp* (England), *lucarne* (France), *sette* (Italy), *winkelhaak* (Netherlands), *devyatka* (Russia), *donde anidan las arañas* (Spain), *wayn yeskon shaytan* (Algeria)

hakam agnabi (حكم اجنبي) – *foreign referee*

The biggest club match in African football is the sulphurous Cairo derby between Al Ahly and Zamalek, which has come to be known as the *classico al Arab* (كلاسيكو العرب). The depth of ill-feeling between the clubs is so profound that their meetings are always overseen by foreign referees, so as to ensure the highest possible standard of officiating and – perhaps more importantly – to negate the risk of the man in the middle being accused of secretly rooting for one of the two teams. Scottish referees with experience of powder-keg Old Firm games are highly prized – Kenny Clark, Hugh Dallas and Willie Collum have all presided over the fixture since the turn of the century. The term *hakam agnabi* has drifted into common speech to refer to any situation where an independent adjudicator is required, such as in a diplomatic dispute or a disagreement between husband and wife.

kora sharab (كوره شراب) – *socks ball*

The traditional breeding ground for Egyptian footballers is *kora sharab*, an informal version of the sport that's played on backstreets and schoolyards using a sock stuffed with sponge and bits of string. As with other folk interpretations of the game from around the world, it's a style of football that places a high premium on trickery and technical skill. *Kora sharab* has its own vocabulary and many of the terms born in its dusty street kickabouts have wriggled their way into Egypt's mainstream football vernacular. A *kora sharab* goal is typically formed using *tobtain* (طوبتين), meaning 'two bricks', which has given rise to the expression that all you need for a game are *tobtain wa kora* ('two bricks and a ball').

See also: *potrero* (Argentina), *tanner ba' player* (Scotland), *sakora park* (Ghana)

sab'at-tamanyat (سبعات و تمنيات) – *sevens and eights*

A *kora sharab* term, *sab'at-tamanyat* describes a drag-back. It comes from a skill exercise taught to Egyptian schoolboys. They would perform a drag-back (dragging the ball towards themselves and then pushing it forwards) in a 'v' movement reminiscent of the number seven in Arabic numerals (٧). That was followed by a kind of 'inverted drag-back' (rolling the ball away and then pulling it back), resembling an Arabic eight, which is an upside-down 'v' (٨). To comprehensively outmanoeuvre an opponent is known as *tar'ees* (ترقيص), which means 'to make someone dance'.

Sifr el Mondial (صفر المونديال) – *The World Cup Zero*

After FIFA decided that the 2010 World Cup would be staged in Africa, Egypt submitted a bid to host the tournament along with Morocco, South Africa, Nigeria and a joint bid from Tunisia and Libya. Nigeria and the combined Tunisia-Libya bid subsequently withdrew from the race. In the first round of voting in Zurich in May 2004, South Africa won 14 votes, Morocco 10 and Egypt none, giving South Africa the tournament and leaving the Egyptian delegation humiliated. The disastrous bid is now referenced at moments of acute national failure, particularly when the organisation of an international event is involved.

West Ham khamsa wahid (ويست هام خمسه واحد) – *West Ham five-one*

In November 1966, West Ham arrived in Cairo for a hotly anticipated friendly game against Zamalek. West Ham had three World Cup winners in their ranks in Bobby Moore, Martin Peters and Geoff Hurst, and had won the European Cup Winners' Cup the previous year. Before the game, they went sight-seeing, riding camels out to the Pyramids of Giza. Unfortunately for Moore and his teammates, they were also treated to a meal the day before the game that left several players feeling unwell. Peters was so ill that he had to be left out of the team. After Hamada Emam had put Zamalek ahead, Ronnie Boyce equalised with a fine goal, controlling the ball on his thigh and sending a shot dipping beneath the crossbar from outside the box. But as the effects of the heat and the previous day's fateful supper began to tell, West Ham wilted. Roared on by 50,000 home fans, Zamalek regained the lead through Emam and further goals from Taha Basry and Abdel Karim El-Gohary took the game beyond the visitors. Emam completed his hat-trick with a late header, setting the seal on a famous 5-1 win, and there was a joyous pitch invasion at the final whistle. In the years that followed, the result – referred to as *West Ham khamsa wahid* – would be cited by fans and journalists as a source of inspiration whenever Zamalek faced daunting opposition.

ya salaam (يا سلام) – *oh wonderful*

If you spend any time on social media, you'll be familiar with the expressive vocal style of Arabic TV commentators, whose animated utterances have reached a global audience thanks to those clips from Arabic-language match broadcasts that pop up on Twitter whenever one of the game's superstars has done something remarkable. *Ya salaam* is a phrase you'll hear, often repeated in tones of mounting incredulity, as Messi tiptoes through a spellbound opposition defence to score.

GHANA

Had it not been for Luis Suárez's goal-line handball deep into extra time of the World Cup quarter-final between Ghana and Uruguay in 2010, the 'Black Stars' would have become the first African team to make the semi-finals at the sport's showpiece event.

The greatest player to have played for Ghana – champions of Africa on four occasions (1963, 1965, 1978 and 1982) – was Abedi Pelé, a three-time African Player of the Year whose trophy-winning exploits with Marseille in the early 1990s broke new ground for African footballers in Europe.

atete nkura – hiding mice

This is the collective name for strikers who are experts at snaffling up chances in the penalty area, but tend to go missing when there are hard yards to be put in elsewhere on the pitch. *Atete* comes from the local Twi language and means 'hiding', while *nkura* means 'mice'. Another lyrical Twi expression is *san bewaami*, meaning 'marry me again', which is the phrase employed when a defender slices an attempted clearance into the air and the ball comes straight back to him.

See also: *quechón* (Panama), *cherry-picking* (United States), *goal hanger* (England), *ficar na mama* (Portugal), *pettu kedakunnavan* (India)

mallam goal – witch doctor goal

When a decisive goal is scored in freak circumstances, it's known as a *mallam goal*. *Mallam* is a Ghanaian term for a witch doctor, so the implication is that some kind of sorcery is at work. Well-known Ghanaian *juju man* Kwaku Bonsam predicted that a May 2016 league game between Asante Kotoko and Hearts of Oak would be decided by a *mallam goal*, although he didn't specify which side would benefit. Kotoko won 1-0 after Hearts of Oak's Burkinabé international goalkeeper Abdoulaye Soulama shinned an attempted pass into his own net in the first half. Bonsam took to the airwaves on Kasapa FM a few days later to denounce Kotoko for not giving him credit. The employment of spiritual assistance to win football matches is euphemistically known as *ways and means* in Ghanaian football circles.

milo – rainbow flick

Milo is the Ghanaian name for a rainbow flick – that supreme display of showboating in which a player clutches the ball between his feet and showily flicks it over an opponent's head before scooting by to collect it. The word owes its origins to a skilful cartoon footballer who appeared in a Nestlé TV advert for Milo chocolate powder in the 1990s.

See also: *lambreta* (Brazil)

mo ni yitso da – *he who has the biggest head*
From the Ga language, this is the cry that will go up when the ball is in the air and needs to be headed away by someone. A player whose aerial game is particularly strong might be known as a *headmaster*.

sakora park – *bare pitch*
Sakora is a Twi term meaning 'bald' and a *sakora park* is a community football pitch without a single blade of grass. Typically covered in sand or dirt, they are the pitches where the vast majority of Ghanaian football players get their first experiences of the sport. A popular format for football matches at neighbourhood level is *small poles*, a game played on an undersized pitch with goals formed by placing two stones about two feet apart. A variant is *four poles*, which is played between only four people, all of whom have their own *poles* (or goal) to defend. Players are restricted to one touch of the ball at a time to develop precision (and heighten tension).

See also: *potrero* (Argentina), *tanner ba' player* (Scotland), *kora sharab* (Egypt)

IVORY COAST

Both of Ivory Coast's successes at the Africa Cup of Nations, in 1992 and 2015, arrived via victories over Ghana in the final and on both occasions marathon penalty shootouts were required to separate the teams, *Les Éléphants* prevailing 11-10 in 1992 and 9-8 in 2015.

The 2015 conquest came six months to the day after Didier Drogba, Ivory Coast's talismanic captain and record goalscorer, had announced his international retirement, having played at three World Cups (2006, 2010 and 2014) and finished on the losing side in penalty shootouts in two Africa Cup of Nations finals (2006 and 2012).

faire voyager – *to send (someone) travelling*
When an attacker throws a defender off balance, he's imagined to have packed his adversary's bags and sent him off on an excursion.

filet est plein – *net's full*
Synonym for when a goal has been scored.

on gagne ou on gagne *– we win or we win*

Getting appropriately pumped up is an essential part of pre-match preparation in Ivory Coast. The phrase *on gagne ou on gagne* reflects a desire to clear all thoughts of defeat from the mind, while players may speak about wanting to *déshabille* ('undress') their opponents with a humiliating victory. Pre-match tub-thumping only goes so far, of course. As a popular saying goes: '*Ya pas hoba-hoba dans ballon*' ('There's no talk in the ball').

pkaka

Pkaka is both a word for a kickabout and a term for rugged play. *Allons pkaka* means 'let's play', but a full-back being tormented by a wily winger might be told by his teammates: '*Il faut le pkaka*' ('You have to kick him').

KENYA

With Kenya having never qualified for a World Cup or gone beyond the first round of the Africa Cup of Nations, football can often seem the poor relation of athletics and cricket in the east African country.

Kenyan footballers to have made the grade in European football include the former Internazionale player McDonald Mariga and Victor Wanyama, who has played for Celtic, Southampton and Tottenham.

kanzu *– long prayer robe*

In Kenya, dinking the ball over an opponent's head is likened to draping them in a *kanzu*, a large robe, usually white or cream in colour, that's typically worn by Kenyan Muslims. You add *na kofia* ('and a hat') if you manage to flick the ball over your opponent's head twice in succession.

See also: *chapéu* (Brazil), *sombrero* (Spain), *baptiser* (Cameroon), *height* (Nigeria), *deff ko watt* (Senegal), *kanyumba* (Zambia)

kukanyaga nyoka *– to step on a snake*

Kenya is home to 126 species of snake, among them the deadly black mamba, puff adder and four types of cobra, so it's no surprise that the country's football dictionary is dotted with serpentine references. To 'step on a snake' is a Swahili expression used to describe an air shot, while a *piga ngoma kimo cha bafe* ('puff adder shot') is a low shot that speeds along the ground.

Kukanyaga nyoka ('to step on a snake') is a Swahili expression used to describe an air shot

kupelekwa shopping – *to send someone shopping*

Used when a goalkeeper is sent the wrong way by a penalty-taker or when a player is flummoxed by an opposing player's dummy. A related term is *kupelekwa marikiti*, which specifically refers to a sprawling fresh food market in downtown Nairobi. *Kukalishwa stool* ('to be sat on a stool') is what happens when a player is left for dead by an opponent and is also used by Kenyan rugby commentators to describe a speedy wing leaving a rival player on the deck.

See also: *llevar a alguien a la escuelita* (Panama), *poslati ga po burek* (Bosnia and Herzegovina), *da go pratya za bira* (Bulgaria), *kohvile saatma* (Estonia), *het bos ingestuurd* (Netherlands), *sendt opp i pølsebua* (Norway), *att köpa korv* (Sweden), *pazara göndermek* (Turkey)

MOROCCO

A 1-1 draw against Bulgaria at the 1970 World Cup in Mexico made Morocco the first African nation to win a point at the tournament, and in 1986 they passed a major milestone by becoming the first team from the continent to advance beyond the group phase.

Nicknamed the 'Atlas Lions', after the Barbary lions that once roamed the Atlas Mountains, they were African champions in 1976.

bayda (بيضة) – *egg*

A nutmeg. Morocco is not alone in likening the act of poking the ball between a player's legs to a bird popping out an egg, with Brazil – *ovinho* ('little egg') – and South Korea – *r kka ghi* (알 까 기), which means 'hatching an egg' – among the other countries who do so.

See also: *caneta* (Brazil), *huacha* (Peru), *salad* (Jamaica), *Gurkerl* (Austria), *jesle* (Czech Republic), *nutmeg* (England), *klobbi* (Iceland), *panna* (Netherlands), *cueca* (Portugal), *yalli* (Senegal), *shibobo* (South Africa), *deya* (Zimbabwe), *lawd daak* (Thailand)

khawya f amra (خاوية فعامرة) – *one empty, one full*

Morocco has a rich history of tricky footballers, from Ahmed Bahja, who showcased his languid dribbles at the 1994 World Cup, to walking *bayda* machine Adel Taarabt. Every self-respecting Moroccan winger has a double stepover in their locker, the local name for which – *khawya f amra* – literally translates as 'one empty, one full '.

See also: *bicicleta* (Argentina), *pedaladas* (Brazil), *caap waa* (China), *marwaha* (Saudi Arabia)

rqayqi (رقايقي) – *maestro*

Reserved for only the most gifted playmakers, *rqayqi* is the name Moroccans apply to talents such as 1985 African Footballer of the Year Mohamed Timoumi.

MOZAMBIQUE

By the time independence came to Mozambique in June 1975, it was too late for the leading players that the country had produced to play in the colours of their homeland. Born in Mozambique, Mário Coluna and the great Eusébio made their names at Benfica and found international fame with Portugal, both players excelling for the team that finished third at the 1966 World Cup.

wupfutela – *seasoning*

The preserve of a particularly confident attacker, *wupfutela* describes a decorous trick or feint added to a finish with the sole aim of showing up the opposition goalkeeper. A player who has succeeded in rounding the keeper might check back or hesitate, giving his hapless adversary a glimmer of hope that the situation might yet be salvaged, only to then stick the ball into the net.

NIGERIA

It took Nigeria until 1994 to reach their first World Cup, but they quickly made up for lost time, finishing top of their group (above Bulgaria, Argentina and Greece) and coming within two minutes of eliminating eventual finalists Italy in the next round before succumbing to the cool brilliance of Roberto Baggio.

With the exception of the 2006 tournament, the three-time African champions (1980, 1994 and 2013) have been to every World Cup since.

cemetery pass

In Britain and elsewhere, a pass that exposes its intended recipient to the danger of a painful collision with an opponent is known as a *hospital pass*. In Nigeria they go one step further. Play a teammate into trouble there and the player receiving the ball is said to be at risk not of ending up in a hospital bed, but in the grave.

See also: *hospital pass* (England)

Dundee United

If you're a Dundee United fan and you ever find yourself in Lagos, you might want to keep your club allegiances to yourself. The reason being that in parts of the country where the Yoruba language is spoken, *Dundee United* is a synonym for 'idiot'. It's thought to stem from a disastrous tour of Nigeria that United undertook in 1972, when they won only one of the five games they played and were beaten by teams including Stationery Stores FC and Kaduna Bees. Manager Jim McLean blamed his team's below-par displays on injuries, poor-quality pitches and, above all, the sapping heat and humidity. An associated theory is that the word *Dundee* reminded locals of the *dundun*, a versatile West African drum that can be manipulated to sound like human speech, thereby helping to forge a connection in their minds between people from Dundee and something that makes a loud, insistent noise.

height
In Nigeria, to beat an opposing player by flicking the ball over their head is to *height* them.

See also: *chapéu* (Brazil), *sombrero* (Spain), *baptiser* (Cameroon), *kanzu* (Kenya), *deff ko watt* (Senegal), *kanyumba* (Zambia)

intercontinental ballistic missile
This ostentatious phrase describes a powerful long-range shot and was popularised by Nigerian commentators in the late 1970s and early 1980s. On the subject of high-tech weaponry, thunder-thighed Nigerian striker Obafemi Martins was nicknamed 'the Weapon of Mass Destruction' after bursting onto the scene as a teenager at Internazionale in the early 2000s.

See also: *pombo sem asa* (Brazil), *pushka strashnaya* (Russia), *evrogol* (Serbia), *bballaejul katteun shoot* (South Korea)

monkey yansh
Monkey yansh means 'monkey arse' and refers to the bruise you're left with after you fall over while playing football on a rock-hard surface. A particularly impressive bruise will be blue or purple in colour, resembling the brightly coloured bottom of a monkey or baboon. *Monkey post*, meanwhile, is the name for an informal match using makeshift goalposts formed of stones or clothing.

NASA pass
A curved pass played with the outside of the foot – a technique of such difficulty it's imagined to require the precision of a NASA engineer.

See also: *de três dedos* (Brazil), *papegøje* (Denmark), *trivela* (Portugal), *shvedka* (Russia), *outfoot* (Pakistan)

Okocha stepover
If there was a metric for measuring the number of smiles spontaneously provoked by a footballer in the course of a game, Jay-Jay Okocha would have topped the charts every season. He mentored Ronaldinho for a year at Paris Saint-Germain and it's hard not to think that some of Okocha's irresistible *joie de vivre* must have rubbed off on the Brazilian during the time they spent messing around at PSG's

Camp des Loges training centre. Okocha had an encyclopaedic skill repertoire that included all manner of dummies and feints. During his time with Bolton, the Nigerian wowed English spectators by using the 'rainbow flick' to take opponents out of the game and he was even known to indulge in the odd spot of mid-match ball juggling. His signature move was a kind of stepover that allied loose-limbed innovation with deadly effectiveness. Generally deployed when Okocha was on the left flank, facing up to a defender (although he would do it all over the pitch), the move began with him using the studs of his right boot to roll the ball forwards. He would then step over the ball with his left foot, lunging in towards the defender, before deftly pivoting and pursuing the ball towards the byline, his adversary invariably left in a pile of tangled limbs behind him. 'I had the thought one day in training to try something different,' Okocha says. 'I succeeded with it, tried it during a game and it worked, so I started doing it more. I'm glad to say that I contributed something.' The Brazilian Ronaldo was another master of the technique, but nobody did it with quite the same springy elegance as Okocha.

SENEGAL

After Algeria's shock win over West Germany in 1982 and Cameroon's ambush of defending champions Argentina in 1990, it was Senegal's turn to make history at the 2002 World Cup, Papa Bouba Diop's goal in Seoul condemning champions France to defeat in the tournament's opening game.

Senegal had lost on penalties to Cameroon in the final of the Africa Cup of Nations earlier that year – their best result at the tournament – and went on to reach the quarter-finals at the World Cup before falling to a golden-goal defeat against Turkey.

deff ko watt – to give someone a haircut
A player who succeeds in lifting the ball over an opponent's head in Senegal is imagined to shave off some hair as he does so. Other technical terms from the Wolof language, which is spoken in Senegal, the Gambia and Mauritania, include *kott* ('feint'), *kadji* ('toe-poke') and *doutt*, which means to beat an opponent with a dribble.

See also: *chapéu* (Brazil), *sombrero* (Spain), *baptiser* (Cameroon), *kanzu* (Kenya), *height* (Nigeria), *kanyumba* (Zambia)

mball camp yi – *put the net in front of the goal*

A team who turn in a defensive display are picturesquely imagined to have gathered the netting from the back of their goal and stretched it across the goalmouth. To score a goal is to *tocc caakh yi*, meaning 'break the net', or *taal thiakhe*, meaning 'set the net on fire'.

See also: *táctica del murciélago* (Ecuador), *Obrona Częstochowy* (Poland), *ući golmanu u krilo* (Serbia)

yalli – *nutmeg*

The Senegalese term for a nutmeg traces its genesis back to the 1964 final of the Coupe de Sénégal between Club Olympique Thiessois (COT) and third-tier US Ouakam. After a 1-1 draw in their first encounter, the replay also finished 1-1 and went to extra time, during which veteran forward Ibrahima Dione scored the winning goal for Ouakam by driving the ball between the legs of COT's distinguished goalkeeper, Yalli Ndieguene. A nutmeg has been known as a *yalli* in Senegal ever since. The word is also used in everyday situations when somebody has been hoodwinked or made to look foolish. An alternative name for a goal scored between the goalkeeper's legs is *butou taate*, meaning 'buttocks goal'.

See also: *caneta* (Brazil), *huacha* (Peru), *salad* (Jamaica), *Gurkerl* (Austria), *jesle* (Czech Republic), *nutmeg* (England), *klobbi* (Iceland), *panna* (Netherlands), *cueca* (Portugal), *bayda* (Morocco), *shibobo* (South Africa), *deya* (Zimbabwe), *lawd daak* (Thailand)

SOUTH AFRICA

Apartheid meant that South Africa spent the best part of 35 years in football's international wilderness, but following readmission by FIFA and the Confederation of African Football, the country hosted and won the 1996 Africa Cup of Nations.

A first World Cup appearance followed two years later and South Africa became the first African nation to stage the tournament in 2010. Siphiwe Tshabalala's thunderbolt against Mexico in Johannesburg opened the cork on the tournament, although his side would become the first host team in the competition's history to go out in the first round.

diski

There's a case to be made that the most eye-catching style of football in the world is played in South Africa, where international isolation during the long years of apartheid allowed a dazzlingly expressive football philosophy to take root. The country's signature style was known as *piano and shoeshine*, a term coined by coach Stanley 'Screamer' Tshabalala to describe the loose, possession-based football played by his Mamelodi Sundowns team of the late 1980s. Showboating in South Africa is not like showboating you've seen anywhere else: absurd, high-stepping stepovers, ludicrously exaggerated fake passes, fiendishly convoluted displays of ball control and all kinds of provocative touches. You even get players precariously perching themselves on top of the ball to goad their opponents into hasty challenges. The word *diski* refers to this highly individualistic approach to the game, born amid the red dust of informal township matches. In 2009 the South African tourist board commissioned Wendy Ramokgadi, a Sowetan choreographer, to devise a *diski dance* for a TV advert that was broadcast around the world in the build-up to that year's Confederations Cup, which South Africa hosted in preparation for the following year's World Cup. The routine he invented was based on an energetic township dance known as a *pantsula* and featured dancers mimicking outlandish football tricks with names like *Table Mountain* (flattening the back and catching the ball on the back of the neck) and *trepa* (flicking the ball from the back of the neck over the head and onto one of the feet). As the World Cup neared, South Africans were encouraged to learn the dance and it was performed at schools, universities, community groups and dance clubs all over the country.

extra strong

Area in a stadium opposite the main stand, where the hardcore supporters gather.

laduma – *goal*

Coined by much-loved commentator Zama Masondo, *laduma* translates as 'it thunders' in Zulu, but has become the default term roared by South African TV and radio commentators when the ball hits the back of the net. Aping the extended '*Goooooool!*' bellow of Latin American commentators, the 'u' in *laduma* is held to achieve a similar effect. Masondo, a former schoolteacher, also invented the expression *ngonyawo lo nwabu* ('feet of the chameleon'), which he used to help viewers confused by slow-motion replays when they first began to appear on screen. 'They thought this was real-time action or that something had gone wrong with their TV sets at first,' Masondo told Ian Hawkey in *Feet of the*

Chameleon: The Story of African Football. 'There was no sense in saying, "Now for the replay," so I came up with a phrase that caught on. I said: *"Ngonyawo lo nwabu."* It means: "Now let's see it again with the feet of the chameleon."'

See also: *mboundja* (Cameroon), *il y est* (Tunisia)

makarapa

A South African football trademark, *makarapas* are elaborately decorated plastic helmets worn by match-going football fans. The inventor of the *makarapa* is Alfred Baloyi, a man from Limpopo province who took to wearing a hard hat decorated in the orange and black of his team, Kaizer Chiefs, after seeing another fan hit on the head with a bottle during a game at Soweto's Orlando Stadium in 1979. At the time, Baloyi made a living cleaning buses in Pretoria, but as word of his invention spread, he was able to go into business selling them. The hand-made plastic hats typically have ornate props protruding from them such as flags, horns, club crests or representations of players. Oversized plastic spectacles complete the look.

shibobo – nutmeg

Shibobo, the South African term for a nutmeg, reached a wider audience in the build-up to the 1998 World Cup in France when it was used as the title of a song by TKZee, a group associated with the *kwaito* genre of African-influenced house music. The song heavily sampled 'The Final Countdown' by Europe and featured 'Bafana Bafana' striker Benni McCarthy on guest vocals. The video showed TKZee's three members – Tokollo Tshabalala, Kabelo Mabalane and Zwai Bala – bouncing around a dusty and deserted Orlando Stadium, interspersed with clips of McCarthy, then aged 20 and plying his trade for Ajax, laying down his rap in a recording studio and wiggling his hips in a goalmouth. The song was a huge trans-African hit. In a case of life imitating art, when McCarthy scored South Africa's first ever goal at a World Cup finals that year, he did it by driving a shot between the legs of Denmark goalkeeper Peter Schmeichel.

See also: *caneta* (Brazil), *huacha* (Peru), *salad* (Jamaica), *Gurkerl* (Austria), *jesle* (Czech Republic), *nutmeg* (England), *klobbi* (Iceland), *panna* (Netherlands), *cueca* (Portugal), *bayda* (Morocco), *yalli* (Senegal), *deya* (Zimbabwe), *lawd daak* (Thailand)

stop nonsense

In a country where humiliating defenders is such a popular hobby, patience unsurprisingly wears thin on occasion. Faced with an attacking player endlessly twiddling his feet around the ball, a South African defender may resort to a *stop nonsense* – a crunching challenge that cleans out both man and ball.

See also: *nabrat na sane* (Czech Republic), *reducer* (England), *Blutgrätsche* (Germany), *to burst someone* (Republic of Ireland), *pakka paer pao* (Pakistan), *enbarash* (Saudi Arabia)

tsamaya

A Sesotho word, *tsamaya* generally describes any showy piece of skill used to outwit someone, but it also refers to a trick in which a player unbalances an opponent by rolling the ball away to one side and then fishing it back.

vuvuzela

Loud, annoying plastic horn.

TANZANIA

The United Republic of Tanzania came into existence in April 1964 when Tanganyika merged with Zanzibar, making the Tanzanian national football team relative newcomers. They have qualified for the Africa Cup of Nations only once, in 1980, when they finished bottom of their group beneath Nigeria, Egypt and Ivory Coast.

kichwa cha mwendawazimu – *madman's head*

Tanzanian equivalent of 'whipping boys', coined by former president Ali Hassan Mwinyi. Lamenting Tanzania's dismal international record, Mwinyi compared the team to a madman who allows barbers to use his head to practise on.

kitasa – *padlock*

A solid central defender who lets nothing past.

See also: *caballo* (Costa Rica), *Holzgeschnitzter* (Austria), *armario* (Spain), *samaam al amaan* (Saudi Arabia)

TUNISIA

Tunisia helped themselves to a slice of World Cup history at the 1978 tournament when their 3-1 victory over Mexico made them the first African team to win a match at the finals.

After two runners-up showings at the Africa Cup of Nations (1965 and 1996), they organised and won the 2004 edition, a fumble by Morocco goalkeeper Khalid Fouhami in the final enabling Ziad Jaziri to prod in the decisive goal in a 2-1 victory.

il y est – *it's there*

Sometimes compressed as *wilyé*, this is the expression roared from the terraces – as well as cafés, bars, living rooms and commentary booths – when the ball hits the net in Tunisia. It came into use during the 1970s and became enshrined in the country's football vernacular during Tunisia's first World Cup appearance at the 1978 tournament in Argentina. In their opening game against Mexico in Rosario, Tunisia were 2-1 up and minutes away from becoming the first African team to win a game at a World Cup. In the 86th minute, with Tunisian fingernails bitten to the quick, Néjib Ghommidh gathered Témime Lahzami's throw-in from the left, turned inside and played an exquisite defence-splitting pass into the path of Mokhtar Dhouib, who motored into the box from right-back and crashed a shot into the roof of the net. On Tunisian TV, Néjib Khattab's crescendoing commentary articulated the relief of the nation: '*Ghommidh pour Dhouib . . . il y est ! Il y est !*' ('Ghommidh for Dhouib . . . it's there! It's there!') A 1-0 defeat by Poland and a 0-0 draw with world champions West Germany brought Tunisia's involvement to an end in the group phase, but Dhouib's goal – and Khattab's commentary – had wrought an unforgettable moment of national communion.

See also: *mboundja* (Cameroon), *laduma* (South Africa)

jbed bih (جبد بيه) – *he's done him*

The Tunisia team of the late 1990s and 2000s, who participated in three World Cups and triumphed as hosts of the 2004 Africa Cup of Nations, were a durable, doughty side, but for all the success they achieved, the players held in the highest esteem in the country are the dribblers. The team that reached the 1978 World Cup contained several players renowned for their ability to outwit an opponent, among them Tarak Dhiab, Hamadi Agrebi and skipper Lahzami. Jameleddine Limam carried the torch in the 1990s, Yassine Chikhaoui in the mid-2000s and Youssef Msakni in more recent times. *Jbed bih* is the expression that leaps to the lips when a jink of the hips takes a defender out of the game. Two dribbles are recalled with particular fondness: Dhiab's right-wing slalom past four defenders during Tunisia's meeting with West Germany at the 1978 World Cup and Msakni's piercing dart down the centre of the pitch before scoring against Morocco at the 2012 Africa Cup of Nations.

mange une hara – *eat a four*

The word *hara* (حارة) is typically used at the grocery to indicate quantities of eggs, which are usually sold in batches of four. One *hara* equals four eggs, two *haras* eight and so on. To concede four goals in Tunisia is to *mange une hara* ('eat a four').

ZAMBIA

Following defeats in the final of the Africa Cup of Nations in 1974 and 1994, Zambia ascended the African throne at the third attempt in 2012 with a penalty shootout win over a star-studded Ivory Coast.

The national team were known as the 'KK 11' during the 1980s, in honour of president Kenneth Kaunda, but subsequently changed their nickname to *Chipolopolo*, meaning 'the Copper Bullets', in a nod to the vast copper mines that sit on the western fringes of the country's second city, Kitwe.

Gabon

One of the great tragedies of African football occurred on 27 April 1993 when a Zambian Air Force DHC-5D Buffalo carrying the Zambia team to Senegal for a World Cup qualifier crashed into the sea after refuelling in Gabon, killing all 30 people on board. The official report, not published until 10 years later, would blame a faulty engine and a fatal error by a weary pilot, but as the investigation dragged on in the months immediately after the disaster, ill-feeling mounted on both sides. In Libreville, where the plane had taken off, there were insensitive protests about Zambian bodies clogging up the local mortuary. The authorities in Zambia accused their counterparts in Gabon of impeding the investigation and there were even rumours that the plane had been shot down by the Gabonese military. Anti-Gabonese sentiment hardened in October that year when a Gabonese referee, Jean-Fidèle Diramba, was blamed for a 1-0 loss to Morocco in Casablanca that cost Zambia a place at the 1994 World Cup. One consequence of the resentment was that for a time in Zambia, the word *Gabon* was used as a derogatory term for something dilapidated or useless. It would take another football tournament, held 19 years later, to bring the countries together. When Gabon co-hosted the 2012 Africa Cup of Nations, Zambia defied the odds to reach the final. With fateful symmetry, the game took place at Libreville's Stade d'Angondjé, just a few miles from where the DHC-5D Buffalo had plunged into the Atlantic almost two decades previously. Having seen their own side eliminated in the quarter-finals, the local fans threw their support behind Zambia, cheering Hervé Renard's team on to a fairytale penalty-shootout win over Ivory Coast.

kanyumba – small house

A player who lofts the ball above an opponent's head in Zambia is imagined to have built a little house over him.

See also: *chapéu* (Brazil), *sombrero* (Spain), *baptiser* (Cameroon), *kanzu* (Kenya), *height* (Nigeria), *deff ko watt* (Senegal)

ZIMBABWE

Previously known as Southern Rhodesia and then Rhodesia, Zimbabwe had to wait almost half a century to reach the Africa Cup of Nations and then qualified for three tournaments in 13 years (2004, 2006 and 2017).

'The Warriors' have never made it to a World Cup and were banned from even attempting to qualify for the 2018 tournament due to an unpaid debt owed to Brazilian coach Jose Claudinei Georgini.

deya – nutmeg

Deya is a shortened form of the local Shona word *mateya*, which means 'rickets' or 'bowlegs', so the cutting implication is that the player who pulls off the nutmeg has exploited some kind of congenital defect in his victim.

See also: *caneta* (Brazil), *huacha* (Peru), *salad* (Jamaica), *Gurkerl* (Austria), *jesle* (Czech Republic), *nutmeg* (England), *klobbi* (Iceland), *panna* (Netherlands), *cueca* (Portugal), *bayda* (Morocco), *yalli* (Senegal), *shibobo* (South Africa), *lawd daak* (Thailand)

kuwarura – laying a carpet

A Zimbabwean team who construct a move with a succession of passes along the ground are said to be 'laying a carpet'.

DODGY KEEPERS – A GLOSSARY OF GAFFES

From the kid picked last in playground kickabouts to the thirty-something veteran whose entire career might be defined by a single handling error, the life of a goalkeeper is a thankless one. As these examples demonstrate, dodgy goalkeepers and disastrous goalkeeping are as universal as football itself.

butou taate – *buttocks goal (Senegal)*
This expression is used when a goalkeeper allows the ball to pass between his legs (and, by extension, his buttocks) and into the net.

cazanda pajaritos – *catching birds (Argentina)*
A goalkeeper who makes a forlorn attempt to gather a high ball is likened to someone leaping around trying to catch birds in Argentina.

Eiergoalie – *eggs goalie (Austria)*
When an Austrian goalkeeper's senses are scrambled and his mistake allows an opposing player to poach a goal, he might be branded an 'eggs goalie'.

huangyou shou (黄油手) – *butter hands (China)*
The expression 'butter fingers' doesn't quite cut it in China, where an errant goalkeeper is imagined to have the greasy stuff all over his sorry mitts.

kul'lyo dhorta (कुल्ल्यो धरता) – *catching crabs (India)*
In India (specifically Goa), a keeper who spills a shot or fumbles a cross brings to mind someone nervously dipping their hands into a rock pool.

lepkevadász – *butterfly hunter (Hungary)*
Flap at too many crosses in Hungary and you're liable to be saddled with this dainty but disparaging sobriquet.

mão de alface – *lettuce hand (Brazil)*
The hands of a gaffe-prone Brazilian goalkeeper are held to possess the same physical characteristics as a lettuce leaf.

pudrunäpp – *porridge-fingers (Estonia)*
Traditional Estonian porridge is made with pearl barley and potatoes and known as *mulgipuder*. Great for filling you up on winter mornings, less useful for repelling swervy 25-yarders.

salir a por uvas – *to go out to collect grapes (Spain)*
If a Spanish goalkeeper strays outside his box in hazardous fashion, it will be observed that he might be better suited to working at a vineyard.

skovtur – *picnic (Denmark)*
The Danish keeper who wanders from his penalty area, meanwhile, is portrayed as having rolled out a picnic mat, plonked down his hamper and settled down for some *al fresco* dining.

uçan manda – *flying buffalo (Turkey)*
It's not quite at the level of Spanish newspaper *AS* labelling David Seaman 'a piece of meat with eyes', but this Turkish term for a hapless goalkeeper is scarcely more complimentary.

zlovyty myshu (зловити мишу) – *to catch a mouse (Ukraine)*
A shot that squirms from the grasp of a Ukrainian goalkeeper might be said to have temporarily assumed the form of a wriggling mouse.

ASIA

Like a magnetic field, Asian football is strongest at its edges, its twin power bases lying in the Middle East (Iran, Saudi Arabia) and the Far East (Japan, South Korea, China).

There's historical evidence that ball games with the feet were played in several Asian cultures – *cuju* in Ancient China, *sepak raga* in 15th-century Malaysia, *kemari* in medieval Japan – but in terms of the modern sport, Asia's breakthrough moment arrived at the 2002 World Cup. Jointly staged by Japan and South Korea, the tournament was a slickly organised, technologically innovative affair in which the Koreans, roared on by fanatical home support, smashed a glass ceiling by becoming the first Asian nation to reach the semi-finals.

From the ornate logograms of Chinese *hanzi* to the bulbous curves of India's Malayalam script, the 2,300 or so languages spoken across the continent are conveyed using some of the most striking and distinctive writing systems in existence.

CHINA

The sleeping giants of Asian football, China have qualified for only one World Cup, going out in the group phase in 2002, and have fared no better at the Asian Cup than a pair of second-place finishes at the 1984 and 2004 tournaments.

More recently, president Xi Jinping's desire to turn the country into a football superpower has encouraged exorbitant spending by clubs in the Chinese Super League.

caap waa (插花) – *arranging flowers*

Neatly capturing the move's essential decorativeness, this is the Cantonese term for a stepover.

See also: *bicicleta* (Argentina), *pedaladas* (Brazil), *khawya f amra* (Morocco), *marwaha* (Saudi Arabia)

caau fei gei (炒飛機) – *stir-fried aeroplane*

An attempt on goal that balloons well off-target is known in Cantonese as a 'stir-fried aeroplane'. Cantonese, which is spoken around Guangzhou in southeast China, as well as in Hong Kong, Macau and many Chinese expat communities, boasts a wealth of quirky football expressions. The term *duk sik* (獨食), literally 'to eat alone', describes a player who's selfish and never passes to anyone. *Mó jiāng* (磨薑), meaning 'grinding ginger', refers to the pain felt by someone playing football on a hard surface who stubs their toe as they attempt to strike the ball.

See also: *palo'e mango* (Colombia), *yaseed hamaam* (Saudi Arabia)

heishao (黑哨) – *black whistle*

Corruption scandals have plagued Chinese football over the past 20 years, teaching fans of the sport in China to be deeply suspicious of referees and the sport's authorities. A three-year government crackdown launched in 2009 led to a purge of high-profile officials, referees and players. Former Chinese Football Association head Nan Yong was sentenced to 10½ years in prison in 2012 for accepting bribes worth more than 1.48 million yuan (£150,000). His predecessor, Xie Yalong, received the same sentence for similar misdemeanours. Former World Cup referee Lu Jun, known as *Jīn shào* (金哨) or 'Golden Whistle' because of his supposed integrity, was also jailed, along with former national team players Shen Si, Qi Hong, Jiang Jin and Li Ming. A total of 58 players and officials received bans from the sport ranging from five years to life. An earlier scandal known as *heishao* ('black whistle') had erupted in 2001. An outbreak of peculiar results in Jia B, the country's second division, prompted a volley of sanctions from the Chinese FA, which in turn yielded public admissions of corruption from several club presidents. Fans chant *heishao* when they suspect a referee of being crooked and will shout *jiaqiu* (假球), meaning 'fake ball', if they believe that the match they are watching has been fixed.

See also: *Calciopoli* (Italy), *dogovornyak* (Russia), *dyvnyy match* (Ukraine), *jual game* (Malaysia)

juesha (绝杀) – *total kill*

Mandarin term for a last-minute goal that changes the outcome of a game. The football equivalent of a basketball buzzer beater.

konghanzheng (恐韩症) – *South Korea-phobia*

Between 1986 and 2010, China went a scarcely believable 27 consecutive matches without victory against South Korea, drawing nine games and losing 18. It was a similar story at junior level. The run finally came to an end when a team coached by Gao Hongbo pulled off a 3-0 win in an East Asian Football Championship match in Tokyo in February 2010. Even then, South Korea had selected a squad composed solely of domestic players, with experienced stalwarts like Park Ji-sung and Park Chu-young absent. China's dreadful record against South Korea gave rise to the expression *konghanzheng*, which suggested that there was some kind of psychological barrier preventing the national team from prevailing against their rivals from across the Yellow Sea.

wuyue shijiu ri shijian (五一九事件) – *19 May Incident*

The World Cup qualifying match between China and Hong Kong that took place in Beijing on 19 May 1985 was make-or-break. The two teams were neck-and-neck at the summit of their group, with China top on goal difference. A draw would have been enough to take China into the next round, while Hong Kong needed to win. China were massive favourites, having finished runners-up behind Saudi Arabia at the previous year's Asian Cup, and with the country striving to assert itself as an international power following the end of the Cultural Revolution, qualifying for a first World Cup was a prized objective. Three years previously a team featuring Rong Zhihang, known as 'China's Pelé', had come within 90 minutes of a place at the 1982 tournament in Spain, only to lose 2-1 to New Zealand in a play-off in Singapore. The 1985 game was also swathed in diplomatic symbolism. Exactly five months earlier, Margaret Thatcher and Chinese Premier Zhao Ziyang had brought an end to years of fraught negotiations by signing the Sino-British Joint Declaration, formalising the process by which Hong Kong would return to Chinese sovereignty in 1997 after 155 years of British rule. Instruments of ratification were exchanged by Britain and China a week after the match. China responded quickly after Hong Kong took a shock 19th-minute lead from Cheung Chi Tak's sledgehammer free-kick, equalising through Li Hui, but when defender Ku Kam Fai put the visitors back in front on the hour, the Chinese had no reply. After the final whistle confirmed Hong Kong's progress at China's expense, fans in the 60,000-strong Workers' Stadium crowd rioted, the violence spilling out into the surrounding streets. Shop windows were smashed, tourists menaced and spat at and buses and cars torched. Chinese football had never experienced mass hooliganism before. Armed police had to restore order and hundreds of people were arrested. The violence became known as the '19 May Incident' and was a source of profound national shame. China coach Zeng Xuelin stepped down days later, never to manage another team, and Li Fenglou, chairman of the Chinese Football Association, tendered his resignation later that year. Chinese embarrassment was exacerbated when Japan thrashed Hong Kong 5-1 over two legs in the next round.

xia ke (下课) – *class dismissed*

Chanted by fans who want a coach to be sacked. This term caught on across China after Sichuan Quanxing supporters shouted it at unpopular coach Yu Dongfeng in 1995.

yau gwai (有鬼) – *there's a ghost*

Another Cantonese term, this is what you shout at a teammate to warn them that they have an opponent on their tail.

See also: *ladrón* (Argentina), *mala leđa* (Montenegro), *polícia* (Portugal), *house* (Republic of Ireland), *gorísh* (Russia)

In Cantonese, you say *yau gwai* ('there's a ghost') to warn a teammate about an approaching opponent

zhongguo tou qiu dui (中国头球队) – *Chinese head-ball team*
One of the explanations offered for China's failings on the international scene is that the country has been too tightly wedded to a Soviet-style selection model that values height and strength over initiative and technical ability. While the push to find China's tallest, quickest and strongest has delivered enduring success in Olympic pursuits such as gymnastics, diving and swimming, the upshot has been that gifted but physically underwhelming football players have sometimes been left on the sidelines. In the early years of the current century, however, a group of tall, athletic footballers came together to give the country a fleeting golden age. The national team finished second at the Asian Cup in 2004, having come fourth in 2000, and under Serbian coach Bora Milutinović they qualified for their first World Cup in 2002. Their archetypal player was captain Fan Zhiyi, a strapping centre-back who was sturdy enough to prosper amid the unforgiving hustle and bustle of the English second tier during a three-year stint with Crystal Palace. Sun Jihai and Li Tie also had spells in England. In the international arena, China made the most of their aerial prowess by successfully targeting opponents with crosses from the flanks and set-pieces (a particularly fruitful tactic against smaller teams from Southeast Asia). China's unsophisticated style of play earned them the moniker *zhongguo tou qiu dui* ('Chinese head-ball team'), but with the team having struggled over the ensuing years, the term has become imbued with a sense of nostalgia. (As a side note, China has always been in peculiar thrall to the rugged nobility of the header. Headed goals were worth extra points in the 1973 Chinese championship and in 1985 they counted double.)

INDIA

Despite being the world's second most populous nation (behind China), India has never sent a team to the World Cup, the national side's peak arriving in 1964 with a second-place finish behind hosts Israel at the Asian Cup.

But improving standards in the 21st century enabled India to return to the Asian Cup for the first time in 27 years in 2011 (with a squad containing the arrestingly named Climax Lawrence) and although cricket continues to hold the country in its thrall, football remains wildly popular.

jalebi (जलेबी)

A *jalebi* is a sweet, spiral-shaped pretzel made from deep-fried flour batter that is dunked in syrup. On the football pitch, a *jalebi* is a player so prone to over-elaboration that he ends up running around in circles.

kul'lyo dhorta (कुल्ल्यो धरता) – *catching crabs*

A Konkani expression from the tiny and football-mad western Indian state of Goa, *kul'lyo dhorta* describes a goalkeeper who allows the ball to squirm from his grasp like a wriggling crab. Another Goan term is *ghot zata* (घट जाता), meaning 'to get frozen', which refers to a player whose nerves betray him at pivotal moments, such as a striker who fluffs his lines when one-on-one with the goalkeeper.

magojastro (মগজাস্ত্র) – *brain weapon*

One of the most enduring creations of legendary Bengali filmmaker and writer Satyajit Ray was Feluda, a cerebral private detective who appeared in many of Ray's stories and two of his films. Feluda was renowned for his mental sharpness and analytical ability, which were described in Ray's writing as his *magojastro*. When a coach of a Bengali team pulls off a tactical coup or makes a game-changing substitution, he's credited with having used his *magojastro*.

See also: *coaching* (France)

paral meen (പരൽ മീൻ) – *striped snakehead*

A *paral meen* is a small freshwater fish found in the backwaters of Kerala that is notoriously difficult to catch. In the local Malayalam football parlance, it's used as a metaphor for a slippery attacker.

pettu kidakunnavan (പെറ്റു കിടക്കുന്നവൻ) – *lying down after labour*

This is a terrace term from the southern state of Kerala. It literally refers to a woman who's bedridden after giving birth and is used to describe a goal-hungry striker who finds it hard to leave the opposition penalty area.

See also: *quechón* (Panama), *cherry-picking* (United States), *goal hanger* (England), *ficar na mama* (Portugal), *atete nkura* (Ghana)

INDONESIA

Then playing as the Dutch East Indies, Indonesia became the first team from Asia to reach a World Cup in 1938, albeit with a squad largely made up of European players. Their 6-0 first-round loss to Hungary in the French city of Reims remains the only match at the finals that they have played.

gajah sepakbola – *elephant football*

Stadion Maguwoharjo, Yogyakarta, October 2014. A curiously uncompetitive Indonesian second-tier play-off match between PSS Sleman and PSIS Semarang had entered the 86th minute and looked to be heading for a 0-0 draw when something truly bizarre happened: both teams started trying to score own goals. Home side PSS Sleman started it, goalkeeper Riyono deliberately allowing Hermawan Jati's back-pass to roll past him and into the net before midfielder Agus Setiawan unambiguously hooked the ball into his own goal from a position wide on the right. Trailing to two goals that they had scored themselves, PSS became a little sheepish and when they next conceded possession, the white shirts of PSIS pounced, quickly ferrying the ball back to their own end and halving the arrears with an own goal of their own, finessed by goalkeeper Catur Adinugroho taking a comedy swipe at the ball as it bobbled past him. A surreal scene accompanied the PSIS kick-off that followed as PSS's players – goalkeeper Riyono included – massed on the halfway line in expectation that they would have to stop PSIS trying to score another own goal. Which they duly did. From kick-off, Fadli Manan turned to face his own goal and coolly passed the ball into the net from a distance of 50 yards, the ball merrily skipping along the bobbly pitch as the hordes of green-shirted PSS players forlornly gave chase. Their transparent attempt to lose the game foiled, PSS began dropping to the ground and feigning injury in the hope that delaying tactics might somehow prevent PSIS from putting the ball into their own net again. But after a delay of four and a half minutes, play resumed. Despite another frantic charge by their opponents, PSIS scored their third own goal, giving PSS a 3-2 win, whereupon the referee finally brought the madness to an end. It transpired that both teams had been deliberately trying to lose in order to avoid a semi-final match against Borneo FC, who were rumoured to be backed by a local mafia. In the end they were both disqualified, while several players and the head coaches from both teams received life bans. The game went down in Indonesian football infamy as *gajah sepakbola*, so named because of the way the two teams had resembled pachyderms blindly charging after the ball in games of elephant football.

gol bunuh diri – *suicide goal*

Melodramatic name for an own goal. A similar expression exists in Japanese: *jisatsu-ten* (自殺点), meaning 'suicide point'.

turun minum – *take a drink*

A quaint turn of phrase, this is an Indonesian expression for half-time.

See also: *going into the sheds* (New Zealand)

IRAN

In the list of the leading goalscorers in international football history, the top 10 features such luminaries as Pelé, Ferenc Puskás and Cristiano Ronaldo, but the surprising figure who sits astride the table is Iran's Ali Daei. The tall, astute striker scored 109 goals in 149 games for the national team, establishing a tally that may never be bettered.

Asian champions on three occasions (1968, 1972 and 1976), Iran have played at five World Cups and scored a famous win over the United States at the 1998 tournament.

grassrolling (غلت خوردن روی چمن) – *diving*

A word spawned on internet message boards (hence its English spelling), *grassrolling* refers to the antics of players who writhe around in apparent agony on the pitch in the hope of winning a free-kick.

See also: *Klinsmann* (England), *Schwalbe* (Germany)

havaa-shi (حواشی) – *sidelines*

Persian name for the gossip, rumour and innuendo that swirl around the margins of the game in Iran. An associated Arabic expression is *taqtaqah* (طقطقه), an onomatopoeic term commonly used to describe social media chatter.

IRAQ

To play for Iraq's national team during the reign of Saddam Hussein was to lead a bleak and terrifying existence, with the dictator's sadistic eldest son Uday personally torturing players for poor performances.

Remarkably, as war rumbled on in Iraq, the national side succeeded in winning the 2007 Asian Cup, captain Younis Mahmoud's 71st-minute header in the final against Saudi Arabia completing one of the most moving and improbable success stories that football has ever seen.

chees, chees (جيس جيس) – bag, bag

Dating from the early 1980s, this is an Iraqi terrace taunt that's aired by fans when their team are beating a rival. *Chees* is a colloquial term for 'bag' or 'net', so the meaning is effectively that the game is 'in the bag'. During the Iran-Iraq war, the Iraqi authorities forbade supporters from chanting it against Al-Jaish, the army club, on the grounds that it was treasonous. When Zico lost his first game as Iraq coach in September 2011, a 2-0 home defeat by Jordan in a World Cup qualifier, fans in Erbil, where attitudes to the national team are ambiguous, chanted: *'Chees, chees, Zico!'*

JAPAN

The launch of the professional J.League in 1992 had a catalysing effect on Japanese football, sparking a sustained upturn that has seen the national team qualify for six successive World Cups (having never previously qualified for any) and win a record four Asian Cups.

In a reflection of the cosmopolitan nature of the country's football culture, Japan's footballing lexicon is crammed full of words borrowed from other nations. English loanwords include *kipa* ('keeper'), *ofusaidotorappu* ('offside trap') and *heading*, which is commonly used as a noun (e.g. 'He scored with a *heading*'). Italian has supplied terms like *bandiera* (meaning 'flag' and referring to a long-serving player) and *ribero* (*libero*), while from Brazilian Portuguese they have lifted *erashiko* (*elástico*) and *boranchi* (a corruption of *volante*, which is a name for a holding midfielder).

dorokusai (泥臭い) – *smelling of mud*

Dorokusai is a word used to describe a goal that owes more to the goalscorer's dogged determination to force the ball over the line than any technical refinement. It's the type of scrappy effort you might expect from Shinji Okazaki (even if the one goal he contributed to Leicester's triumphant Premier League title run-in in 2016 was a textbook overhead bicycle kick against Newcastle). A hard-working player like Okazaki might be referred to as an *ase kaki-ya* (汗かき屋), which literally means 'someone who sweats'.

ēkyūketsuban (永久欠番) – *retired number*

A concept borrowed from Japanese baseball, *ēkyūketsuban* refers to the practice of honouring a former player by retiring his shirt number. The most high-profile Japanese club to have withdrawn a shirt number in honour of a player are Yokohama F. Marinos, who announced in 2011 that no player would wear their number three shirt again following the unexpected death of their former centre-back Naoki Matsuda from a heart attack at the age of 34. Japanese clubs routinely withdraw the number 12 shirt from circulation in dedication to their fans. A sought-after squad number – generally seven, 10 or 11 for the Japanese national team – is an *ēsunanbā* (エースナンバー), which means 'ace number'.

kachiboshi o ageta (勝ち星を上げた) – *to earn a winning star*

Poetically, victorious teams in Japan are sometimes said to have picked up a 'winning star'.

kusabi no pass (クサビのパス) – *wedge pass*

A *kusabi no pass* is a vertical pass played down the centre of the pitch to the feet of a forward player, who receives the ball with his back to goal. Hold-up play, which is considered a distinct element of the game in Japanese football, is known as *posutopurē* (ポストプレー), meaning 'post play', while a target man is called a *posutopureiyā* (ポストプレイヤー) or 'post player'.

mukaitenshūto (無回転シュート) – *non-spin shot*

As footballs have become lighter and their surfaces smoother over the past 15 years, innovative ways of striking them have emerged. A favoured technique of modern free-kick takers is to 'stun' the ball by arching the back, dipping the head over the ball at the point of impact and striking through it with the outside of the foot. Struck in this manner, the ball does not spin, instead remaining 'still' in the air, and acquires a wicked, fluttery trajectory that can involve multiple swerves in different directions. Similar to a 'knuckleball' pitch in baseball, the technique is known in Japan as a *mukaiten shoot* and Japanese midfielder Keisuke Honda is one of its foremost practitioners. He served notice of his dead-ball ability with a breathtaking free-kick against Hong Kong in an Olympic qualifying match in May 2007, the ball gliding to the right and then suddenly swerving to the left, leaving goalkeeper Li Jian helplessly flat-footed. Three years later he lit up the 2010 World Cup with a terrific effort against Denmark in a group game in Rustenburg. The Adidas Jabulani ball had been sharply criticised for its unpredictability, but Honda displayed his ability to control it with a 35-yard shot from wide on the right that soared over the wall and dipped viciously past Thomas Sorensen. An associated term, also used in baseball, is *furinuita* (振り抜いた), which means 'swung out' and describes a clean strike.

See also: *folha seca* (Brazil), *banaanipotku* (Finland), *la maledetta* (Italy)

mukan no teiō (無冠の帝王) – uncrowned emperor
An 'uncrowned emperor' is a team or player whose ability has not translated into silverware. A Japanese example might be Yoshito Ōkubo, who's one of the J.League's record marksmen but has never won a team honour in Japan.

shireitō (司令塔) – control tower
Also meaning 'leader' or 'boss', a *shireitō* is a central midfielder or playmaker who coordinates his team's play and controls the tempo of the game.

See also: *regista* (Italy)

shugoshin (守護神) – guardian deity
They may be cursed more often than any other player on the pitch, but goalkeepers do have their uses. A particularly inspired performance between the posts might see a goalkeeper in Japan hailed as his team's 'guardian deity'.

MALAYSIA

While the Malaysian national team may be something of a sideshow as far as top-level Asian football is concerned, having never progressed further than the group stage of the Asian Cup, the country's passion for the sport is fanatical.

The Malaysian capital, Kuala Lumpur, has been the seat of the Asian Football Confederation since 1978.

curi ayam – *stealing chicken*

In everyday conversation in Malaysia, the phrase 'stealing chicken' describes doing something surreptitiously or in an underhand manner. In football terms it refers to the actions of a striker who loiters close to the opposition's goal, constantly flirting with the offside flag, in the hope of procuring a goal-scoring opportunity. *Kaki ayam*, which literally means 'chicken foot', is a Malaysian idiom for being barefoot and describes someone playing without footwear in a street kickabout. An inept player is known as a *kaki bangku* or 'stool-foot' (i.e. someone with a wooden stool for a foot). An error-prone goalkeeper could be labelled a *tangkap ayam*, which means 'chicken-catcher'.

jual game – *game sold*

An accusation of corruption, *jual game* is something that might be heard at the end of a match when a team have taken a beating or dubious goals have been scored. Rampant corruption in the domestic game means Malaysian football fans have learned not to trust what they see with their own eyes. The country's biggest match-fixing scandal, in 1994, saw over 100 players – including several internationals – arrested by police in nationwide raids, with dozens subsequently banned from the game.

See also: *Calciopoli* (Italy), *dogovornyak* (Russia), *dyvnyy match* (Ukraine), *heishao* (China)

referee kayu – *blockhead referee*

Common term of abuse directed at referees in Malaysia and Singapore. An alternative is *referee bodoh*, which simply means 'stupid referee'.

See also: *pískat hovna* (Czech Republic), *corbeau* (France), *sędzia kalosz* (Poland), *sudyu na milo* (Russia)

PAKISTAN

In spite of a population of just under 200 million people, Pakistan has barely caused a ripple in global football terms.

Dire mismanagement at the Pakistan Football Federation resulted in football in the country effectively being put on hold in 2015, which sent Pakistan plummeting to 201st in the FIFA rankings alongside the likes of Montserrat, San Marino and the Turks and Caicos Islands.

Faisalabad style

Pakistan's eastern Faisalabad region is renowned for producing lanky centre-backs whose style of play encompasses thudding headers, blunt clearances and very little in between. A team who play in the *Faisalabad style* are a team whose approach is based on long balls and knock-downs.

outfoot

A neat compression, *outfoot* is a pass or shot played with the outside of the foot. Another efficient Pakistani coinage is *linkman*, which is the name for a deeply-lying playmaker.

See also: *de três dedos* (Brazil), *papegøje* (Denmark), *trivela* (Portugal), *shvedka* (Russia), *NASA pass* (Nigeria)

pakka paer pao – go with a strong foot

This Urdu expression will be bellowed from the technical area when a coach has had enough of an opponent running rings around his defenders and wants somebody to cut him down to size. A *two man* is a challenge where two players sandwich the ball-carrier at the same time.

See also: *reducer* (England), *Blutgrätsche* (Germany), *to burst someone* (Republic of Ireland), *stop nonsense* (South Africa), *enbarash* (Saudi Arabia)

QATAR

Jaws hit the floor across the football world in December 2010 when Qatar, a tiny oil-rich state on the sun-scorched Arabian Peninsula with a population of under three million, was announced as the host nation of the 2022 World Cup.

Qatar have played at nine Asian Cups, reaching the last eight in 2000 and 2011, but will be making their World Cup debut in 2022.

foul thawb (فاول ثوب) – tunic foul

The *thawb* is the long, white tunic worn by men in Qatar. In informal kickabouts a *foul thawb* is called when a player uses his *thawb* to prevent the ball being passed between his legs by an opponent.

See also: *sotana* (Argentina), *dimije* (Bosnia and Herzegovina), *kupite mu pregaču* (Croatia)

mujannisoon (مجنسون) – naturalised players

Qatar's vast oil and gas wealth has enabled the country to establish itself as a major player in world football by striking lucrative sponsorship deals with glamorous European clubs, hosting training camps and prestige friendlies, and tempting well-known players to wind down their careers in the Qatar Stars League. But while Qatar succeeded in securing the right to host the 2022 World Cup, the one thing that its money has not yet been able to buy is a successful national team: having missed out on a place at the 2018 World Cup, Qatar will be the first country to make their tournament debut as hosts since Italy in 1934. In other sports Qatar has successfully raised its standing by naturalising players from other countries. Saif Saaeed Shaheen, formerly known as Stephen Cherono, won steeplechase gold for Qatar at the 2003 and 2005 World Athletics Championships after defecting from Kenya. The Qatari handball squad that reached the Men's World Championship final in 2015 included players born in France, Spain, Bosnia and Herzegovina, Montenegro, Iran, Syria, Egypt, Tunisia and Cuba. Naturalising players in football has proved less straightforward. In 2004 the Qatar Football Association made an ambitious move to naturalise three Germany-based Brazilian players – Aílton, Dedé and Leandro – only for FIFA to tweak its eligibility rules so that a non-native player seeking to switch allegiance to a new country must have either lived there for at least two years or have a parent or grandparent who was born there. (The residency requirement was increased to five years in 2008.) Undeterred, Qatar has succeeded in naturalising a whole host of players over the years since. The country's most-capped player and all-time leading scorer is Uruguay-born Sebastián Soria, and the national team's starting line-up has often featured more naturalised players – or *mujannisoon* – than home-grown players. Structures are in place to prevent Qatari clubs from fielding too many non-Qatari players in domestic games, with teams only allowed to have four such players in their squads. A scheme known as *albitaqat alsawda'* (البطاقة السوداء) or 'black card', which allowed clubs to register one additional non-Qatari player, was scrapped in 2017.

See also: *UB40s* (Jamaica), *farbowane lisy* (Poland)

SAUDI ARABIA

The engine room of Middle Eastern football, Saudi Arabia has celebrated three Asian Cup triumphs (1984, 1988 and 1996) and witnessed its national team qualify for five World Cups (including four in a row between 1994 – when they reached the last 16 – and 2006).

Saudi great Sami Al-Jaber is one of a select group of players to have scored at three World Cups, having found the net at the tournaments of 1994, 1998 and 2006.

al eyab al entihari (الاياب الانتحاري) – *the suicidal return leg*
This describes the situation facing a team who, having lost the first match in a two-legged tie, are obliged to go all-out for victory in the return fixture.

enbarash (انبرش) – *to roll out*
Saudi term for a hard sliding tackle that leaves an opponent sprawled on the deck, the idea being that the player taken down has been laid out like a carpet.

See also: *nabrat na sane* (Czech Republic), *reducer* (England), *Blutgrätsche* (Germany), *to burst someone* (Republic of Ireland), *pakka paer pao* (Pakistan), *stop nonsense* (South Africa)

jahfali (جحفلي) – *last-minute goal*
Al-Hilal were trailing 1-0 to Saudi arch rivals Al-Nassr in stoppage time of extra time in the 2015 King Cup when a corner from the right was headed back across goal by substitute Ahmed Sharahili and centre-back Mohammed Jahfali bravely threw himself between two yellow-shirted opponents to head in an equaliser. Having escaped defeat by the skin of their teeth, Al-Hilal went on to win the cup on penalties and Jahfali's name has since come to be used colloquially as a synonym for a dramatic late goal.

See also: *Fergie time* (England), *Zona Cesarini* (Italy)

marwaha (مروحة) – *fan*
When an attacker subjects an adversary to a burst of stepovers, his legs are pictured to have assumed the form of an electric fan's furiously whirring blades.

See also: *bicicleta* (Argentina), *pedaladas* (Brazil), *khawya f amra* (Morocco), *caap waa* (China)

mazhariya (مزهرية) – vase

A goalkeeper who remains rooted to the spot as the ball flashes past him into the net is likened to a vase, his apparent inability to move rendering him a mere object of decoration.

A goalkeeper who doesn't move as a shot flies past him is called a *mazhariya* ('vase') in Saudi Arabia

samaam al amaan (صمام الأمان) – safety valve

Arabic term for a trusty centre-back. The English equivalent would be 'stopper'.

See also: *caballo* (Costa Rica), *Holzgeschnitzter* (Austria), *armario* (Spain), *kitasa* (Tanzania)

yaseed hamaam (يصيد الحمام) – to hunt pigeons

To send a shot sailing over the crossbar.

See also: *palo'e mango* (Colombia), *caau fei gei* (China)

SOUTH KOREA

South Korea are Asia's most successful World Cup team, having qualified for 10 editions of the competition. As co-hosts with Japan in 2002 they became the first Asian nation to reach the World Cup semi-finals, a team meticulously organised by Guus Hiddink benefiting from some iffy officiating to beat Italy in the second round with a golden goal by Ahn Jung-hwan, and seeing off Spain on penalties in the quarter-finals, before losing to perennial party-poopers Germany in the last four.

The national team's fans, known as the 'Red Devils', are famed for their hypnotic choreographies and militarily organised chanting.

bballaejul katteun shoot (빨랫줄 같은숏킥) – clothesline shot
A powerful shot that follows a consistent trajectory, such as a rising strike into one of the top corners, is known in South Korea as a 'clothesline shot'. But sling your clothesline carelessly and it risks transforming into a *daegigwon-dolpa-shoot* (대기권돌파슛) or 'outer-space shot', which is the name bestowed upon an effort that drifts way over the crossbar.

See also: *pombo sem asa* (Brazil), *pushka strashnaya* (Russia), *evrogol* (Serbia), *intercontinental ballistic missile* (Nigeria)

bbeung chuk gu (뻥 축구) – long-ball football
The root of this term is the word *bbeung*, which is held to echo the sound a ball makes when it's been struck with a player's full might. England – poor old England – are still felt to embody *bbeung chuk gu* in South Korea and are sometimes teasingly referred to as *Bbeungland*.

See also: *route one* (England), *bakrom* (Norway), *långa bollar på Bengt* (Sweden)

ddong-ball (똥볼) – poop ball
Slang term for a mishit pass, shot or clearance. A player prone to this type of miscalculation might be dubbed *ghe bal* (개발), which means 'dog foot'. *Ddong-ball* also describes an embarrassing misstep in everyday life.

geomi-son (거미손) – spider hands
When every attempt on goal by a team finds one of the goalkeeper's hands and every cross seems to stick in his gloves, the man between the posts is imagined to possess *geomi-son*, a term that evokes both multiple limbs and glue-like palms.

Lee Woon-jae, who went to four World Cups with South Korea, was known as 'Spider Hands'. In Thailand the equivalent expression is *mue gaao* (มือกาว), meaning 'glue hands'.

jeonseol-eh pocketmon (전설의 포켓몬) – *legendary Pokémon*

As *Pokémon* fans know all too well, some monsters are harder to find than others, with the rarest of all falling into the 'legendary' category. In South Korean football, this rueful sobriquet is applied to players with huge talent who are rarely seen on the pitch because of injury.

leejeu shijeol (리즈시절) – *Leeds season*

When people get nostalgic about Leeds, they invariably hark back to the Don Revie glory years or the time when David O'Leary's turn-of-the-century tyros briefly fought it out with Europe's finest in the Champions League. But in South Korea, where the Premier League is followed with forensic devotion, Leeds-related wistfulness has focused on one player. The term *leejeu shijeol* specifically refers to Alan Smith, the tigerish home-grown striker with the blond curtains who bade a tearful farewell to Elland Road after Leeds were relegated from the top flight in 2004 and went on to become an unexpectedly run-of-the-mill central midfielder with Manchester United, Newcastle, MK Dons and Notts County. Brought into the world on Korean online football forums, the phrase *leejeu shijeol* migrated into everyday speech as a general metaphor for happier, more hopeful times.

See also: *doing a Leeds* (England)

ui-jeok-jil (의적질) – *Robin Hood behaviour*

Ui-jeok-jil describes the fortunes of a team who succeed in beating the strongest sides in their division, but struggle to break down the weaker teams, effectively stealing from the rich and then being pickpocketed by the poor.

THAILAND

Thailand's most successful Asian Cup was their first, the 'War Elephants' finishing third as hosts of the 1972 tournament after losing on penalties to South Korea in the semi-finals.

The team's traditional strip is all red, but in recent years they've also worn blue, yellow (to mark King Bhumibol Adulyadej's 80th birthday in May 2007) and black (following the king's death in October 2016).

gii mong (ที่โมง) – what's the time

Anxious not to incur punishments from Thailand's football authorities for singing abusive songs at referees, Thai football fans have come up with an ingenious solution. Rather than chanting *kii gong* (ขี้โกง), which means 'cheat', they sing *gii mong*, which sounds almost identical but has the completely anodyne meaning of 'what's the time'. It started in around 2014 with fans of Buriram United, who have long felt that their sworn foes Muangthong United receive preferential treatment from referees. Buriram's supporters took to holding up cardboard cut-outs of clock faces at their team's Thunder Castle ground – along with large placards spelling out '*gii mong*', just to be crystal clear about what they were singing – during games officiated by referees of dubious character. And The Man couldn't do a thing about it.

kai deak (ไข่ แตก) – to break the egg

When a player scores his team's first goal in a match, he's imagined to have cracked the 'egg' represented by the zero in their half of the scoreline.

lawd daak (ลอดดาก) – through arse

A nutmeg. Sounds more painful than it is (unless something's gone badly wrong).

See also: *caneta* (Brazil), *huacha* (Peru), *salad* (Jamaica), *Gurkerl* (Austria), *jesle* (Czech Republic), *nutmeg* (England), *klobbi* (Iceland), *panna* (Netherlands), *cueca* (Portugal), *bayda* (Morocco), *yalli* (Senegal), *shibobo* (South Africa), *deya* (Zimbabwe)

pao (เป๋า) – referee

A colloquial term for the referee, *pao* comes from *Pao boon jin* (เปาบุ้นจิ้น), which was the Thai name for a long-running Taiwanese television drama about a morally unimpeachable judge that proved immensely popular in Southeast Asia in the 1990s. Starring Taiwanese actor Jin Chao-chun, the show was based on the life of Bao Zheng, a legendarily fair-minded government official during China's Song dynasty (960–1279) who became a symbol of justice in the Chinese-speaking world. A Thai referee might also be referred to as *ajarn* (อาจารย์), meaning 'professor'.

VIETNAM

South Vietnam played at the first two Asian Cups in 1956 and 1960, coming fourth on both occasions, but there has been Vietnamese representation at only one subsequent tournament. Vietnam co-hosted the 2007 event alongside Indonesia, Malaysia and Thailand, and went the furthest out of the quartet, losing to glory-bound Iraq in the quarter-finals.

chọc khe – hit through the hole

Term employed when a playmaker succeeds in threading a pass through a narrow gap in an opposition defence, giving a teammate a clear run on goal.

See also: *Česká ulička* (Czech Republic), *caviar* (France), *Zuckerpass* (Germany), *lissepasning* (Norway), *ciasteczko* (Poland)

ngả bàn đèn – bicycle kick

The Vietnamese term for a bicycle kick literally means 'smoking opium position'. It's felt that the body position of a player who attempts the technique – whether an overhead bicycle kick or a lateral scissors kick – mirrors the traditional reclining pose adopted by someone smoking opium in a Chinese-style opium den.

See also: *chilena* (Chile), *chalaca* (Peru), *Fallrückzieher* (Germany), *hjólhestaspyrna* (Iceland), *rovesciata* (Italy)

taca-dada

Abbreviated version of *tạt cánh đánh đầu*, which means 'cross the ball, header'. An ironic echo of *tiki-taka*, it will be uttered sarcastically when a goal arises from some unapologetically rough-edged build-up play.

NATURAL TALENT – EXPRESSIONS INSPIRED BY THE ANIMAL KINGDOM

Look closely and you'll find animals everywhere on the football pitch – the cat between the posts, the midfield terrier, the fox in the box. Gather together all the creatures from the various animal metaphors used to describe the sport and you'd have a menagerie to rival Noah's Ark.

aile de pigeon – *pigeon's wing (France)*
In the terminology of French football, an *aile de pigeon* is a volley played with the heel.

atete nkura – *hiding mice (Ghana)*
This phrase comes from Ghana's Twi language and describes strikers who go missing as soon as there's work to be done outside the opposition penalty area.

bal yapmayan arı – *bee without honey (Turkey)*
A Turkish player who runs around a lot without contributing anything to his team's cause is likened to a bee who flits from flower to flower without producing any honey.

bubamara – *ladybird (Bosnia and Herzegovina)*
Coined in the 1970s in honour of the old footballs with the black and white panels, this term now serves as a general nickname for the ball.

buffelstoot – *buffalo push (Belgium)*
A *buffelstoot* is a header struck with impressive force.

caballo – *horse (Costa Rica)*
If you're a big, uncompromising Costa Rican player with a kick that could flatten a small building, chances are you'll be known as a *caballo*.

cola de vaca – *cow's tail (Spain)*
Closely associated with the former Barcelona and Brazil striker Romário, the *cola de vaca* is a trick in which a player uses his instep to cradle the ball and sweep it past an opponent.

curi ayam – *stealing chicken (Malaysia)*
A striker will be said to be 'stealing chicken' in Malaysia if he's always making a nuisance of himself in the opposition box.

el scorpión – *the scorpion (Colombia)*
Invented by the eccentric René Higuita, the 'scorpion kick' is the goalkeeping equivalent of stopping the ball on the goal-line and then kneeling down to head it into the net.

fox in the box *(England)*
A wily striker, the kind who regularly manages to be decisive despite his heatmap typically showing nothing more than a handful of yellow blobs in the opposition's penalty area.

frango *– chicken (Brazil)*
A goalkeeping blunder is known as a *frango* in Brazil, while a serial fumbler of shots will find himself dubbed a *frangueiro*.

geomi-son (거미손) *– spider hands (South Korea)*
Laudatory epithet for an unbeatable goalkeeper.

Kampfschwein *– battle pig (Germany)*
This gloriously German (if not especially flattering) expression denotes a tough-tackling midfielder.

kukanyaga nyoka *– to step on a snake (Kenya)*
In Kenya, where treading on a snake is an everyday hazard for many, this term is trotted out when a player takes a swipe at the ball and connects with only fresh air.

monkey yansh *(Nigeria)*
Meaning 'monkey arse', this is a name for a brightly coloured bruise sustained by someone who falls over while playing football on a hard surface.

palomita *– little pigeon (Argentina)*
When a footballer takes flight to score with a diving header in Argentina, it's known as a *palomita*.

papegøje *– parrot (Denmark)*
For reasons obscured by the sands of time, a pass or shot played with the outside of the foot is called a 'parrot' in Denmark.

ratón *– mouse (Chile)*
Timorously peeping out at the match from the safety of their own penalty area, a defensive team in Chile will be scornfully compared to a mouse.

Schwalbe *– swallow (Germany)*
An act of simulation is known as a 'swallow' in Germany due to the perceived resemblance between the bird of that name and the body position of someone taking a dive.

yaseed hamaam (يصيد الحمام) *– to hunt pigeons (Saudi Arabia)*
Fire an effort over the crossbar in Saudi Arabia and you might find yourself accused of endangering the local birdlife.

AUSTRALASIA

Australia and New Zealand are the only teams from the Australasia region to have made it to a World Cup, but Tahiti's shock victory at the 2012 Oceania Nations Cup took the tiny French Polynesian island to the following year's Confederations Cup in Brazil. Although Eddy Etaeta's team lost their three group games – 6-1 to Nigeria, 10-0 to Spain (a record for a senior men's FIFA competition) and 8-0 to Uruguay – they returned to the South Pacific with an army of new admirers.

Inevitably, British English provides the framework for the way that football is talked about in Australia and New Zealand, but local influences – chiefly immigration from southern Europe and the vernaculars of the region's other popular sports – give the game's Antipodean argot a character of its own.

AUSTRALIA

In search of some stiffer competition after years of lording it over their rivals in Oceania, Australia jumped ship in 2006 and joined the Asian Football Confederation. Within nine years they were champions of their adopted continent after James Troisi's extra-time goal sank South Korea in the final of the 2015 Asian Cup, which took place on home soil.

The 'Socceroos' progressed beyond the group phase of the World Cup for the first time in 2006, losing to a soft stoppage-time penalty against eventual champions Italy in the round of 16.

individual brilliance
The trademark utterances of well-known pundits are as familiar to football fans as the catchphrases of our nearest and dearest. Alan Hansen's 'diabolical defending'. Andy Townsend's 'not for me'. Andy Gray's 'you just don't save those, Martin'. Watch a programme featuring former Australia midfielder turned

TV pundit Ned Zelić and you're highly likely to hear the expression *individual brilliance*, which is Zelić's term of choice when he's waxing lyrical about the skill levels within a particular team. He has trotted out the phrase so insistently that it's become something of a go-to term in Australian football coverage. The well-travelled Zelić, whose former clubs include Borussia Dortmund, QPR, Auxerre, Urawa Red Diamonds, Wacker Tirol and Dinamo Tbilisi, also likes to see teams play with *imagination and fantasy*. His Fox Sports colleague Andy Harper coined the phrase *spawning salmon* to describe a player rising gracefully for a header.

shoot farken

The expression *shoot farken* ('fucking shoot') lingers in the background of Australia's football lexicon as an example of the mangled English spoken by immigrants who moved to the country from southern Europe in the second part of the 20th century and quickly grasped the cultural significance of the f-word, but struggled to pin it in the appropriate place in a sentence. For second- and third-generation Australian immigrants, the phrase *shoot farken* is something they might associate with people from their parents' generation animatedly watching football on TV. Generally used ironically, it's now the name of an Australian sport and pop culture website.

slice of cheese

In August 2014, Tasmanian side South Hobart hosted Tuggeranong United in a first-round match in the inaugural edition of the FFA Cup, Australia's premier knockout competition. Canberra club Tuggeranong progressed on penalties after a 1-1 draw in front of 1,472 fans at Hobart's KGV Park and although it represented an upset, the match would probably have passed off without anyone paying too much attention had it not been for the efforts of the local commentary team. With the competition in its infancy and broadcasting guidelines not strictly enforced, South Hobart decided to stream the game live on their website, placing their faith in amateur commentators Callan Paske, Damian Gill and Trent Cornish to call the action. Occasionally breaking into giggles as they described passages of play, the trio seemed to take particular boyish delight in referring to the yellow card as a *slice of cheese*. Footage of the match went viral and the phrase *slice of cheese* became a part of Australia's football lingo.

See also: *gorchichnik* (Russia)

246

to kick a goal

Just as football in the United States must jostle for position with the country's home-grown sports, so Australian football has had to carve out an existence for itself in opposition to its unruly housemates rugby union, rugby league and, in particular, Australian Rules football. As a codified sport, Aussie Rules pre-dates association football: a committee set up by Tom Wills, an Australian educated at Rugby School in England, devised a set of rules for it in May 1859, over four years before the founding fathers of the Football Association sat down to codify football at a Covent Garden pub in 1863. The inventors of the Australian version of the sport cherry-picked elements of football (and the nascent game of rugby football) played at various English public schools and modified them to suit the dry, firm pitches of Australia. A fast, visceral and hugely popular game, Aussie Rules embodies a certain rugged perception of Australian masculinity that stands squarely at odds with the subtleties and swan dives of the soccer pitch. Echoing the provocative title of former Australia midfielder Johnny Warren's 2002 biography, football was traditionally perceived by fans of Aussie Rules as a pastime for 'Sheilas, wogs and poofters', and the popularity of the round ball continues to mystify many of those who like their shorts short, their aerial battles vertiginous and their fisticuffs as frequent as possible. Unsurprisingly, the language of Aussie Rules occasionally floats across the football divide, such as when a goalscorer is said to have *kicked a goal*.

NEW ZEALAND

There's no escaping rugby union in New Zealand, where even the nickname of the nation's football team – the 'All Whites' – carries an echo of the oval-ball game.

New Zealand lost all their games at their first World Cup in 1982 and drew all their games at their second World Cup in 2010. Although Ricki Herbert's side went home after the group phase in 2010, they ended up being the only unbeaten team at the tournament.

going into the sheds

A term shared with the two rugby codes, *going into the sheds* is a manly metaphor for returning to the changing rooms at half-time. A team leading at the interval of a match might be said to be in a positive frame of mind *going into the sheds*.

See also: *turun minum* (Indonesia)

munted

When a 6.3 magnitude earthquake struck Christchurch in February 2011, it left a legacy of devastation, flattening buildings, splitting roads open and claiming 185 lives. It was the most deadly natural disaster to have hit New Zealand since the 1931 Hawke's Bay earthquake, and local officials struggled to articulate the extent of the destruction. But as the city began to pick itself up, an utterance by mayor Bob Parker struck a chord. 'Our main sewer trunk is seriously *munted*,' Parker told journalists one day. 'I believe that is the technical term.' *Munted*, meaning 'knackered' or 'broken', became the default word for anything damaged in the quake. Before long it was being printed on T-shirts and although it wasn't a new coinage, it was voted New Zealand's Word of the Year for 2011 by a prominent community of blogs called Public Address. It was subsequently picked up by football fans and is now used to describe anything from an injured player to a substandard playing surface. 'You seen the pitch, mate? Absolutely *munted*.'

BIBLIOGRAPHY

Books

Paddy Agnew, *Forza Italia: The Fall and Rise of Italian Football* (Ebury Press, 2007)

Phil Ball, *Morbo: The Story of Spanish Football* (WSC, 2011)

Alex Bellos, *Futebol: The Brazilian Way of Life* (Bloomsbury, 2002)

Marc Bennetts, *Football Dynamo: Modern Russia and the People's Game* (Virgin, 2008)

Dominic Bliss, *Erbstein: The Triumph and Tragedy of Football's Forgotten Pioneer* (Blizzard Media, 2014)

Jimmy Burns, *La Roja: A Journey Through Spanish Football* (Simon & Schuster, 2012)

Andreas Campomar, *¡Golazo! A History of Latin American Football* (Quercus, 2014)

John Cross, *Arsene Wenger: The Inside Story of Arsenal Under Wenger* (Simon & Schuster, 2015)

Alex Ferguson with Paul Hayward, *My Autobiography* (Hodder & Stoughton, 2013)

John Foot, *Calcio: A History of Italian Football* (Harper Perennial, 2007)

Cris Freddi, *The Complete Book of the World Cup* (HarperSport, 2006)

Eduardo Galeano, *Soccer in Sun and Shadow* (Nation, 2013)

David Goldblatt, *The Ball is Round: A Global History of Football* (Penguin, 2007)

Ian Hawkey, *Feet of the Chameleon: The Story of African Football* (Portico, 2009)

Uli Hesse, *Tor! The Story of German Football* (WSC, 2013)

Fan Hong and Lu Zhouxiang, *The Politicisation of Sport in Modern China: Communists and Champions* (Routledge, 2013)

Raphael Honigstein, *Das Reboot: How German Football Reinvented Itself and Conquered the World* (Yellow Jersey Press, 2016)

Graham Hunter, *Barça: The Making of the Greatest Team in the World* (BackPage Press, 2012)

Zlatan Ibrahimović with David Lagercrantz, *I Am Zlatan Ibrahimović* (Penguin, 2013)

Gary Imlach, *My Father and Other Working-Class Football Heroes* (Yellow Jersey Press, 2005)

Simon Kuper, *Football Against the Enemy* (Orion, 1996)

Eva Lavric, Gerhard Pisek, Andrew Skinner, Wolfgang Stadler (eds), *The Linguistics of Football* (Gunter Narr Verlag Tübingen, 2008)

John Leigh and David Woodhouse, *Football Lexicon* (Faber and Faber, 2006)

Sid Lowe, *Fear and Loathing in La Liga: Barcelona vs Real Madrid* (Yellow Jersey Press, 2013)

James Montague, *When Friday Comes: Football, War and Revolution in the Middle East* (deCoubertin, 2013)

Julian Norridge, *Can We Have Our Balls Back, Please? How the British Invented Sport* (Penguin, 2008)

Leonam Penna, *Dicionário Popular de Futebol* (Nova Fronteira, 1998)

Martí Perarnau, *Pep Confidential: The Inside Story of Pep Guardiola's First Season at Bayern Munich* (BackPage Press, 2014)

Andrea Pirlo with Alessandro Alciato, *I Think, Therefore I Play* (BackPage Press, 2014)

Wayne Rooney, *My Decade in the Premier League* (HarperSport, 2012)

Peter Seddon, *Football Talk: The Language and Folklore of the World's Greatest Game* (Robson, 2004)

Paul Simpson and Uli Hesse, *Who Invented the Stepover?* (Profile, 2013)

Rory Smith, *Mister* (Simon & Schuster, 2016)

Rob Smyth, Lars Eriksen and Mike Gibbons, *Danish Dynamite: The Story of Football's Greatest Cult Team* (Bloomsbury, 2014)

Gianluca Vialli and Gabriele Marcotti, *The Italian Job* (Bantam Press, 2006)

David Wangerin, *Soccer in a Football World* (WSC, 2006)

Richard Williams, *The Perfect 10* (Faber and Faber, 2007)

Jonathan Wilson, *Angels with Dirty Faces: The Footballing History of Argentina* (Orion, 2016)

Jonathan Wilson, *Inverting the Pyramid: The History of Football Tactics* (Orion, 2014)

Jonathan Wilson, *The Outsider: A History of the Goalkeeper* (Orion, 2012)

David Winner, *Brilliant Orange: The Neurotic Genius of Dutch Football* (Bloomsbury, 2001)

Articles

James Appell, 'The Dark Heart of Russian Football' in *The Blizzard* (issue 0, March 2011)

Eduardo P. Archetti, 'The *Potrero* and the *Pibe*: Territory and Belonging in the Mythical Account of Argentinean Football' in Nadia Lovell (ed), *Locality and Belonging* (Routledge, 1998)

Martin da Cruz, 'The Not-So Crazy English' in *The Blizzard* (issue 24, March 2017)

Patrick Dessault, 'Deschamps-Suaudeau' in *The Blizzard* (issue 4, March 2012)

Richard Giulianotti and Gary Armstrong, 'Drama, Fields and Metaphors: An Introduction to Football in Africa' in Gary Armstrong and Richard Giulianotti (eds), *Football in Africa: Conflict, Conciliation and Community* (Palgrave Macmillan, 2004)

Karel Häring, 'Antonín Panenka' in *The Blizzard* (issue 6, September 2012)

Uli Hesse, 'Learning to Press' in *The Blizzard* (issue 11, December 2013)

James Horncastle, 'The Man Who Made Calcio' in *The Blizzard* (issue 2, September 2011)

James Horncastle, 'Verona's Great Romance' in *The Blizzard* (issue 0, March 2011)

Benjamin Perasović and Marko Mustapić, 'Torcida and Bad Blue Boys: From Hatred to Co-operation and Back' in Christian Brandt, Fabian Hertel and Sean Huddleston (eds), *Football Fans, Rivalry and Cooperation* (Routledge, 2017)

Lars Sivertsen, 'The Mind Has Mountains' in *The Blizzard* (issue 3, December 2011)

Colin Udoh, 'Football's Only Part of It' in *The Blizzard* (issue 11, December 2013)

Newspapers, magazines, websites and blogs

Athletic News
Birmingham Mail
The Daily Mail
The Daily Record
The Daily Telegraph
The Economist
Evening Standard
The Guardian
The Independent
The Liverpool Echo
Manchester Evening News
The Scotsman
The Scottish Sun
The Times
FourFourTwo
When Saturday Comes
World Soccer
BBC
In Bed With Maradona
Phrases.org
The Set Pieces
STV
Deftly Hallowed
The Gentleman Ultra
The Language of Football
The Tanner Ba'
They Fly So High
Unusual Efforts
Djazairess (Algeria)
TN (Argentina)
The FFA Cup (Australia)
Folha da Manhã (Brazil)
Lance! (Brazil)
Terceiro Tempo (Brazil)
Camfoot (Cameroon)
CBC (Canada)
China Daily
La Nación (Costa Rica)
Ekstra Bladet (Denmark)
Jyllands Posten (Denmark)
DR (Denmark)
El Comercio (Ecuador)
Le Monde (France)
L'Équipe (France)
France Football
So Foot (France)
Bild (Germany)
Süddeutsche Zeitung (Germany)
Bundesliga.com (Germany)

Ghana Soccernet
Ghana Web
Detik Sport (Indonesia)
La Gazzetta dello Sport (Italy)
La Repubblica (Italy)
Parola del Giorno (Italy)
Storie di Calcio (Italy)
The Gleaner (Jamaica)
Japanese Football Association
Medio Tiempo (Mexico)
Ahdaaf (Middle East)
Algemeen Dagblad (Netherlands)
Volkskrant (Netherlands)
Onze Taal (Netherlands)
Correio da Manhã (Portugal)
Mais Futebol (Portugal)
O Jogo (Portugal)
Russian Football News
The Moscow Times
Galsen Foot (Senegal)
AS (Spain)
El Mundo (Spain)
Marca (Spain)
Mundo Deportivo (Spain)
LaLiga.es (Spain)
Sport (Spain)
Zwoelf (Switzerland)
The Chicago Tribune (United States)
The LA Times (United States)
The New Yorker (United States)
Pittsburgh Post-Gazette (United States)
Paste (United States)
Sports Illustrated (United States)
SB Nation (United States)
Soccer America (United States)
Big Soccer
CNN
ESPN
Eurosport
FIFA.com
Futbolgrad
Goal
Google Translate
Online Etymology Dictionary
RSSSF
UEFA.com
Vice Sports
Wikipedia
YouTube

ACKNOWLEDGEMENTS

When I started working on this project, in addition to English I spoke French, a smattering of Portuguese and some GCSE-level Welsh, so it was clear from the outset that I was going to need a lot of help. The extensiveness of these acknowledgements is a testament to the extraordinary generosity from which I have benefited throughout the process of putting the book together.

The book you're holding started life as a glossary of French football terms in issue 21 of *The Blizzard* and I'm indebted to Jonathan Wilson, editor of that august publication, both for badgering me to write something for it and then for very kindly sharing the contents of his contacts book with me once I found myself with a book to write.

I owe particular debts of gratitude to Hugo Steckelmacher, Uli Hesse, Matt Barker, Sam Kelly, Jack Lang and Mohamed Moallim, all of whom spent the best part of a year unable to peer into their inboxes without fear of finding an email from me asking a pernickety question about a translation or a spelling or the correct positioning of an accent. Thank you all for your patience, insight and good humour.

Massive thanks also to Marcus Alves, Aidan Hamilton, Raphael Honigstein, Gabriele Marcotti, Serafino Ingardia, Simon Kuper, Carlos Santos, James Appell, Artur Petrosyan and Sid Lowe for sharing their considerable expertise and kindly agreeing to read over sections of the text.

One of the joys of working on this book was forming connections with journalists, broadcasters, translators and football lovers from all over the world, a great many of whom shared my enthusiasm for rustling up quirky words and obscure turns of phrase. With a deep breath, thanks to Joel Richards, Diego Escalera, Andrew Downie, Luciano Monteiro, Alex Bellos, Rupert Fryer, Adam Brandon, Carl Worswick, Ralph Hannah, David Leon Bardi, Martin da Cruz and Luis Vargas for their assistance with the South American section.

In North and Central America, I was grateful for the help of John Molinaro, Richard Whittall, Michael Krumholtz, Laianer Arias, Fernando Palomo, Tom Marshall, Nino Mangravita, Adam Svoboda, Simon Preston, Nigel Myers, Grant Wahl, Joe Prince-Wright and Graham Parker.

The assistance of three experts on the history of Southampton Football Club – David Bull, Gary Chalk and Duncan Holley – proved invaluable across a number of entries in the European section. Costas Bratsos provided me with enough material from Greece for an entire book. Metodi Shumanov did the same for Bulgaria.

Other European football experts to have kindly shared their time and knowledge include Bobby Bendekovits, Florian Vetter, Kristof Terreur, Saša Ibrulj, Aleksandar Holiga, Michal Petrák, Kim Michelsen, Aet Süvari, Ari Virtanen, Rich Nelson, Philippe Auclair, Vincent Duluc, Thomas Schmidt, Giorgio Alafogiannis, Tomasz Mortimer, Simon Evans, Magnús Már Einarsson, Miguel Delaney, Ciarán Ó'Raghallaigh, Ori Cooper, Keith Bailie, Thore Haugstad, Brendan Husebo, Michał Pol, Tom Kundert, Emanuel Roşu, Igor Novikov, Gosha Chernov, Alex Jackson, Jonathan Northcroft, Alec Ross, Vladimir Novak, Lukáš Vráblik, Miran Zore, Johanna Frändén, Mämä Sykora, David Lemos, Alper Öcal, Uğur Karakullukçu, Vadim Furmanov and Seiriol Hughes.

Mark Gleeson, Aliou Goloko and Salim Masoud Said helped to put me in touch with football journalists from all over Africa. Thanks to Peter Rundo from Dundee United for sharing newspaper clippings on the club's ill-fated tour of Nigeria. Maher Mezahi, Antoine Battiono, Njie Enow Ebai, Leocadia Bongben, Dickson Yala, Muhammad Y Gamal, Tarek Talaat, Fiifi Anaman, Michael Oti Adjei, Pierre Ephèse Kouamé, Celestine Karoney, Abdellah Aârab, Mohamed Amine El Amri, Oluwashina Okeleji, Mamadou Koumé, Michael Mwebe and Farouk Abdou graciously guided me through the landscape of African football.

In Asia, Andrew Mullen and Patrick Johnston helpfully passed a number of useful contacts my way. In Masayuki Tanabe, Ben Mabley, Sean Carroll and, in particular, Dave Phillips, I was able to call upon the services of a veritable brains trust on the language of Japanese football. Big thanks to Ahmed Hashim, Wael Jabir, Hamoudi Fayad and all the other lads from the Ahdaaf website for painstakingly helping me to piece together a glossary of Arabic football terms.

For advice and ideas on Asian football, thanks also to Cameron Wilson, Rowan Simons, William Bi, Tobias Zuser, Siddharth Saxena, Leslie Xavier, Rayson Tennyson, Marcus Mergulhao, Dwaipayan Datta, Antony Sutton, Hamed Momeni, Hassanin Mubarak, Haresh Deol, Gary Koh, Umaid Wasim, Steve Price, Taejeong Kwon, Dominick Cartwright and Erick Bui.

Finding region-specific football vocabulary in Australasia was more problematic than I had anticipated, but thankfully Joe Gorman came out to bat for Australia and the hive mind of the Wellington Phoenix fans on the Yellow Fever forum pitched some ideas my way from New Zealand.

Working for AFP, I was fortunate to be able to tap into a global network of reporters. Thanks in particular to Pablo San Roman, David Legge, Fanuel Jongwe, Ziad Bouraad, David Harding and Quy Bui. For contacts, useful links and general guidance, thank you to Marcus Christenson, Adam Hurrey, Archie Rhind-Tutt, James Montague, Marc Joss and Peter Clark. Thanks very much to Richard Furlong for generously giving me permission to cherry-pick elements from his fantastic website, The Language of Football. Thanks to Daniel Rooseboom de Vries from the Freestyle Football Federation for variously confirming and shooting down my theories about the language of freestyle football.

A huge thank-you is due to my agent, Melanie Michael-Greer, who effectively delivered this project fully formed into my lap and has been a steadfast source of support throughout. At Bloomsbury, thank you to Sarah Skipper and Matt Lowing, who proved to be a dream of an editor – patient, trusting and enthusiastic in equal measure. This book would not be the same without the work of Dan Leydon, whose fantastic illustrations, though black and white, bring so much colour and warmth to these pages. I'm also indebted to Hamish Ironside for his eagle-eyed proofreading.

Thanks to my friends for not disowning me when deadline-induced panic turned me into a hermit. And lastly, thank you to my wonderful, funny and endlessly supportive family. This book is for you.

INDEX

Page numbers in italics are illustrations.

'At last, the definitive guide to football phraseology across the world. The richness of the game's language shines through in this addictive glossary. Sparky and very funny.'

Paul Hayward, *Daily Telegraph*

'*Ein super Buch!*'

Raphael Honigstein, ESPN and the bestselling author of *Das Reboot*

'A fascinating and necessary work.'

Jonathan Wilson, founder of *The Blizzard* and the bestselling author of *Inverting the Pyramid.*

'Amusing and informative in equal measure. Who knew Dundee United commanded such disdain in Nigeria?'

Oliver Kay, *The Times*

'Funny, erudite, rich in detail and endlessly readable. Perfect for anyone who thinks they already know about the language of football.'

Barney Ronay, *The Guardian*

'Like Eskimos with their many words for snow, Brazilians – who else – have at least five ways to describe that cheekiest skill, the nutmeg. *Do You Speak Football?* is full of such delights. Quirky, addictive, stuffed with anecdote, it's far more than a glossary – revealing the character of countries and the story of the game through how the world talks about its favourite sport. An essential book in World Cup year and, befitting one focusing on language, the writing is precise, light and often lovely. A treat.'

Jonathan Northcroft, *Sunday Times*

In Russia, an ungainly footballer is called a *derevo* ('tree')